Theology in Revolution

1

alba house DIVISION OF THE SOCIETY OF ST. PAUL
STATEN ISLAND, N.Y. 10314

GEORGE DEVINE

Editor of the Proceedings of the
College Theology Society

Theology in Revolution

With ecclesiastical permission.

Library of Congress Catalog Card Number: 71-110590

Designed, printed and bound in the U.S.A. by the Pauline Fathers and Brothers of the Society of St. Paul at Staten Island, New York as a part of their communications apostolate.

© 1970 by the Society of St. Paul, Staten Island, N.Y. 10314

SBN: 8189-0176-4

Also by the Editor:

Our Living Liturgy. Chicago: Claretian Publications, 1966.

Why Read the Old Testament? Chicago: Claretian Publications, 1966.

To Be A Man (ed.) Englewood Cliffs, N.J.: Prentice-Hall, Inc., 1969.

Acknowledgments

The editor of this volume, himself a member of the College Theology Society and concerned with the vitality of that Society, wishes to thank all of those within and outside of the Society who have contributed to the successful publication of this volume of the College Theology Society Proceedings, based on the Society's last annual convention in Chicago, April 6-8, 1969.

The book could not have appeared without the encouragement and confidence which the editor received from the Board of Directors of the Society, especially the President, Rev. Mark Heath, O.P.; the secretary, Sister Maura Campbell, O.P.; and the treasurer, Brother C. Stephen Sullivan, F.S.C.

The editor's burden has been lightened and his task made more enjoyable by numerous individuals who have, in myriad ways, aided in various aspects of the Proceedings project, including Sister Katherine T. Hargrove, R.S.C.J.; Mr. and Mrs. Peter Lind Hayes; Mr. Victor Berardelli; Mrs. Robert Hair; Mrs. Shirely Lazarus; Rev. Mark Hurtubise, S.J.; Mr. William J. Toohey; Mr. Peter R. Flynn; Miss Anne M. Buckley; Miss Sally T. Abeles; Prof. Mary Perkins Ryan; Prof. William Radtke; Mr. John Smith, and a number of the editor's students and colleagues.

The physical production of the book and its appearance are due to the fine work of Alba House, the publishing division of the Society of St. Paul.

Lastly, the editor wishes to thank all those who have been around and with him throughout this endeavor, but especially his wife Joanne, and his son George IV.

— George Devine

Contents

I Introduction

GEORGE DEVINE

The Age of Aquarius

A new era in American theatre began on the evening of April 29, 1968, when an audience in New York's Biltmore Theatre was introduced to a revolutionary experience, heralded by the announcement, "This is the dawning of the Age of Aquarius . . ." Since then, if *Hair* has signaled a revolution on Broadway (and Geary Street), it is even more significant that it arises from a revolution in life itself.

Revolution! The word is proclaimed with bravado, or whispered in fear. And its meaning is laboriously debated.

Analogies to the Industrial Revolution miss the mark. So, too, do references to political and military revolutions of history ancient and recent. Whether the revolution is violent or non-violent, a good or a bad thing, seems to be a matter of opinion. And opinions are almost as myriad as persons themselves.

To some, the revolution is necessarily urgent, violent and reckless. Its principles are to be found in the Thoughts of Chairman Mao, and its heroes to be found in Che Guevara and Ho Chi Minh. Accordingly, it is the salvation of mankind, or the worst threat to civilization, in so far as beauty — or ugliness — is in the eye of the beholder.

To others, it is hot, then cool, then hot again, depending upon the circumstances: a demand for reparations by James Forman, a march led by Ralph Abernathy, a petition dissenting from a Papal encyclical, a confrontation in Chicago.

To History, a tired old man who smokes his pipe and slowly scratches his head, it may be merely a more active part of the passing parade, already destined to become less significant, less exciting, less remembered than the events yet to come.

In any event, no one who has lived through the past decade —
indeed, the past five years — would gainsay the oft-sung words of
Bob Dylan, "The times, they are a-changin'. . ."

We know that the number of human beings below the age of
twenty-five continues to grow geometrically, and that, as Margaret
Mead has pointed out, this is a generation whose experiences,
anxieties and hopes will necessarily be vastly different from those
of their elders . . . even those elders who have not yet reached
the incredible age of thirty.

They are different, we are told, because their world differs
so greatly from the one which most of us knew even a few years
ago. Because of a complex series of technological developments,
the planet which we inhabit is much smaller than ever before. Air
trips from New York to Chicago are now shorter than train or
bus trips from New York to Washington. And those Californians
who, in the infant days of television, watched three-week-old
kinescopes of Ed Sullivan's Christmas show every January, now
find themselves able to watch asronauts live from the Moon.

Yesterday's child read of faraway places like Iwo Jima, or
heard the crackling voice of Edward R. Murrow from London.
Today's child sees the VietNam war being fought in his living
room, in living color. And the closer the child is to the magic
age, the more he wonders about his own direct involvement in a
war that other people will watch in their living rooms . . . or one
that will be fought in a few hours by pushbutton.[1]

The changes of which we have spoken here are relatively
superficial, however, in the terms of the overall revolution which
has become characteristic of our time.

For the revolution is chiefly in the hearts and minds of human
beings. And, however this revolution may have been occasioned
by circumstances, it is more important than the circumstances
themselves.

1. George Devine, "Changes," in *To Be A Man* (Englewood Cliffs, N.J.:
Prentice-Hall, Inc., 1969).

The revolution — viewed from any perspective — has brought us a new generation which refuses to be docile, insists on asking "why?", demands an honesty which its own prophets often find hard to achieve.

The children of the revolution barrage their elders with questions. At the same time, they are unreceptive to answers, all the while secretly hoping to be barraged with them. They excoriate those who do not fulfill the highest ideals, yet seldom is their urgent pragmatism able to make room for the same ideals. In the Western world, they are the most financially prosperous generation in history, and the one most concerned with the economic well-being of the underprivileged. And if they are self-contradictory, perhaps it is because they live in a self-contradictory world.

For some of them, the answer is a deep involvement with the world, its progress and its problems: the Peace Corps, VISTA, the service professions, an increasing desire to prepare oneself for assistance to others. And for some, it seems that the tack taken is not unlike the "optimism of withdrawal" of which Teilhard wrote,[2] a disgusted, alienated dropping out, if not turning-on.

For still others, the answer may seem to lie in the "age of Aquarius," that magical, mystical era of "harmony and understanding" wherein the ills of modern civilization may be cured by the *sphragis* of a flower and the ebullient proclamation of *love,* possibly combined with the all-important utterance of *om.*

Critics will be quick to point out that the utterances of *om,* despite the soothsayers of the 1967 march, failed to make the Pentagon turn orange and levitate six feet above the ground as promised, that Claude, the hero of *Hair,* winds up going into the Army, and that most of today's young revolutionaries are sowing their last wild oats before that all-too-soon day when they buy monthly commutation tickets for the 8:17 out of Hoboken.

But be that as it may, the revolution is here. Hardly, it seems,

---

2. Pierre Teilhard de Chardin (tr. Norman Denny), "The Grand Option," in *The Future of Man* (Evanston, Ill.: Harper & Row, 1964).

the violent revolution praised by some and feared by most. But a drastic change from the world of even the very recent past, when cherished verities were as warm and protective as Linus' blanket and the Powers that Be were never challenged.

It is in some ways good; it is in some ways bad. But it is here.

It is here when Gene McCarthy can rock the fortress of the Democratic Party, when already-fired professors are begged by administrators to accept apologies and return to the campus, when an Archbishop will advise parishioners to remain in their pews and pay courteous attention to black militants demanding a chunk of the parish till, and when a theologian will tell his listeners, "Well, we really can't be sure about that at all."

If there is one thing that theologians *must* be sure about, it is that an age of revolution demands a theological expression which takes the revolutionary character of the times into account. A few years ago, we might have said that we must pay attention to the revolution going on outside of classrooms, away from ivy-covered *academe,* and far from the protective arms of Holy Mother Church. Now, all of these once-insulated premises are the *locus* of the revolution itself, and there is no getting away from it. As a result, today's theologians and religious educators must be fully aware of the times, even though they will often be very much disturbed by them.

Teachers have long insisted that their students not only have the freedom to dissent, but the intellectual obligation to know just what it is that they are dissenting from. Pedagogues must now (if they have not already) be sure to apply the requirement to themselves. The teacher, especially the teacher of religion, may often see so much in the revolution that genuinely incarnates the revolutionary spirit of the Gospel message, and tragically enough, it will often be side-by-side with elements which do great violence to that same message. The teacher, though he be tempted to reiterate Cicero's *O tempora! O mores!* and be done with it, must speak in the context of the times, and speak to those who live in them.

It is not an easy task. It means understanding of more than the times themselves, but indeed an understanding of persons — of students, and of self. It is to this end that the current efforts of the College Theology Society, and this volume of the Society's annual Proceedings, are offered. As will become evident to the reader, the first division of this book will be concerned, in the main, with the revolution of a world entering the unchartered 1970's; the second will be more taken up with the myriad responses of theologians and religious educators to the signs of the times, and their assessments of the responsibilities that await them.

II   Changing Churches in a Changing World

REV. ANDREW M. GREELEY

1 Dynamic Theology - Today and Tomorrow

I am not sure that sociologists are in a position to tell theologians how to practice their craft. However, I propose to discuss four of the major themes that I see running through American society, for, say, the rest of this century, themes to which I think theologians and theology teachers will have to address themselves. I don't doubt much that these are the themes that will be most pertinent in American Society. As a sociologist I can speak of them with some confidence, but when I try and link these themes to theology, as I will in the second half of each section of my remarks, then I am on very thin ice, and I acknowledge this and leave it to theologians to judge how thin the ice may be.

The four unit ideas I wish to discuss are (1) person, (2) community, (3) sex, and (4) the sacred and the city. The first unit idea that I see operative for the rest of the century is the unit idea of person. Stephen Spender, the British poet, had an extraordinarily sensitive article in the March 30, 1969, New York *Times* magazine, and compared the recent student revolts in the United States, France and in Czechosolovakia. He said they all had one thing in common; they represented each in their own way a search on the part of the students for self-realization, for self-fulfillment, for life as opposed to the restrictions, negativism, the death they perceive in the organized society around them. If Spender is right, and I think he is, then the student revolts were merely the tip of the iceberg that the personalist revolution really is.

For the first time in human history, the fulfillment, the development, the enrichment of the individual human personality has become the most important goal, indeed, the only goal that a whole generation of people are willing to accept as a valid end for human effort. Any organization, any social structure which does not concede primary importance to the fulfillment and enrichment of the human personality is simply going to be rejected by the young people of today and by everybody in the years to come. Now, through most of Christian history we have paid some sort of lip service to the value and dignity of the person. However, the dignity of the individual person as the operating principle of human endeavor is something rather new.

My generation of liberals, moderates, radicals, progressives, whatever we were, didn't care much about whether we were loved or not. We wanted to get things done. We wanted to form Christian family movements and labor schools. We wanted to have active participation in the liturgy; we wanted to crusade for integration (remember the good old days when we crusaded for integration?); we wanted to accomplish social change. Whether we loved or not, whether we were *able* to love or not were issues that were not raised. But today the social change, the change of structures is viewed by most young people as being quite secondary to the establishing of loving, open human relationships. This is not to say that they are very good at it but that they are the first ones in history who, as a large group of people, indeed almost the unanimous group of their generation, place self-fulfillment, self-realization at the very top of their list of goals.

This emphasis on love, of course, upsets many in the older generation. Several summers ago, Father Eugene Kennedy, the Maryknoll psychologist, and I were wandering through the Orient haranguing captive audiences of missionaries and we came to a certain country, which will remain nameless, and to the center house of a mission community, which will remain nameless, save that it was not a Maryknoll center house, and there we encountered a bishop from a certain Western European country, which we will also keep nameless. Now this bishop, as bishops will, fell to discussing other bishops. He fell, in fact, to discussing the American bishops and he told us what he thought of American bishops.

"To tell you the truth, Father, I don't think very much about them at all," he said. "That man Sheen, for example; he was a marvelous orator. He gave us a splendid talk at the Council about poverty, but, of course, himself staying all of the time at the Rome Hilton." "But," he added, "the thing I really don't like about him, Father, is his choice of language."

And I said, "Language, My Lord?" (in this Western European country you call bishops My Lord, because they are.)

And he went on, "Well, yes, Father, he uses the wrong kind of words for a bishop altogether. Everything is love; love this, love that, love everything else. Well, now, Father, a bishop shouldn't be using that word, don't you know. After all, it's primarily matrimonial in meaning."

Any of you who know Eugene Kennedy or have read his books can imagine the difficulty I had in keeping him quiet under such circumstances. But, in fact, whether the older generation likes it or not, personal love, personal fulfillment through love, love as a condition for fulfillment, these have become the primary and essential ethical and religious issues of our time. Freud, Kierkegaard, the existentialist, Paul Tillich, these are the prophets, the prophets of the personalist revolution . . . a revolution which may be one of the greatest cultural breakthroughs, the greatest leaps forward the human race has ever made. Why? Because our generation of liberals and radicals, interested as we were in institutional reform, won. We won most of the things we wanted to win and then discovered that for all our victories the world wasn't a much better place; having won, we discovered that we had failed. It seems to me that the personalist generation is concerned about distrust, suspicion and fear, and its emphasis on openness, honesty and authenticity probably is far wiser and will accomplish far more towards making the world a better place than we did — at least if they are capable of living up to their own ideology.

Now what are the goals of personalism? It seems to me that they are many, but at least some of them are fairly clear. The personalist stresses the need for curiosity. The personalist is fulfilled only by learning, only by growing. He can only grow if he is curious. Personalism stresses playfulness. It rejects, at least in its best manifestations, soberness, sobriety, dullness. Only when we are able to be playful can we be speculative and creative. The personalist insists on freedom from ritual, and by ritual he means not liturgy but the repetition of foolish behavior. Such as, in my business, for example, the language exam for the Ph.D or, even more embarrassingly, the idea that academic grades in college have any relevance for anything that matters. This is the sort of ritual that the personalist wants no part of.

The personalist insists upon an environment in which people are free, and indeed, motivated to grow in self-esteem; to have more respect for themselves, their own dignity and their own lovability. The personalist wants to reject fear as a primary motivation in people's lives. He perhaps is willing to concede that fear of the Lord is the beginning of wisdom but it is only the beginning and should not be, in his view, the main motivation for human behavior. He wants to create a situation in which everyone is able to make a meaningful contribution to society, where people enjoy a sense of personal efficacy, that is to say that they control in some way or other their own destinies. He wants a situation where people are able to exercise, to commit themselves to responsible concern for others. He wants a situation where people can have diffused relationships with members of other status groups. I mean a situation in which young people are able to relate not only to other young people but to middle-aged people and old people, and where students are able to relate to professors, not merely as student-professor but as one human being to another. Diffused relationships across status lines are of high importance in the personalist's view of the world he wants to make.

What does the Church have to respond theologically to this world? It seems to me that we have a great richness and to ignore this richness would be blindness. For the personalist thrust is rooted in the dynamic of the Resurrection promise. The idea of fulfillment, the enrichment of the person only came into the world when mankind believed that growth and progress were possible. As Brian Wicker points out, "The Christian is merely the humanist who is sure of the ground on which he stands." He believes in the Resurrection and he therefore knows that self-fulfillment need never end whereas the agnostic humanist has to concede that eventually self-fulfillment is futile because it is crushed by the ugliness of death. But I think we can go further than this. The promise of the Resurrection not only underpins personalism but personal growth anticipates the Resurrection.

There is one thing we know from psychology, particularly from clinical psychology, *viz.*, that personality growth involves death and re-birth. St. Paul's words that "we must put off the old man to put on the new" and that "we must die to the former self in order to rise in Christ Jesus," were profoundly accurate in their psychological insight. And the Lord's words, "he who loses his life shall find it," are also insightful in the psychological realm because human growth, particularly that kind of growth that emerges through the therapeutic process, is a death and a resurrection. We die to our defenses, we die to our fears, we die to our suspicions and distrusts and anxieties. Moreover, as any of us who have gone through it know, it is a terrible, painful death, but we have to go through that death in order to rise again to love and trust and openness and to the best that is in ourselves. The systematic defenses with which we cramp our warmth and generosity and goodness must be put aside and they can only be put aside through an experience rather like death. Easter comes only after Good Friday, and this is a profoundly important myth of all human growth. By myth I don't mean something false but something that symbolizes. All human growth, all human resurrection presumes first a Good Friday.

Now for most of human history the growth of the human personality was cut short very early in the game. At five or six, or ten or twelve or nineteen or twenty. But in contemporary society, because of the breakthroughs we are making in understanding the human personality, growth can go on indefinitely; as Nevitt Sanford has said, "We are never too old to grow." That means we are never too old to die and to rise again and that means that an increasing proportion of the human race is going to go through a Good Friday, Easter Sunday experience throughout their lives.

It seems to me that when this happens it will be much easier for us to believe in a resurrection, because we will have experienced it as part of the human condition. We will realize that to be human means to die and to rise again. And so the idea that at the end of the process there is an ultimate Resurrection will not seem so very difficult to accept at all.

It's interesting in passing to note how much of our training in our spirituality in the past was interested in cutting off our growth. In limiting us behind certain barriers, in fixing us in certain categories, in cutting us off, literally, to the possibility of death and resurrection. If this prediction of mine or projection be right, if the resurrection experience is going to become more and more widespread in the human race through psychological discoveries and progress, then the Church, built around the mystery of the Resurrection, ought to be able to speak very profoundly to this most difficult of human questions: death, resurrection, death and then, finally, resurrection. My own personal hunch is that for many in our generation and many more in the generation after us, when the Lord finally comes and touches our hand, as He did the hand of the son of the widow of Naim, or when he says as he said to Lazarus, "Come forth," the experience will come, not exactly an anti-climax, but as something with which we are very familiar because we have gone through it so many times before.

This, then, is my first unit idea: self-fulfillment as death and resurrection, and the Church because of its conviction of the Resurrection is uniquely able to provide a theological context for the greater understanding of the dimensions of the personal revolution.

The second unit idea which I see at work is the idea of community. To be a person means to be a person with and for others. We cannot die and rise again save in relationships. Marriage, the most primal of relationships, is a paradigm of death and resurrection, for if a marriage is to be happy, both people have to die to their fears and their distrusts. They have to put aside not only the physical barriers to love but, far more important and far more difficult, they must put aside the psychological barriers. Their suspicions, their distrust of themselves, their feelings of inadequacy, their defense mechanisms have to be overcome or the relationship will not grow. Marriage is the paradigm of all relationships; the family the paradigm of all community. If we are to die and rise again it must be in a relationship with each other. The community then provides the psychological context in which we are not only able to be ourselves but in which we are forced to be ourselves. You see, the marriage relationship creates a demand. It demands that we be the best that we are capable of being. Friendship is not total acceptance. Love is not total acceptance. Love is rather a demand for the best that is in ourself. So community relationships call upon us, they challenge us, they demand of us that we die in order that we may rise to be what we are.

Sometime ago, one hundred and fifty to two hundred years ago, man began a pilgrimage. He left behind the peasant, farming community and began his migration to the industrial metropolis. He left his rural cottage in part because the population explosion gave him no room to live. He left it also because he wanted a better life. He wanted the good life and the city seemed to offer that to him. And the pilgrimage was a success. The industrial metropolis made possible a level of affluence and abundance undreamed of in any other time in the world's history. But man had to pay a price for this affluence. He left behind the warmth and the intimacy and the social support of that little peasant village. There is no need however, to romanticize our peasant past as some of the great sociologists of the nineteenth century came dangerously close to doing.

I don't know how many of you have visited the place of your ancestral origins. I have. I have seen the actual house in Ballendrae, County Mayo, Ireland whence my granddaddy sprang about a hundred years ago. All I can say is that it is a darn good thing for me that granddaddy sprang. The peasant village was narrow, it was uncomfortable, it was rigid, it did not leave much room for spontaneity and creativity. In Ireland it was also very wet and damp. Almost all the time. Nevertheless, even though we do not want to go back to it, we left something behind there. We've tried ever since the moment we started, really, to recreate in the big cities some of the warmth and the intimacy and the social support of the peasant village. Modern man, particularly the *young* modern man, having read all about the quest for community, is prepared to demand that he have his cake and eat it too. He wants the affluence and the comforts of an industrial society but he also wants the warmth, intimacy and social support of the old community. The various ecclesial communities which, in my judgment, are inaptly called the underground church, the communities of hippies and young radicals, the new utopian communities which are springing up all around the country, splendid, bizarre, insane groups like Ken Kessey's "Merry Pranksters," all of these, each in its own way, represent the determined search of modern man for community. We must, in passing, note some of the dangers of community. For any time in the past when there was a question of who was more powerful, the person or the community, it was the community. The community dominated the person and the person did not have much freedom or distance vis-a-vis the community.

There is, as anybody who has been in an ecclesial community knows, a tremendous danger even today of the community dominating the person. The danger is made even more serious because the techniques of group dynamics make it much easier to manipulate other people. Indeed, now we can even manipulate them in such a way that we can persuade them half the time that they are free. Community can destroy privacy, destroy creativity, destroy individuality. It need not; but the point is it *can* and it must be watched with caution and reserve. I must say that while I have the highest faith in the processes of group therapy and in the utility of sensitivity-training in certain circumstances, it does seem to me that sensitivity-training has become, for many people in the Church, a panacea which it is not capable of being, and for others, a means for disturbed people to engage in aggressive and manipulative behavior. The nearly mad enthusiasm of some Catholics for sensitivity training ought to be a serious warning to all of us that the quest for community can get badly fouled up and do an incredible amount of harm. But despite the dangers in communitarianism, it's one of the important cultural thrusts of our time and it represents great potential for human growth and for religious growth, which, in the final analysis, are the same thing.

What resources does the Church have with which to respond to the quest for community? First of all, I think we can say that we know more about community than any other organization in the world, because we have been presiding over communities for almost seventeen hundred years: religious communities which, at least in their initial thrusts, were successful in balancing the question of individual freedom versus common good. No matter how the religious communities may have deteriorated through time, there was nonetheless in their beginning, in the insights of their great founders, an understanding of how a person and society could blend with due respect for both. We have in St. Paul, secondly, this passionate concern for freedom from the Law. I think that to social scientists looking at it from the outside St. Paul was revolting against a structure which was outmoded, which was oppressive, which was tying people down to useless ritual. He was trying to replace the Law with a community based on love and trust. And in this theology of freedom versus the Law, we may very possibly have an extremely useful platform on which to stand when we address ourselves to the communitarian challenge.

If we look at the Lord's life, we can see what a splendid convener of community he was, because, particularly in dealing with his apostles, he showed his mastery at those two arts which any convener of community must possess: the art of challenge and the art of reassurance. This is what it means to lead a group. We must challenge those who are our colleagues. Challenge them to be the best of what is in themselves. Challenge them to die the death that is necessary for resurrection, but at the same time, when they are going through the agony of suffering and dying in order that they may rise again, then we must encourage them, reassure them, create an atmosphere of comfort and want and confidence that they can indeed rise to a new life. I must say that sometimes, in being a convener of a community myself, I am very good at challenging and very good at reassuring. We do need desperately, in our modern communities, people who are very good at reassuring. We have a notion of our Church as not merely or not even principally an organized structure but rather a people on pilgrimage for whom the structure exists merely as a service and the leaders of the structure as servants. In these theological themes and above all on the theme that we are held together by love: "by this all men shall know you are my disciples that you have love for one another," we have, I think, the rudiments of a theology of community which, if we develop it, will place us in an extraordinarily strategic position in responding to modern man's quest for community. It always seems to me so tragic that we who have known so much about community for so long find ourselves now, at a time when the world is searching for community, spending so much of our time in reforming canon law. Canon law is important and needs to be reformed but why, oh why, have we not been able to say more to those who are looking for community? We, who in our position know so much about it!

The third unit idea is closely related to the first two: the unit idea of sex. I don't know how many of you saw the movie "Belle du Jour"; it was a "B," which immediately assured its success at the box office. At any rate it was an extraordinarily interesting story. I take it to be a modern version of the Osee myth, a tale in which the heroine was not able to engage in any sort of meaningful love with her husband because of a profound feeling of evil and worthlessness. To punish herself for this failure and this feeling of evil, she degraded herself by becoming a prostitute, a *belle du jour,* a lady of the day. But despite that fact, that one of her gangster consorts even seriously injured her husband, the husband refused to be turned away from her love, or from his love for her. The power and the persistence of his love finally overcame her feelings of worthlessness and shame and she was able to respond to him. Now this Osee theme in modern dress seems to me to be terribly important as a symbol of the challenge the sexual revolution presents to the Church. By sexual revolution I don't mean there are more people engaging in intercourse before marriage now than there were twenty-five years ago. Frankly, I don't believe that. It seems to me that chastity has never been a very popular virtue and if we are engaged in a sexual revolution one wonders what the standards of comparison were. London in the time of Regency? Paris in the time of Louis XIV? Puritan New England in the time of the bundling phenomena? I very much doubt there is any more sex or any less sex now than at any time in history. By sexual revolution I mean something much different and ultimately much more important. We have come to the end of three millenia of dualism.

Ever since the appearances of the great world religions, a thousand years or so before Christ, man has thought of himself as a spirit imprisoned in a body. The spirit was good, the body was evil. Sex pertained to the body; sex, therefore, was evil. Even Christianity, while it had a rather different approach to reality, was not able to effectively triumph over dualism, and it was the dualism philosophy they absorbed from their society, rather than any doctrines of Christian faith; this is what turned so many of the early Fathers into religious puritans. As puritans they were no different than the secular philosophers in the world around them. They thought sex was evil and every other educated man in society thought it was evil too. But after three millenia of this dualism, there came along a man named Sigmund Freud whom we probably will have to get around to canonizing one day. And Freud said that sex was not something to be ashamed of but he said something much more important than that. He said that sex was not a drag on the human spirit but, on the contrary, a terribly important stimulus to the expansion of the human spirit. That was the sexual revolution, because with that one insight Freud struck a mighty blow against dualism. The residue of dualism is still with us but on the wane, because now we see sex is not an encumbrance to the spirit but ideally is a stimulus to its growth.

Belle du Jour was able to grow because she was finally able to respond to her husband's sexual affections. Similarly most human beings grow, if they grow at all, in the sexual relationship. All human beings, whether they are involved in marriage relationships or not, grow in a way that is profoundly affected by their sexuality.

Despite the marvelous value of this Freudian insight, there is a good deal of confusion, simplicism, silliness and nonsense in the present time in the transition away from dualism and once again towards a deep respect for the human body. One of the reasons for it is that we have no coherent meaning system to set a context which would enable us to cool the sexual revolution. I use "cool" here in the sense that Marshall McLuhan uses it when he says, "Sex will be cooler in years to come." He doesn't mean that it will be less fun; he means rather that it will be seen as more of a part of life. It will be integrated and diffused into the rest of life, and not so sharply segregated from it as is presently the case. We need, I think, if we are to accomplish this cooling of sex, a whole meaning system into which the insight of the sexual revolution can be placed.

Now I would suggest that such a meaning system is at the disposal of Christianity. Sex is the strongest urge in the human personality towards both personhood and community because the sex instinct moves against shame. Very clearly it forces us if we are to engage in sexual relationships to overcome physical shame, but it also and more importantly forces us to overcome psychic shame. For if our sexual relationship is to be satisfactory, we must begin to believe in ourselves. If we are to give ourselves totally to somebody else, we've got to have some conviction, at least tentative, about our own worth. And when we tentatively make that gift and the other accepts it and demands more of us, then we have an even stronger stimulus and challenge to more growth. So the sexual urge forces us to both personhood and community. We can resist it, we can hide behind our shame, we can hide behind our self-hatred, our timidity, our defensiveness, our narrowness, our complacency. We can hide behind it. We can lose ourselves in the twisted roots of our own self-hatred and yet, if we do, rather quickly the joys and the pleasures of sex come to an abrupt end. We may occasionally have moments of passion but the joy of a pervasive sexual relationship is destroyed when shame and self-hatred prevent us from having faith in ourself and faith in the other.

Marriage, or indeed any friendship, and all friendships have a sexual dimension to them, demands that we overcome our shame.

Marriage doesn't necessarily guarantee this but at least it creates a brief moment when it is possible. I've seen in many marriages a situation arising where a reasonably satisfying level of the sexual relationship begins to demand of people that, having put aside their physical shame, they now put aside their psychological shame. This is the critical moment in their life. If they can follow up that urge to put aside psychic shame, to make an act of faith in themself and to allow the other's act of faith to break through, then the possibilities of growth are limitless. In most instances I fear the possibilities are rejected, at least in part, but when we see these possibilities, we realize the tremendous power of sex to facilitate human growth. In passing, I intend to remain a celibate and this rhapsody about the possibility of sex in human fulfillment has nothing to do with whether one happens to occupy a bed at night with a member of the opposite sex because all friendship has a profoundly sexual dimension to it, all friendship grows through self-disclosure. All relationships are rooted in our body and self-revelation is essentially a sexual act. When we let others know about what we really are, we are disclosing ourself to them, we are revealing ourself to them, we are unveiling ourself to them, we are surrendering ourself to them. And in their response to this free, if frightened, gift, we begin to see what we are and begin to value what we are. Marriage is merely a paradigm of all friendships. Thus, too, the sexual union in marriage is merely the paradigm of the sexual dimension, the surrendering, the giving of the totality of oneself which happens in every friendship.

Now what can the Church say about sex? Well we can quote St. Augustine who said it is no more than a venial sin, or we can quote our Lord and St. Paul who, when they were looking for a human phenomenon that would most accurately express the nature of love between Christ and his Church, talked about the marital union. We can look at the Old Testament where the relationship between God and his people were described constantly in terms of the relationship of married lovers, the spouse pursuing his unfaithful wife. This sexual imagery pervades the Old and New Testaments.

I often think that if a person from another planet came and was told about the Freudian revolution, and was then made to read our Scriptures, he would feel quite confident that we were the ones who would be most agile and most eager to respond to the challenge of the sexual revolution. Alas, he would be wrong, because he would have found out that all we have been able to do so far in response to the sexual revolution is to prescribe the forms that are acceptable for family limitation. It has always struck me as interesting, ever since I began to study comparative religions, to realize what the symbolism is that most of us witness on Holy Saturday because in any religion the world has ever known, when you plunge a lighted candle into water, you are symbolizing sexual intercourse, and in every dream analysis that any psychoanalyst has ever engaged in, the lighted candle and the water represent marital intercourse. Now I am a little amused at the generations of Irish monsignors who did that right up there on the altar without knowing what they were doing. Most of us didn't know it. But the important point is that the people who put that symbolism in there knew what it stood for and they said the best way we have of symbolizing the union between Christ and his people that is consummated with the Resurrection is the consummation of love between a man and wife. Indeed, I think if we told that man from Mars of this symbol at the high point of our year of worship, he would scarcely believe that the only response we have made to Sigmund Freud is in things like *Humanae vitae.*

The third theme then is sex. Sex which drives us to both community and personhood. Sex which theologically symbolizes the love for Christ in his Church.

The fourth unit idea and the last one I will discuss is the idea of the sacred. Now I have news for you: God is alive. Not only alive and well in Argentina; He is alive and well everywhere. God is alive but science is dead. I'm not quite sure when science died but sometime in the last four or five years, when the death of God theologians were copping off all the newspaper publicity, science quietly died . . . assassinated, I suspect by a conspiracy headed by Paul Tillich, Franz Kafka, Soren Kierkegaard and Sig-

mund Freud. At the big secular university campuses today you
have to search very long and hard to find, outside of the philosophy
departments, a viable, logical positivist. My students accuse me
of being an empiricist, and that word around the University of
Chicago is double plus un-good. A positivist, a scientist in the
sense of scientism as a philosophy, an empiricist are viewed not
only suspiciously but contemptuously by the best of our students
at the best universities. From their viewpoint science has failed.
Even many of those who are students in the hard sciences and
who acquire skills as physicists and chemists reject agnosticism,
scientism, empiricism, and positivism as philosophies of life.

The younger generation is revolting against the inhumanity
and the failures of bourgeois, rational, liberal, positive science.
And so astrology, witchcraft, contemplation, vegetarian dieting,
meditation, the whole works are now flourishing around our
land. We go to the university book stores and what do we find?
One book store has a solid shelf from floor to ceiling filled with
books on witchcraft which people are buying and which I am
afraid they are practicing. (We recently had some unpleasantness
out at the University of Chicago [in the Sociology Department, as
a matter of fact] and an organization called Women's International Terrorist Corps in Hell, or WITCH, had a — I think they
call it a "sobot" — in front of the departmental office to put
a hex on the chairman of the Sociology Department. They screamed
and wailed and croaked and chanted implications and incantations
and slogans like, "Fie on thee, Morris Janowitz; a hex on thy
strategy." I don't know whether it worked or not. Nothing has
happened to Mr. Janowitz yet. If it does there are going to be
a lot of very frightened agnostics around our University.)

The psychedelic revolution, rock and roll, drugs, witchcraft,
astrology, the whole dramatic turn among the younger generation
is non-rational. It is, in fact, a turn to the sacred. From their
viewpoint science has failed and so once again they are ready
to try the mystical and the sacred. And of course it gets bizarre.
There were people who, in 1968, climbed up to Mt. Shasta in
California to await the end of the world. It didn't come. Whether
they wore white robes, as the eschatologists of the past did, I

don't know. The signs of the death of science, the death of the
rational are all around for those of us who want to see them.
It means, it seems to me, that the work of a great many theologians
to make Christianity relevant to scientific man — the work of
people like Bultmann, Cox, Bishop Robinson, the early Cox, in
any case — this work must now, for whatever intellectual wisdom
it has, be said to be precisely that which it set out not to be, irrelevant, because it is pretty hard to find scientific man on the
university campus. He has been replaced by something new; perhaps something very old — mythological man or, even worse,
superstitious man. One of my colleagues remarked to me, "You
know, before many more years are over, the Catholic Church is
going to end up as one of the staunchest defenders of unaided
human reason. We have battled with human reason for four
centuries and we are going to end up defending it when the choice
is reason or astrology." Then he smiled and said, "Of course,
that's not an unusual position for the Catholic Church because
we spent most of our first fifteen hundred years defending reason."
And then he shook his head and said, "But, my heavens, we are
sadly equipped to defend it now."

Now do I exaggerate? Perhaps for the point of emphasis,
somewhat. And yet, there is great restlessness among the younger
generation, great dissatisfaction with the organized, scientific, secular, profane world they see. The psychedelic revolution with
its emphasis on the primordial, the ceremonial, the mystical, the
sensual and the esthetic represents a revolt against rationalism, a
revolt that is widespread and profound and is going to be with
us for a long time.

It fascinates me in many ways: the hippies and the Merry
Pranksters are putting on vestments and we're taking them off;
we have stopped saying the rosary and they're wearing beads;
we are putting aside our Roman collars and they're donning
turtlenecks and Nehru jackets; we are urging our bishops to have
no part of pectoral crosses and they are wearing neck jewelry;
we are making our new low-church liturgy as symbol-free as
possible and they are creating their own liturgy which is filled
with romantic poetry and symbolism. This is another manifestation

of what I once called Greeley's Law. Greeley's Law goes as follows: As soon as everybody else starts it, Catholics stop it.

Why the revolt against reason? Why the turn to the sacred? It seems to me there are a number of reasons. The young people see that science has not been able to solve the problems of the world; that naive faith that the world is getting better has proved deceptive; that war, injustice, pollution, the inhumanity of relationships in the great corporate structures, none of these things have been eliminated by science. Indeed science has not even made much dent on them and may have made them worse. Secondly, they see that the rational society, the organized society, the scientific society has not been able to respond to the hungers of the human heart. And so they say, perhaps much too hastily, "Science is dead, we want no part of it." Many a poor sociologist who puts a table on the board is described not only as an empiricist by his students but even worse as a *naive* empiricist. The point that is relevant, and most of us knew it all along, is that reason at best is a constitutional monarch. Once it tries to become a tyrant, lording it over man's hunger for the mystical and the orgiastic, once it tries to squelch man's need to contemplate and his need to celebrate, his need to dream and his need to experience, then reason is in trouble. For either reason rules as a constitutional monarch or it will be overthrown as a tyrant and a dictator. Reason has tried during the last one hundred years or so to rule as a tyrant and psychedelia is the revolution against this tyranny.

Now what does the Church have to respond? We have two very strong traditions: the tradition of liturgy and the tradition of mysticism. Curiously enough, these are two traditions which seem in many things to be weakening precisely at the time when the world outside is most seriously concerned about them. Mr. Callahan informed us two or three summers ago that liturgy was no longer relevant and an increasing number of the bright, progressive young Catholics were saying the same thing, as though they simply do not recognize the resurgence of the liturgy in the world of the psychedelic. And mysticism. My heavens, who has seen a Catholic mystic lately? There are all kinds of revolutionary people in San Francisco, on the near north side of Chicago and in New York who are contemplating for hours each day, and how many of us still make our morning meditation? If we do not meditate or reflect, if we respond to mankind's hunger for the mystical and the mysterious with group discussion homilies, it seems that we have ignored not only some of the best in our own tradition but we have ignored one of the deepest hungers of modern man. So in our liturgical and mystical traditions, about which we seem to know so precious little today, we have I think more than adequate material to respond to the new quest for the sacred.

So these are four of the major themes which I see in the United States today, in particular in the younger population in the United States, themes which ought to delight theologians because if these are the problems that modern people have, if these are the challenges that modern college students are looking for, then theologians ought to be able to have a field day because there is a richness of resource with which they can respond to these questions that they have not even begun to tap.

In conclusion I might ask, "Why aren't these things recognized? Why haven't Catholic theologians, Catholic hierarchal leaders really read the signs of the times? Why don't they realize that the world is asking questions again to which their own tradition can speak directly, brilliantly, inspiringly?" I'm not sure of the answers to that but I have a hunch it is because we are losing our nerve. We see so much of the old Church we used to know falling apart. We see so much confusion and chaos and change. We seem so eager to believe that the worst is about to happen. Some of us seem to have so much invested in believing in disaster that we cannot lift up our eyes and see the signs on the horizon. Signs which are not like Scriptural clouds, no bigger than a man's hands, but signs which are, in fact, huge thunderheads coming down upon us at a frantic pace.

AVERY DULLES, S.J.

2 The Magisterium and Authority in the Church

Speaking as a theologian who is not a member of the official *magisterium*, I might fairly begin by admitting that theologians, as a class, have traditionally experienced an ambivalent relationship toward higher teaching authority — a mixture of love and hate, respect and resentment. The theologian is often protected by the *magisterium* when unfair charges are made against him by the laity or by his colleagues. Sometimes, however, he has to defend himself against members of the *magisterium*. As a spokesman for the Church, the theologian considers it his business to understand, explain, present, and defend Catholic doctrine. But he is also the critic, the innovator, the explorer — and in these capacities he is likely to chafe under the curbs of authoritative teaching, especially when the authorities decide against his own opinion.

In an amusing passage, the English convert, Ronald Knox, while still an Anglican, argued, tongue in cheek, for the abolition of bishops:

It has come to be seen that bishops and archbishops are not, as was commonly supposed hitherto, the vehicles of any extraordinary grace, which they passed on one to another, like a contagion, by the laying on of hands, but only another of these obstacles, which make the race of life so agreeable a pursuit. They exist to supervise our doctrines, and find them unscriptural, to control our religious practices, and forbid their continuance, thus enabling us to snatch a fearful joy while we are about 'em: in short, to give the Christian profession that spice of martyrdom, which it has so sorely lacked since the abolition of the amphitheatre.[1]

A certain "spice of martyrdom" has indeed been added to the lives of some theologians in recent months, and in view of the well publicized incidents no one will be inclined to question the urgency of our theme in this volume.

The problematic position of papal and episcopal teaching authority in our day has been set forth by no less an authority than Cardinal John Heenan: "Today what the pope says is by no means accepted as authoritative by all Catholic theologians. An article in the periodical *Concilium* is at least as likely to win their respect as a papal encyclical. The decline of the *magisterium* is one of the most significant developments in the post-Conciliar Church." [2]

The reasons behind this decline of the official *magisterium* are numerous and complex. We live in a revolutionary age, when the official spokesmen of any group have a hard time winning credibility. Whether in business, in government, or in the Church, people generally rely far more on reporters and analysts who hold no official position than on company officials, who are presumed to be poorly informed, and perhaps even hypocritical.

This prejudice against official spokesmen — widespread in all walks of life — is even intensified in the case of the Church, since the members of its *magisterium* are not chosen by the consent of the governed or by any demonstrated capacity in doctrinal matters. The gulf between intellectual competence and decisive power has become, at times, too wide for comfort. Why, people ask, should the right to commit the Church publicly be placed in the hand of officers who notoriously lack the requisite skill? [3]

1. Ronald Knox, *Essays in Satire* (New York: E. P. Dutton, 1930) pp. 48-49. I have modernized Knox's archaic spelling.
2. "The Authority of the Church," *The Tablet* (London) 222 (18 May 1968) p. 488.

In this situation little is to be gained by fervent appeals to the official charisms which allegedly go with the episcopal office or by passionate insistence on "religious submission of mind and will." The curtailment of open debate and criticism in the Church merely increases the suspicion that its teachings may be intellectually indefensible. It is often objected that the ecclesiastical conception of teaching authority is all too juridical, and neglects the fact that an assent to teaching cannot be a matter of merely voluntary obedience; it demands grounds for honest conviction.[4]

A full answer to questions such as these would involve us in a long discussion of ecclesiology, and would vastly exceed the limits of the present chapter. I mention the objections merely to put my remarks in context. On the basis of these prenotes I should like to address myself to three main points: (1) the existence in the Church of unofficial or non-hierarchical teaching; (2) the importance of official or hierarchical teaching; (3) the desired relationship between these two types of teaching.

1. Non-Hierarchical Teaching in the Church

As a basic paradigm of the Church, the validity of which can scarcely be challenged, let us take the Pauline image of the Body of Christ. In First Corinthians, chapter 12, Paul insists that the life of the Church is sustained by a great variety of ministries and competences, including those of apostles, prophets, teachers, and administrators. While these ministries are not all on the same

3. Regarding the process by which the Church, driven by the need to cope with heresy and various other pressures, gradually confined the teaching office to bishops, Tollinton remarks: "So the scholar surrendered his rights to the bishop, and when the bishop was also a scholar, all went well. But when he was not, the surrender, though inevitable, had its dangerous consequences." R. B. Tollinton, *Clement of Alexandria: A Study in Christian Liberalism* 2 (London: Williams & Norgate, 1914) p. 229; cf. R. P. C. Hanson, *Origen's Doctrine of Tradition* (London: S.P.C.K., 1954) p. 108.

4. Cf. R. A. McCormick, S.J., "Notes on Moral Theology," *Theological Studies* 29 (1968) pp. 714-18.

level of dignity, none of them is so exalted that it has no need of the rest. Just as the eye cannot say to the hand, "I have no need of you," so too, Paul implies, the apostle cannot do without the prophet, or the teacher without the administrator. There is a reciprocity of dependence of each upon the others. Again in Ephesians, Paul returns to the same theme, listing the ministries of apostles, prophets, evangelists, pastors, and teachers. All of these ministries, he says, contribute to the building up of the entire body in love (Cf. Eph. 4:11-16).

Applying this doctrine to the modern situation, one might say that the bishops, as one order in the Church, cannot claim for themselves the totality of teaching power. Providence ordains that there should be other teachers, including charismatics (such as prophets) and scholars (such as theologians). Each type of minister has his own gift and must be allowed, as the phrase has it, to "do his thing."

In the documents of Vatican II, this organically diversified view of the Church was accepted. *Lumen gentium,* in Chapter 2 (no. 12) declared that the People of God as a whole is a living witness to Christ and shares in his prophetic office. In Chapter 4 this was further specified by the statement that the laity are sharers in the "priestly, prophetic, and kingly offices of Christ," [5] and that they should exercise their freedom as sons of God in expressing themselves about things of concern to the Church, making full use of their "knowledge, competence, or outstanding ability." [6]

The Pastoral Constitution, *Gaudium et spes,* frankly recognized that humanity is entering a new age and thus intimated that new styles of teaching authority are to be expected. Fresh avenues of knowledge, it stated, have been paved by the rapid advances of the human and social sciences as well as by natural science and technology.[7] Theological inquiry must keep in close contact

5. *Lumen gentium* no. 31; W. M. Abbott, S.J., ed.; *The Documents of Vatican II* (New York: Association Press, 1966) p. 57.
6. *Lumen gentium,* no. 37; Abbott, p. 64.
7. *Gaudium et spes,* no. 54; Abbott, p. 260.

with these other sciences and seek to collaborate with them in the better understanding of the faith.[8] In the complex world of our day, said the Constitution, it would be a grave mistake to imagine that the hierarchy is omniscient. "Let the layman not imagine that his pastors are always experts, that to every problem which arises, however complicated, they can readily give him a concrete solution, or even that such is their mission." [9] In order to cope with the rapid changes presently occurring, the Church has to rely on laymen well versed in various specialties. "With the help of the Holy Spirit, it is the task of the entire People of God, especially pastors and theologians, to hear, distinguish, and interpret the many voices of our age, and to judge them in the light of the divine Word." [10] For this reason, continued the Constitution, "It is to be hoped that many laymen will receive an appropriate formation in the sacred sciences." [11] Finally, echoing *Lumen gentium,* the Pastoral Constitution declared: "Let it be recognized that all the faithful, clerical and lay, possess a lawful freedom of inquiry and thought, and the freedom to express their minds humbly and courageously about matters in which they enjoy competence." [12]

It seems evident, therefore, both from Scripture and from the official documents of the modern Church, that sound doctrine does not in every case flow down to the theologians and the laity from the top officials in the Church. If the Spirit dwells in the entire Body, enlivening all the members and breathing as He wills, doctrinal initiatives can begin from below as well as from above. Alert Christians, listening to the many voices of our age, may be expected to have something intelligent to say to the hierarchy.[13]

---

8. *Gaudium et spes,* no. 62; Abbott, p. 270.
9. *Gaudium et spes,* no. 43; Abbott, p. 244.
10. *Gaudium et spes,* no. 44; Abbott, p. 246.
11. *Gaudium et spes,* no. 62; Abbott, p. 270.
12. *Ibid.*
13. This point is forcefully made by Norbert J. Rigali, S.J., "Right, Duty and Dissent," *Catholic World* 208 (Feb. 1969) pp. 214-17, esp. p. 217.

The theologian, then, cannot be rightly regarded as a mere agent of the hierarchical teaching authority. His task is not simply to repeat what the official *magisterium* has already said, or even to expound and defend what has already become official teaching, but, even more importantly, to discover what has not yet been taught.[14] He must seek to discern and to formulate "what the Spirit is saying to the Churches" (Apoc. 2:7). Paul VI, after alluding to this biblical phrase, went on to speak of the theologian's task of interpreting "the general mental outlook of our age and the experiences of men" and his duty to transmit his insights to the hierarchy for the enrichment of the entire Church.[15]

2. Hierarchical Teaching in the Church

The second problem with which I wish to deal grows out of the points already made. If the Church is not a purely juridical society, in which all sound teaching flows down from the highest officers, but a Spirit-filled Body such as I have described, is there really any need or room for an institutional hierarchy? Cannot the society allow itself to be directed by the various movements stirred up here and there, now and again, by the Holy Spirit, and learn to live with both the tensions and agreements which seem to be the lot of such a body? Does the Church really need a juridical power to adjudicate conflicts of opinion? Can any juridical power, in fact, effectively settle such conflicts?

Questions such as these cannot be solved by purely abstract reasoning, without some attention to the kind of basic constitution which was historically given to the Church. Yet there are factors in the nature of the Christian faith which seem to call for some official teaching authority in the Church. To begin with, one may point out that the Church is not simply an association

14. *Ibid.*
15. Paul VI, "Address to the International Congress on the Theology of Vatican II, *Libentissimo sane animo*" (Oct. 1, 1966); A.A.S. 58 (1966) 889-96, p. 892. E.T., *The Pope Speaks* 11 (1966) 348-55, p. 352.

for the advancement of religious knowledge. It differs radically from a professional group, such as the American Historical Society. The Church is a witnessing community. It is bound together not simply by a common method but by a common creed. Its corporate existence and its life of witness, worship, and service are premised on what God is believed to have revealed in Jesus Christ.

The Christian faith was communicated in the first instance not to any particular individual but to the Church as a group. Any individual person, even though he be a pope or a bishop, is capable of losing the faith. Only the Church as a society enjoys the divine promise of indefectibility. In other words, the faith inheres in the Church inseparably.

For the Church to perdure in the world as Christ's authentic witness it must have some way of publicly expressing its faith. From the earliest centuries, it has repeatedly had to define itself against heretical distortions, such as Gnosticism in its various forms. In modern times this danger of falsification continues to haunt the Church. For instance, the "German Christians" in the 1930s sought to popularize a Nazified version of the Gospel. In our own country some have sought to find Biblical warrant for white or black racism. Or, to take a less extreme example, have understood the axiom "Outside the Church no salvation" in a harsh and unacceptable way, apparently consigning to perdition all but Roman Catholics. Against aberrations such as these, the Church needs ways of authentically expressing its genuine faith. At the present time, when the stresses and strains on traditional faith have grown to new intensity, the Church, if it lacked a *magisterium*, would rapidly cease to stand for anything determinate. It might be overrun by the forces of public opinion. Thus the times call not for a dismantling but for a rehabilitation of the *magisterium*.

The difficult questions about the *magisterium*, for most Catholic Christians, relate not so much to its existence as to its nature. It is not easy to say who has the right to speak for the Church, what matters lie within the scope of its competence, how great is the binding force of its decrees, and what are the responsibilities of those who find themselves in disagreement. In this chapter

I shall focus my attention on the first question: who constitute the members of the *magisterium?*

The primary members of the *magisterium,* it would seem, are those who exercise the pastoral ministry on the highest level. The bishops, since they are charged with the supervision of the preaching and sacramental life of the Church, became involved in doctrinal questions in the early centuries. It was their task to admit or exclude from the sacraments, to license preachers, and to regulate catechetical schools. Thus it was natural that doctrinal disputes were referred to them for adjudication. Especially after the conversion of Constantine their position in the Church was assimilated to that of senators in the Roman Empire.[16] Since that time they have always been regarded as the supreme spokesmen of the official teaching of the Church.

Vatican Council II, far from restricting the teaching authority of bishops, raised it to unprecedented heights. Partly to offset the excessive papal centralization of the preceding century, the Council invoked the principle of collegiality and assigned to the universal episcopate the supreme jurisdictional and magisterial powers which Vatican I had recognized in the Roman pontiff. "The order of bishops is the successor of the college of the apostles in teaching authority and pastoral rule." [17] "The episcopal order is the subject of supreme and full power in the universal Church." [18] By thus extending to the bishops collectively the powers previously ascribed to the pope, the recent Council inevitably raised the question, no longer of papal, but now of episcopal, absolutism. As we have seen in the first section of this paper, the Council made it clear, in numerous documents, that the public teaching of the official *magisterium* is only one of many elements in the total witness of the Church. The hierarchy does

16. Francis Dvornik, *The Ecumenical Councils* (Twentieth Century Encyclopedia of Catholicism, 82) (New York: Hawthorn, 1961) 9-14. Cf. his article, "Councils, General, history of," *New Catholic Encyclopedia* 4:373-77.

17. *Lumen gentium,* no. 22; Abbott, p. 43.

18. *Ibid.*

not have exclusive, absolute, or unlimited doctrinal authority.

The primary task which faces the post-Conciliar Church is to find a proper relationship between the juridically supreme teaching power of the bishops and the equally undeniable right of the faithful in general, and competent experts in particular, to exercise their doctrinal responsibility. The decline of the *magisterium,* to which Cardinal Heenan refers, is partly due to the fact that the universal episcopate has not yet achieved a satisfactory working relationship with the intellectuals and theologians in the Church.

3. Relationship Between *Magisterium* and Theologians

Lest the relationship be totally misunderstood from the outset, it must be recognized that there is a qualitative difference between the authentic *magisterium* of the hierarchy and the doctrinal *magisterium* of the scholar. The bishop and the theologian, while they are both teachers, have different roles. The bishop's task is to give public expression to the doctrine of the Church and thus to lay down norms for preaching, worship, and Christian life. His concern, therefore, is primarily and directly pastoral. The theologian, on the other hand, is concerned with reflectively analyzing the present situation of the Church and of the faith, with a view to deepening the Church's understanding of revelation and in this way opening up new and fruitful channels of pastoral initiative. To be faithful to his vocation, the theologian often has to wrestle with unanswered questions and to construct tentative working hypotheses which he submits to criticism from his colleagues. His goal is not to spread doubt and confusion — though he is often accused of seeking to do so — but rather to face the real questions and to pioneer as best he can the future paths of Christian thought and witness.[19]

---

19. On the distinction between the teaching powers of bishops and theologians see especially: L. Orsy, S.J., "Academic Freedom and the Teaching Church," *Thought* 43 (1968) pp. 485-98; R. A. Mackenzie, S.J., "The

Because of this difference in vocation it is clear that the theologians should not seek to substitute themselves for the public teaching authority in the Church, nor should the bishops turn over their teaching responsibility to the theologians. Only the bearers of the official *magisterium* can formulate judgments in the authoritative way. They may of course accept and approve the work of private theologians, but when they do so it is they — not the theologians — who give official status to the theories they approve.

The bishop's task, therefore, does not require him to be a theologian in his own right. He is not supposed to reduplicate, on a higher and more authoritative level, what the theologian does in a less official way. Still less is he supposed to decide doctrinal questions without paying any heed to what theologians are saying. He has no charism which operates mechanically or magically, even though he fails to take measures to avoid mistakes. In order to make good doctrinal decisions the *magisterium* has to bring the best and most creative available theological talent to bear upon the problem which is to be decided. It has to listen to what the professional thinkers are saying to lead the dialogue, to engineer a measure of consensus, to discern the spirits at work, and to render pastorally sound decisions.

Speaking of ecclesiastical government in general, Congar remarks that the Church has traditionally been governed by conciliar procedures, not by solitary personal decisions.[20] Cyprian, who was a theologian, a bishop, and a saint besides, enunciated the principle: "I have made it a rule, ever since the beginning of my episcopate, to make no decision merely on the strength of my own personal opinion, without consulting you [the priests and deacons] and without the approbation of my people." [21] In another

Function of Scholars in Forming the Judgment of the Church," *Theology of Renewal* 2 (ed. L. K. Shook, New York: Herder & Herder, 1968) pp. 118-32.

20. Y. Congar, O.P., *Jalons Pour une Théologie du Laïcat* (Unam Sanctam 23) (2nd ed., Paris: Cerf, 1954) p. 338. E.T., by Donald Attwater, *Lay People in the Church* (Westminster, Md.: Newman, 1957) p. 237.

21. Ep. 14:4. Ed. G. Hartel, *C.S.E.L.*, III/2, p. 512.

letter Cyprian wrote: "Bishops must not only teach but also learn, for the best teacher is he who daily grows and advances by learning better." [22]

In his address to the International Congress on the Theology of Vatican II, in 1966, Paul VI acknowledged the dependence of the *magisterium* on the work of theologians:

> Without the help of theology, the *magisterium* could indeed safeguard and teach the faith, but it would experience great difficulty in acquiring that profound and full measure of knowledge which it needs to perform its task thoroughly, for it considers itself to be endowed not with the charism of revelation or inspiration, but only with that of the assistance of the Holy Spirit . . . .
>
> Deprived of the labor of theology, the *magisterium* would lack the tools it needs to weld the Christian community into a unified concert of thought and action, as it must do for the Church to be a community which lives and thinks according to the precepts and norms of Christ.[23]

Occasionally the *magisterium* issues pronouncements without adequate theological consultation. In spite of all efforts to enforce acceptance by appeals to the authority of office, these pronouncements become an embarrassment to the Church. Some years later they have to be corrected or retracted, and as a result the general confidence of the faithful in the *magisterium* is undermined. An obvious case in point would be the series of responses issued by the Pontifical Biblical Commission during the aftermath of the Modernist crisis. Many of these decrees are now dead letters. In the long run, it would have been better for the authority of the *magisterium* if more liberal scripture scholars had been called in to share in the drafting of these responses. The same may be said of certain Encyclicals of the anti-Modernist period,

---

22. Ep. 74:10. *C.S.E.L.*, III/2, p. 807.
23. *A.A.S.* 58 (1966) p. 892f.; *The Pope Speaks* 11 (1966) p. 352.

such as *Spiritus Paraclitus* and even sections of *Humani generis*
which have, in retrospect, proved unduly restrictive, and were
not reaffirmed by Vatican Council II.

As Karl Rahner has noted, there is nothing in the nature of
the case which requires that the episcopate should always be
a conservative force, and that the theologians should represent
the radical or critical wing.[24] Ideally, bishops and theologians
should appear as brothers in a single unified community of faith
and witness. The highest officers, no less than the theologians,
should be concerned with adapting the Church to the needs of
the times, and with leading it forward into God's future. This is
an important part of the pastoral office, which too often conceives
of its task in a negative and restraining way. On the other hand
the theologians, no less than the official *magisterium,* should be
concerned with faithful obedience to the word of God as it
comes to us through the Bible and the monuments of tradition.
In recent times theologians have tended to become increasingly
venturesome in advancing new and untried theories. Not surprising-
ly, the bishops, conscious of their responsibility to safeguard the
ancient Christian heritage, have become increasingly suspicious
of creative theology. Many bishops habitually consult only the
more conservative theologians — those who are likely to represent
the state of theology a generation ago.

As a result, a vicious circle has been set up. Theologians,
distrustful of the procedures by which official decisions are
reached, are increasingly critical of the *magisterium.* Often they
feel that they cannot conscientiously defend one or another of
its pronouncements. If they are not permitted to voice their
dissent within the Church they turn increasingly to secular publications and news media. Some theologians, feeling that they cannot operate successfully under the *aegis* of the hierarchy, prefer
to pursue a purely academic kind of theology in secular institutions.

The increasing independence of theology from the *magisterium,*

24. K. Rahner, S.J., "Theology and the Magisterium," *Theology Digest*
(sesquicentennial issue, 1968) 4-16, p. 15.

while it is not entirely bad, could seriously weaken the corporate witness of the Church. While preserving its scientific integrity and autonomy, theology should be conscious of its ties with the *magisterium*. The theologian cannot properly perform his task unless he is solicitous of keeping his solidarity with the Church, to which the Christian revelation has been primarily committed. He must feel co-responsible, as Suenens would say, for its teaching, and therefore anxious that his personal charisms of wisdom and knowledge should redound to the benefit of the whole Church, making it better able to articulate its faith.[25]

In order to restore a proper working relationship it might be desirable to institutionalize to some degree the participation of theologians in the Church's decision-making processes. Some interesting models for such institutionalization can be found in the middle ages, when the theologian was considered to have quasi-hierarchical status. In many medieval texts, as Congar points out, the *ordo doctorum* is listed after the *ordo cardinalium,* the *ordo episcoporum,* and the *ordo praelatorum,* i.e., as an instance of the hierarchy.[26] The university theology faculties played a normal role in the settlement of theological disputes and in the formulation of official doctrine. Thus the decrees of the Council of Vienne (1311-12), by order of Pope Clement V, were not made official until they had been submitted to the universities.[27]

It might be profitable to study anew the medieval conception of the General Council with a view to assessing its positive value for our times. Of many medieval councils one may say what Brian Tierney says of the Fourth Lateran Council (1215) — that it "was not simply a synod of bishops but an 'assembly of estates' to which all the constituent elements of the Church were sum-

25. Cf. L.-J. Suenens, *Corresponsibility in the Church* (E.T., by Francis Martin) (New York: Herder & Herder, 1968), Chap. 6, "The Coresponsibility of Theologians."

26. *Vraie et Fausse Réforme dans l'Église* (Unam Sanctam 20) (Paris: Cerf, 1950) p. 516.

27. *Ibid.,* p. 517.

moned either in person or through representatives." [28] Not in-
frequently at the medieval councils non-bishops in attendance
were given the right to exercise a deliberative vote. When some
opposition was voiced to this procedure at the Council of Con-
stance (1415), Cardinal Pierre d'Ailly, among others, argued for
the view which eventually prevailed. In the course of his famous
speech, he particularly urged that theologians should have the
power to vote:

> One cannot exclude from decisive vote the doctors of
> sacred theology, civil and canon law, especially the theo-
> logians, who have received the authority to preach and teach
> everywhere. This is no small authority over the faithful. It
> greatly exceeds that of an individual bishop or an ignorant
> abbot or titular.[29]

In the later middle ages the papacy was in danger of being
excessively enslaved by the *magisterium* of theologians and by
the interventions of secular princes. Since the sixteenth century,
the Church has been understandably anxious to keep the freedom
of the *magisterium* to go against the desires and opinions of any
particular group. In some non-Catholic bodies, the highest officers
have so little doctrinal power that the group as such can hardly
utter anything but platitudes. The prophetic freedom of the
magisterium in the Catholic Church is an asset which should
not be lightly bargained away under pretext of democratization.
It is good that the Church, through its highest officers, should
be able to take a strong stand, if necessary, against the tide
of public opinion. If the Church could no longer champion
an unpopular cause, the salt would quickly lose its savor.

28. Brian Tierney, *Foundations of Conciliar Theory* (Cambridge, Eng.:
    University Press, 1955) p. 47.
29. J. D. Mansi, ed., *Sacrorum Conciliorum . . . Collectio* (Venice, 1784)
    27:561. Cf. H. Küng, *Structures of the Church* (E.T., by Salvator
    Attansio) (New York: T. Nelson, 1964) p. 88.

Without introducing complicated juridical procedures that would paralyze the *magisterium,* the modern Church should seek better ways of assuring that official doctrinal decisions are regularly made in the light of the best theological advice available. In practice the bishops cannot fulfill their teaching office without wide consultation and consensus on the part of scholars and intellectuals of various schools of thought. Vatican Council II achieved splendid results because the most talented theologians of many nations were involved in the drafting of the more important documents, and because the successive drafts were submitted to the criticism of numerous experts, including even non-Catholic theologians, before being brought on the Council floor.

To recommend how the theologians of a particular country might relate themselves more effectively to its national hierarchy demands careful thought and creative experimentation. In principle it might be possible to send theologian representatives, chosen by professional societies or by university and seminary faculties, to take part in national synods or bishops' conferences. It might also be possible for the draft declarations of such meetings to be submitted to criticism and review by the theological community, or by other competent experts, before being formally promulgated. Such procedures would not, in my opinion, undermine confidence in the value of such declarations; it might on the contrary win them added support.

There is no reason in principle why the names of theologians who collaborate with the hierarchy on official statements should be kept secret, as though only the words of bishops were graced with the unction of the Holy Spirit. Nor is there any good reason why disagreements among bishops on doctrinal questions should be kept secret. In American political life the conflicting views of senators and congressmen are public knowledge, and this does not result in any disrespect for duly established laws.

Whether voting powers should be given to non-bishops when they meet with bishops in ecclesiastical councils is a question that cannot be answered in the abstract. In the last analysis, voting in Church councils is valuable as a means of discerning the exis-

tence of a consensus. For some questions it might be important
to find out whether the consensus is present not simply among
bishops but among theologians and other experts. Since Church
councils do not ordinarily operate on a basis of simple majorities,
one could provide against the contingency that a majority of the
bishops might be voted down on some doctrinal question by a
majority of theologians together with a minority of bishops. The
fact that the deliberative vote, even in modern ecumenical Councils, has never been confined to the bishops, indicates that theologians and others could be invited to express their adherence by
a deliberative vote. In this way they would become more evidently
participants in the *magisterium* of the Church.

In conclusion, then, who constitute the *magisterium?* If we
think of the *magisterium* as a function, rather than as a determinate body, we can leave the answer somewhat vague. The highest
officers of the Church — the pope, the other bishops, and perhaps
certain other prelates — by virtue of their office, have general
charge of the Church's teaching as well as its worship and discipline. But these prelates are not, by themselves, the teachers. In
order to teach effectively they must "tune in" on the theological
wisdom that is to be found in the community, and bring it to
expression. Thus the theologians are not totally external to the
magisterium, considered as a function or process.

All of this could perhaps be summarized in a metaphor. One
may say that in the Church of God there is an abundance of light
provided by the gospel of Christ and the inner illumination of the
Spirit. In the total Church this light is widely diffused among individuals and groups which are differently gifted. The task of the
hierarchy in any given region, and in the world at large, is to
gather up all this radiance of light and bring it into focus. The
official teaching of the Church emanates indeed from the episcopate,
but not from the episcopate alone. The popes and bishops are
rather the lens by which the light, issuing from all who are competent by faith and scholarship, is brought to a focus and expressed. By gathering up and concentrating the diffused light, the
hierarchy intensifies its splendor, and enables it to be refracted,

with greater power, into the world. All the members of the Church, and especially those who seek to understand and teach the faith, must contribute, in their distinctive ways, to the public doctrine of the Church, in order that the Church may continue to be, in this troubled and divided world, the light of the nations and the catalyst of reconciliation.

EDWARD D. O'CONNOR, C.S.C.

3 The Pentecostal Movement Among Catholic College Students

There is a special difficulty about defining the Pentecostal Movement in the Catholic Church, due to the fact that it has no peculiar ideology whereby it may be identified. When you ask, "What is the leading idea that guides or inspires this movement?" the answer is simply that it has none, other than those doctrines that have guided and inspired Christianity from the beginning. Of course it places a certain emphasis on the idea of the Holy Spirit, but no more so than you find in some parts of the New Testament. It is only by contrast with the neglect of the Holy Spirit in the past that one can say that the Pentecostal Movement emphasizes him. In fact, *many* of the great Christian doctrines seem to mean more to the Pentecostals than to the average Christian; but they are the same doctrines.

Likewise, the Pentecostal movement is not characterized by a methodology or a technique. It is not, for example, a sort of Christianized sensitivity program or group dynamics. Pentecostals do hold informal prayer meetings much more than other Christians; but prayer meetings were around before Pentecostalism, and are held by others than Pentecostals. For the rest, Pentecostals do the same things, religiously speaking, that other Catholics do: they go to Mass, receive the sacraments, and say pretty much the same prayers as others. They spend a great deal more time in prayer, and in the reading of Scripture, than the typical Catholic; but this is not a method, but a result of the Pentecostal movement.

Is it then possible to speak of Pentecostalism as a movement at all? Indeed it is; there is no possible doubt but that it is a movement, which began at an identifiable time and place, has spread with a manifest continuity from one person to another, and is readily distinguishable from other movements, as well as the lack of movement, which can be seen in the Christian world alongside of it. But what characterizes this movement is not what its members think, or what they do, but what has been done to them. Pentecostals are not people moving (i.e., by their own determination) in a certain direction, but people who *have been moved*. They have been moved by the death and resurrection of Christ, and by the sending of the Holy Spirit — these same great events of Salvation History which are the foundation of all Christianity but which leave so many Christians unmoved. The difference between Pentecostals and other Christians is comparable to the difference between the apostles before and after Pentecost (in fact, that is precisely why they are called Pentecostal Christians). The descent of the Holy Spirit did not give the apostles a new Gospel other than that which they had already been preaching for some three years but it gave them light to appreciate that Gospel, and a power to preach it, which they had not had before.

I realize that this comparison sounds invidious, and this I regret. I do not mean, for example, to suggest that only Pentecostals have received the Holy Spirit; this is certainly not the case. I admit also that the comparison needs considerable qualification and supplementation. But when this has been done, the comparison remains substantially valid. Pentecostalism is not characterized by an idea or a method, but by an experience — an experience of the reality and the power and the goodness of God. Pentecostals are Christians to whom St. Paul can say, "Now you have come to know God, or rather to be known by him" (Gal. 4:9).

There is a certain quasi-visible sign by which the Pentecostal movement can be identified, namely, the return of the charisms that we have tended to associate with the primitive Church. The most common of these charisms is the gift of tongues — that is, the power to pray and to praise God in a tongue that one has not learned naturally. Fairly common also are the charisms of interpretation of tongues and of prophecy, and the word of wisdom and knowledge. The gift of healing and the gift of miracles have also appeared, but they are more rare.

These charisms are in a certain sense spectacular, and have drawn attention to the Pentecostal movement, giving it also its second name, "the charismatic renewal." In truth, the term *spectacular* is somewhat inappropriate, because these gifts normally function in a quiet way, and those who use them rightly do not seek to create a sensation. All I mean by this term is that there is something visible and remarkable about the charisms which compels people to pay attention and take a stand. If a man prays quietly and loves his fellow man dearly, that does not make news, even though it is the most precious fruit of Christianity. But if someone is reported to be working miracles or speaking in strange tongues, you cannot help but take note of him. You are put more or less under compulsion to take a stand. Either you must declare, "The hand of God is here," and follow this judgment out to its consequences, or you must say, "The man is an imposter," and seek to be rid of him. But you can hardly remain indifferent.

So it is that the Pentecostal movement has been marked by the renewal of charismatic activity. But it would be a mistake to identify the mark with the reality itself. The charisms are a sign but not the substance of the Pentecostal movement. The substance lies in an experience and a movement that occurs in the innermost depths of human hearts: an experience of the power of God, like that of which Christ said, "Wait here in the city until you are clothed with power from on high" (Lk. 24:49), and a movement of love — of that love which "is poured forth in our hearts by the Holy Spirit, who has been given to us" (Rom. 5:5).

I said that the Pentecostal movement began at a definite time and place. I mean that only in the sense possible to an historical movement involving multitudes of people. Origins inevitably have a certain complexity and diffuseness. In truth, this movement is tributary to many, many different streams that we could never finish tracing back. But to speak in the rough terms appropriate to human history, we can say that in the American Protestant church the Pentecostal movement began at the turn of the century. In the Catholic Church it can be traced to a number of beginnings, most of which fall within the past ten years. But the main stream began in the fall of 1966, with two young professors at Duquesne University in Pittsburgh. They were active in various liturgical, apostolic and retreat projects at the University and in the city, and were praying that the Holy Spirit might fill them with his gifts to make their work more effective. Their prayer was answered far beyond their expectations, and had repercussions in the lives of a circle of people around them. From Duquesne, the movement spread to Notre Dame and to the student parish at Michigan State University. From these centers, and from other independent sources, it has spread across the country, and now is found from Massachusetts to Oregon, from Florida to California, and at innumerable places in between. It seldom seems to get very big in any one locality — most prayer groups number perhaps between 30 and 50 people (however, in Ann Arbor, Cleveland, and Chicago there are exceptionally large groups which number in the hundreds), but new sparks keep spreading the fire to new places with great rapidity. The main centers of the movement at the present time seem to be at Ann Arbor and at the University of Notre Dame but this, too, is probably a transitory situation. A national meeting of some 50 leaders from all over the country was held at Ann Arbor in January of 1969, and another one was held at Notre Dame for the weekend of April 25, 1969, at which several hundred attended.[1] Because the movement started at the college level, and spread first of all at that level, a rather high percentage of its adherents are college students. But it is spreading now to all brackets and social classes; it includes the young, the aged, and the middle-aged; students and professors, professional men and day laborers, priests and religious of many communities.

The key to the Pentecostal movement is what is known as the

---

1. In fact, over 400 registered for it, in addition to numerous casual visitors not registered.

"Baptism in the Holy Spirit." Sometimes this occurs in one over-whelming and unforgettable experience, when the power of the Holy Spirit seems to descend upon a person as the glory of God descended upon the Tent of Meeting in the desert. The person finds himself filled with the presence of God, transfused with the love of God, and overcome with the power and the glory of God. He may weep for the sheer joy of the experience, or burst out in the praises of God, speaking, perhaps even singing, in a new tongue. More often, however, the baptism comes quietly and "not so as to be observed by men." In the language of Gerard Manley Hopkins, "It gathers to a greatness, like the ooze of oil crushed." Only by the effects it leaves can one detect that it has taken place. One cannot say "Here is where it happened," or "there," but simply, "Lo, the Kingdom of God is (already) within you." Between these two extremes, the variations and gradations are numerous.

Ordinarily, the baptism in the Spirit is, as it were, mediated to a person by the testimony and the prayers of others who have already received it. They gather around him and lay their hands on his head, praying for the Holy Spirit to descend and fill him. But not rarely a person receives the baptism simply by hearing others speak about it, or even while reading a book.

It is by its effects on people that the Pentecostal movement will ultimately have to be judged. The orthodoxy of its inspiration only shows that it *may be* good. The upright character and good sense of its adherents gives us a certain *a priori* confidence in their witness. But the question, whether the Holy Spirit has really intervened here, can only be decided on the basis of the effects. "By their fruits you shall know them," said Christ when he warned against false prophets (Mt. 7:15ff.). I will speak here only of fruits of which I myself have been a personal witness. Even these are so abundant that I can do no more than give samples.[2]

---

2. Different people are of course affected in different ways. In the summary that is to follow, I don't mean to give the impression that all these

KNOWLEDGE OF GOD

The most radical effect can only be called simply the *knowledge of God*. For those who have been touched by the Holy Spirit in the Pentecostal experience, God is no longer a vague, distant figure, but a reality they have encountered. He has *demonstrated* his reality to them. "He is really real!" is a phrase used very often, as human language is tortured in the effort to express that which cannot be put into words. "At that moment, I really knew that God exists," says Jim B. about the time when a friend read him a passage from Scripture that pierced him to the heart.

Instead of the doubts that plague most believers,[3] the Pentecostals are impressed and overwhelmed by the reality of God who has met them with such power. They have been touched somehow by his presence. Many people *believe* in the presence of God, but are not effectively influenced by it. But these people tend (in varying degrees, of course), to live and abide in it, as an atmosphere that engulfs them, and a weight that presses constantly upon them.

Likewise, God is no longer a peripheral figure on their horizon; he has established himself right at the center of their lives and their thought. They turn to him spontaneously. When they have a decision to make, they ask, "What does God want of me here?" When anything happens to them, their characteristic ques-

---

effects are found in all people, or that any given effect is realized to the same degree in everyone. I am merely collecting in one survey statements which have struck me as the typical effects of the Pentecostal experience, with the understanding that they are realized in varying degrees and with different modulations in different persons.

3. Later on, doubts may, and frequently do, occur, about the reality of the Pentecostal experience. This is altogether normal; for when a transitory grace has passed, one can no longer even remember the grace itself (since no idea, no image, is adequate to it), but only something associated with it. But the lasting effect of the experience is to leave people with a remarkably firm conviction about the existence of God, even when it does not deliver them altogether from the temptation to doubt.

tion is, "What is God trying to say to me?" Not that they seek superstitiously, by contrived imagination, to force meanings upon coincidences; but aware that God is in all things and governs all events by his Providence, they do not let their minds stop at the human event, but always seek by faith to reach the Lord of History who lies behind it.

One student declared, "I have always tried to be faithful in giving God a part of my life. But now I see that he is not content with a part; he demands everything. And by his grace, I'm going to give him everything."

A girl from St. Mary's College said, "I used to consider myself very religious. I tried to offer God everything I did. But now he has made me realize that I was hiding him behind other people. He is not content to be left in the background; he demands to be right in the center of the stage. He wants to be loved in himself, directly, not just in other men."

These people know God as a person; they have a personal relationship with him. One senses personal familiarity in the way they speak of him. He is not just an entity about whom they have learned some lessons; nor the ground of being to which they subscribe. In attempting to say what the Spirit has done to them, many have used such expressions as, "For the first time in my life, I really knew God. Previously, I had known *about* him, but that's not the same as knowing *him*."

It is as though someone had opened a secret door in the center of their being, and, like Alice stepping through the looking glass, they had entered in and discovered a whole new world they had never known was there. They had heard of it, indeed, but as something strange and unreal, unrelated to their experience. Now, suddenly, they find themselves within it, able to move about in it.

In particular, they know his love. They *know* that they are loved. In a personal, experiential way, they have felt his love embracing and sustaining them. As a result, they are able to respond to him also with true love. Whenever good Christians speak of loving God, often what they really mean is, "I know I ought to love him, I want to love him, and I try to love him."

They love him in intention. But many will frankly and sometimes desperately admit, "I don't know what it means to love God. I don't know whether I love him or not. How can you love someone you have never met?" What usually passes for the love of God does not look much like that which we call love in human relationships. When a man and a woman are in love with one another, they know it; they know what love is. But our love of God usually bears very little resemblance to this. It has not the warmth or strength, the consuming character of human love. It is a pure act of will, without passion.

Many people will defend this state of affairs by saying that the substance of love does not consist in emotions but in an act of will. The test of our love of God is not whether we feel it, but whether we keep his commandments. Of course, this is true; Christ himself gave us this criterion (Jn. 14:15, 21), and every one of us must expect periods in which his love for God manifests itself in no other way than obedience. However, it is also true that love is more than obedience. An employee may obey an employer whom he detests, likewise a soldier his commanding officer; this is not love. And when love is strong, full and rich, it does not normally remain confined in a pure act of will, but arouses harmonics in the emotions. No doubt St. John of the Cross and St. Teresa of Avila tell us that in its highest and purest form, the love of God leaves the emotions untouched, because they are too gross for it; but that is not the problem of the ordinary Christian. It is rather because our love of God is so weak and rudimentary that it appears as sheer volition. It is real enough to bring us salvation, but so under-developed that it does not show its true face. If we loved another human being in this way, we would hesitate to call it love. Many Christians never discover that it is possible to love God by anything better than this pallid intention. But where the Holy Spirit has descended in power, people love God with love that is unmistakable. They love God with warmth and affection, as a man loves a woman or a child his parents. God becomes truly and very dear to them.

This knowledge and love of God are often concretized in a deep sense of God's fatherliness. The *Our Father,* recited slowly and thoughtfully, is a favorite prayer at Pentecostal meetings, and many other prayers are addressed to God as Father. A priest told me the greatest grace he had received through the movement was that of *realizing* that God is our Father. He had always known this and believed it, but now he *experienced* it, and felt towards God the attitude of a son toward his father. Is this not what St. Paul meant when he wrote, "God has sent the Spirit of his Son into our hearts, crying '*Abba,* Father'" (Gal. 4:6)?

The same priest added that this grace likewise enabled him to look upon other men as his brothers in a way he never had before. He had done so, of course, by faith and deliberate resolution but it used to require a deliberate and difficult effort to treat disagreeable persons as brothers, whereas, now, in a more spontaneous and powerful fashion, he felt a brotherly affection for them.[4]

The knowledge and love of God show up in the way people speak about him. Most people, and especially most Americans, are very diffident in speaking of God. Pious parents will tell their children about him, and priests, rabbis and ministers are expected to speak about him to their congregations.[5] Apart from these cases, adults seldom speak about God to one another. If they do, it is usually in a discussion or an argument; but to speak simply of God as a reality well known and unquestioned, as a person dear and familiar, about whom we gladly share our thoughts among our friends — this is an experience unknown to most men.

Such is not the case with the people of whom I am speaking. They are willing and glad to talk about God. College students talk about him to their campus acquaintances — to their roommates, and classmates, to casual acquaintances and to old friends. They are willing to stand up before a strange group, even on oc-

4. I should add that the priest in question is well known to me, and has always been widely regarded as a very kind and loving father. From such a person, this testimony has all the more power.
5. At least they used to be expected to speak; today, it might be safer to say that if at times they do speak about God, one accepts this as their professional duty!

casion an unsympathetic group, and speak not timidly and dif-
fidently, but with as much boldness and enthusiasm as they will
show the following Friday at a pep rally. Conviction rings through
their speech. When you hear them, you sense the reality God has
for them. At the same time, however, they do this without the
artificial pressure or proselytizing insistence of fanatics. Their
very conviction lets them also be relaxed and sensitive to the
reactions of the hearer, willing to bide time, if need be, until he is
ready.[6]

As a result, they spread the word to others effectively. There
is almost never a prayer meeting at which some new people are
not in attendance, drawn by the confident, pressing message of
those who were in the group before them. Many people have been
brought back to God and to Christ and to the Church through
this quiet missionary activity.

People who speak about God professionally today so often
speak in despairing tones. Religion as they have known it seems
to be vanishing, and their frantic efforts to reanimate it are
scorned by a youth that finds God-talk irrelevant. Their feverish
search for a new language in which to speak of him, and new
symbols in which to worship him, are like desperate efforts to
save an expiring man; and some of course have given up and
conceded that God is dead.

I was lecturing about the movement once to a theology faculty
(not at Notre Dame), when one young professor, obviously
expecting to find reinforcement for one of his own projects, in-
quired, "Are these people creating a new language in which to
speak of God?" I was dumbfounded for a moment, because, to
my knowledge, nothing of the sort had ever been contemplated.
They are not creating a new language, because they have found
the reality! Of course all language is inadequate to describe God;

---

6. It is true that not all the Pentecostals evince such tact; sometimes, especially in their initial enthusiasm, they are guilty of an excessive insistence
that irritates. But usually this disappears rather quickly. At least, I find
this to be true in general about Catholics. I am not sure about others.

for the same reason, all language, within certain limits, is equally acceptable. The important thing is not to polish up words but to encounter the reality. Once a person has found God, he can talk about him in almost any language.

On another occasion I was having lunch with a Pentecostal minister who began to speak about how wonderful God was, and how great it is to be alive today. His face glowed as he reflected on the good things God is doing, and the power with which he is ruling over all the world. It struck me then that almost the only people who speak this way today are those who have been touched personally by the Holy Spirit. They feel a joy and confidence that makes such a contrast with the melancholy tones in which most theologians and ministers of religion bewail the disappearance of God from human life, or the disintegration of the Church.

The sense of God and of the value of prayer among the Pentecostals today is all the more remarkable in view of the fact that our age is preoccupied with the social gospel. Humanism, secularism and activism permeate much that is preached in the name of Christianity today. Modern men, and college youth, in particular, have a difficult time with the idea of worship and prayer, with contemplative values, because their thoughts have been directed almost exclusively to concern for the needs of neighbor by a philosophy that reduces the love of God to social service. Yet it is often among people raised in such a climate, and formed in its attitudes, that the Holy Spirit is touching hearts and making them know God and the depths of his loving personality.

Those who are being thus affected are by no means confined to the introverts, the disillusioned, or the "natural" contemplatives. On the contrary, many of them were enthusiastic activists and socialites. But like St. Paul at Damascus, they have found their false worlds suddenly shattered by encounter with the truth and reality of God, which tears away the webs behind which they have hidden him, and reveals to them the shallowness and emptiness of views they had held with passionate faith. It is certainly no human persuasion that has brought this about. By theological arguments to bring a secular humanist to acknowledge that God has a claim on our attention and devotion *in himself,* and not just through the world, is a slow, difficult, and usually fruitless task.

I have often preached [7] about the presence of God and the divine indwelling. My experience, which I believe other priests will confirm, is that it is very hard to bring the average Christian [8] much conviction on these topics through preaching. He may believe what you tell him, but the ideas seldom take much of a hold. Most of what you say is quickly forgotten; or if it is remembered by a few, it is as a belief held onto by an effort of will, and acted upon sporadically.

With those who have been touched by the Holy Spirit, the case is almost reversed. They already know, by their own experiences, the reality of which you speak; it isn't necessary to persuade them. They have already drunk from the stream of living water that springs up within them; indeed, they have been plunged into it. Preaching and instruction are still useful for them, but have a different function — that of articulating for them something that is a matter of deep but obscure personal experience; of helping them to understand that which has actually taken place in them; and finally of reminding them of a truth which they too can be tempted to forget (for they have not been delivered from the regime of faith, and the trials which it entails).

The difference can be compared to the contrast between trying to start a car when the engine isn't working, and driving the car when it is. In the first case, you shove to the point of ex-

---

7. Not, however, to the group among whom the Pentecostal movement at Notre Dame began. I had never had any occasion to preach to any of them.

8. In order to avoid any possible misunderstandings, let me recall here that there are many extraordinary Christians outside the Pentecostal movement, and what is being said here applies perfectly well to them. But usually they occur to isolated individuals, who suffer a great deal for lack of support. What is striking about the Pentecostal movement is to find so many people together who know experientially what is spoken of.

haustion in order to make the car roll a few feet. But when the engine finally takes over, the car spurts forward with immeasurably more energy than you could put into it. When you preach about spiritual matters to people who have not been opened to them by the Holy Spirit himself, you generally find that they will go just about as far as you can push them and their inertia is so great that you can't push them very far, or impart any real momentum to them. But after the Holy Spirit has acted they begin to move under their own power; the source of energy is within. The preacher has the gentler role of guiding; he no longer has to push.[9]

Who is it then that has taught these people in a way no human teacher can? Who is it that has opened within them those valves no human hand can touch, releasing the fountains of living water? I do not believe it can be anyone other than he who said to the Samaritan woman, "If you but knew the gift of God, and who it is that speaks to you, you would have asked him and he would have given you living water . . . And the water that I will give will become . . . a spring of water, welling up unto life everlasting" (Jn. 4:10, 14).

When Jeremiah foretold the new covenant that God was going to make with his people he characterized it thus:

This is the covenant which I will make with the house of Israel after those days, says the Lord: I will put my law within them, and I will write it upon their hearts; and I will be their God, and they shall be my people. And no longer shall each man teach his neighbor and each his brother, saying, "Know the Lord," for they shall all know me, from the least of them to the greatest, says the Lord (Jer. 31:33-34).

Only in the Kingdom of heaven will this covenant be fully achieved. But already, here and now, though men still need to be taught

9. In the early months of the movement, I was sometimes tempted to exclaim to myself, "Well, those things you have been preaching all these years are true after all!"

by one another, there is a secret knowledge of God which no man can impart to another, which each must receive directly from his personal contact with God. It is this knowledge (which has always been known in the Church, and has been in a special way the goal of contemplative life) that is the chief fruit of the Pentecostal movement, and the chief source of its dynamism.

PRAYER

The experimental knowledge of God given by the Holy Spirit seems to be a root out of which many other effects proceed. Perhaps the most important of these occurs in the life of prayer. Pentecostals spend a great deal of time in prayer. Most of those with whom I am acquainted go to Mass and Communion daily. Some also meet together each day for Lauds and Vespers. Many make a daily meditation of half an hour or even more. The prayer meetings themselves, which are held at least once a week, generally last a couple of hours. When there is some special need, it is quite common for nearly everyone in the group to offer an extra hour of prayer for this intention. One student felt that he ought to talk about the Pentecostal experiences with a certain professor who was not very open to such things; he prepared for this spontaneously by making an hour of adoration. In the Fall of 1967, Father Connelly and I were to go see our bishop, who had some serious doubts about the movement. We asked the students to pray that all would go well. By taking turns, they kept an all-night vigil of prayer in Farley Hall chapel the night before our visit.[10] On several other occasions the same thing has been done.

But it is not only the quantity of their prayer which is impressive; it is much more the spirit and style. They take very

10. As a result of this meeting, on October 17, 1967, the Bishop told us that, although he could not give an official approbation to the movement, he found nothing to condemn in it, and gladly sent his blessing to all who participated in it.

seriously the promise of Christ, "Whatever you ask for in prayer, believing you shall receive" (Mt. 21:22). They pray with the confidence of those who know that their heavenly Father hears them always and will refuse them nothing. They go to him for their most ordinary and everyday needs, as well as for the great and "impossible" things. Often their prayer is answered in a way that is almost palpable. They frequently have stories of how they have been freed from illness, found missing articles, and obtained other favors they had eagerly sought through prayer. Most of these stories cannot be told in detail without becoming tedious; moreover, they are about things so commonplace as to be meaningless except to the individual concerned. But occasionally there is a more dramatic instance, such as the following.

In the fall of 1967, after a prayer meeting, some one proposed to have a weekend retreat. Almost unanimously the group agreed to do this. But when they discussed the various places where it might be held, none appeared suitable. Old College was too small; Moreau Seminary too big; the parish hall that had been used for Antioch weekends was no longer available. And so it went. Then someone suggested, "Wouldn't it be nice if we had a house up on Lake Michigan?" Everyone agreed enthusiastically that this would be ideal and promised to pray that God would provide such a place. I vividly remember overhearing this discussion, and wondering at the boldness of this request, which seemed almost like tempting God; but I said nothing and waited to see what would happen.

About two weeks later word was brought to us through a friend that a couple in Ganges, Michigan, had offered us the use of their house for our retreat.[11] It was large enough for nearly thirty

---

11. There is no mystery about how these people came to make this generous offer. They were attending a meeting of the Full Gospel Business Men, at which someone mentioned that some Notre Dame students were looking for a place to hold a retreat. But this does not detract from the providential fact that so unlikely a request was so precisely answered.

people to stay overnight and was located a little over a mile from the lake. As it turned out, not only was this offer an answer to our prayer, but an answer to theirs also. They had moved into this house several years before with the idea of using it for retreats; but almost no one had taken advantage of it. Finally they had begun to pray that God would give them a sign whether this was according to his will. We were that sign.[12]

Perhaps the most remarkable thing about the prayer of this group is the degree to which it is impregnated with the praise of God. Anyone who has done much study in the field of prayer knows that the prayer of praise is the most difficult form of prayer for most people. If they pray at all, it is usually to ask God for something they need. Only a few even remember to thank him for favors received (one out of ten, according to biblical sociometrics). But to praise God doesn't even come into the mind of most people, and often remains meaningless for them even when it has been explained. In the Pentecostal group many have declared that they never in their life offered a prayer of praise before receiving the baptism in the Holy Spirit. But now the praise of God seems to predominate in their prayer. Spontaneously they burst into exclamations of praise; they sing hymns of praise with great spirit. The goodness and glory of God have impressed them so profoundly, his greatness, wisdom and power have hit them so hard, that they are glad to praise him. They don't need a theory as to *why* man ought to praise God; the way they know him makes them *want* to do so. They want to tell all the world how great and good he is; they feel a need to tell God himself what they think of him. The Apocalyptic vision of the court of heaven, in which

---

12. In the spring of 1968, Jim B. and Pete E. began to pray that God might provide a place where they could live in order to carry on the apostolate to which they wished to dedicate themselves. A few weeks after they began to pray, a house was made available to them rent-free by a man in South Bend, who did not know them, nor that they were seeking a house, nor anything about the Pentecostal movement. He simply felt that he would like to use this house for God somehow, and offered it to Father Robert Connor of *Opus Dei,* who in turn referred him to us.

thousands of thousands sing, "Worthy is the Lamb to receive power, and divinity and wisdom and strength and honor and glory and benediction" (Apoc. 5:12), represents their spirit very well, especially when they are gathered for a prayer meeting.[13]

Occasionally a person who has been quite reticent about speaking of God is so touched by the Baptism in the Spirit that he cannot say enough about him. Previously, if he dared to pray in public at all, he put words together hesitantly and laboriously, one by one. Afterwards, however, the praise of God pours out of him like water from a geyser; the warmth and spontaneity of his language are eloquent witness to the power of that which touched him.

One of the earliest published articles about the Pentecostal movement was entitled "People having a good time praying." [14] This is journalistic, but reflects a truth. The Holy Spirit does transform prayer from something difficult and burdensome to something glad and joyous. One young woman declared, "I used to find it hard to pray, then afterwards, I felt good because I had done what was right. But now I feel good *while* I pray." [15] This joy in prayer does not take away all the burden from it, and does not last forever. It is a transitory grace, like that of the apostles on Mt. Tabor. It is not meant to be permanent; for every disciple of Christ is called to take up the cross and follow him up the hill of Calvary. But while it lasts, it teaches us effectively as nothing else can, how good God is to those that love him, and how truly Christ meant what he said, "Come to Me, all you that labor and are burdened, and I will give you rest" (Mt. 11:28).

I am convinced that some grace of infused contemplation has been given to quite a number of these people. This is what explains

---

13. The exclamation, "Praise God," has been a trademark of the Pentecostal denominations for many years, especially as a response to anything good that comes into their lives, and Catholics have adopted it also with great alacrity.
14. *National Catholic Reporter,* May 17, 1967.
15. Cf. K. and D. Ranaghan, *Catholic Pentecostals,* Glen Rock, N.J.: Paulist Press 1969, p. 81.

the joy with which they pray, and the fact that, with little or no previous training in mental prayer, many of them suddenly find themselves able to pray for extended periods of time simply by placing themselves in the presence of God and abiding there quietly, wordlessly, lovingly.[16]

LOVE OF SCRIPTURE

One of the most striking effects of the Holy Spirit's action has been to give people a new love for the reading of Scripture. This is an aspect of Catholic life that has been deficient in recent centuries,[17] and which a new biblical movement under the leadership of recent popes (and vigorously seconded by the Vatican Council) has tried to rectify. The fruits of their efforts, while noteworthy, have been far from satisfactory.

In the Pentecostal group at Notre Dame, and elsewhere too, so far as I have observed, an intense desire to read Scripture has arisen in almost every member. Nearly all carry small pocketbook editions of the New Testament around in their pockets and purses, to be read frequently during the day as there is occasion. Many, even among the undergraduates, bought the expensive new Jerusalem Bible, which appeared just a short time before the movement got started.[18] They don't read Scriptures as a duty, but

16. Again and again, I have noticed classical principles of spiritual theology being verified in, or rediscovered by, people who have never studied that subject.

17. While frankly regretting this situation, we ought also to bear in mind what brought it about. Scripture can be abused by those who read it in the wrong spirit. Abusive and gravely injurious interpretations of Scripture in the late Middle Ages and sixteenth century led the Church to discourage the private reading of the Bible by unqualified persons. And we can expect that as private reading again becomes common, new abuses will occur.

18. It costs $16.00 a copy, which is no slight outlay for a college student. I have found that most other college students sell their Bibles to a used book agency as soon as their Scripture course is over.

because they love it. They don't study it as a textbook. They find in it light, power, nourishment and encouragement. It is a book that comes to life for them. One student remarked, "The words seem to leap off the page and take hold of your heart." [19]

That this is really so is indicated in many cases by their remarkable retention of what they have read. Certain ones seem to have this faculty to an amazing degree. They recall from memory a passage that meant so much to them that it burned itself into their mind on a single reading. Or a well-known passage, which had grown dull through familiarity, they will suddenly see in a fresh light that recharges it with meaning.

Jim C. has a special gift of this sort. In his account of the night that he was first prayed over, he tells how various passages of Scripture came to his mind, one after another, shedding light on the problems he was facing. I still recall vividly how he used to cite the words of St. Paul, "We are fools for Christ" (I Cor. 4:10), as indicating the spirit in which one must accept the gift of tongues. It was certainly what one might call an extrapolated interpretation or application of the text; yet I am convinced that it was perfectly and deeply authentic. He had laid a finger on the deep spiritual attitude which needs to be realized in any close follower of Our Lord's, and is exercised very specially in the gift of tongues. On another occasion, Jim remarked that it was precisely in view of charisms such as were being received in this group that Christ had said, "Do not rejoice in this that the spirits are subject to you; but rejoice that your names are written in heaven (Lk. 10:20).

19. Jim B. tells how someone read a text of Scripture to him one day, at a time when Jim looked scornfully on such a practice, as well as on the entire movement. "At that moment," says Jim, "I knew why it is said that the Word of God is like a two-edged sword that pierces right to the heart (Heb. 4:12). For in the whole Bible, from Genesis to Apocalypse, there is not another text that described so accurately my spiritual state at that moment; for the first time in my life, I really knew that God existed."

Jeanne D. has for years been one of those rare Catholics who make it a practice to read a chapter of the Bible every day. The day after receiving the Baptism in the Spirit, she sent her husband off to work and her children to school, and then sat down with her Bible as usual and began to read the Acts of the Apostles. She had read this book several times before; but now, it was as if a veil had been taken away from it. The stories recorded there were charged with new color, force and meaning. Entranced, she continued reading, racing ahead with excited curiosity, turning to passage after passage among her favorites, to see how they looked now. All day long she kept this up until it was time to prepare supper, and didn't interrupt her reading except for the most indispensable tasks, such as caring for the baby. The phone did not ring that entire day (that was in itself a most extraordinary occurrence in their household) and she thanked God for it, because she would have regretted the interruption.[20]

The day after he was prayed over, Gerry R. spent four hours reading his Bible. He kept this up every day for two weeks, even though he was at the time carrying a full load of classes, attending prayer meetings, talking to numerous students about the Holy Spirit, and engaged in several extra-curricular activities. After two weeks, he realized that he would have to moderate his reading in order to study for his classes; so for the rest of the semester, he limited himself to only two hours of Scripture a day! Some faculty members who heard about this were concerned that it might do serious harm to his studies. I was a little worried myself, and I knew that if the students suffered academically because of their Pentecostal involvements, it would provoke the complaint that they were neglecting their duties. Shortly after the final examination, I asked Gerry, who was due to graduate, how he had done in his courses. "It was the best semester I've ever had," he replied. "I got an A in every class!"

20. A woman in Cincinnati wrote, "After all these years I now read the Bible and find it a great source of consolation. In fact, I can hardly wait until my chores are finished and I can sit down and study it. I read and reread some of the passages and especially like the Psalms."

TRANSFORMATION AND DEEPENING

The majority of the people in the Pentecostal movement were, so far as I can judge, genuinely good people before the Holy Spirit came in a new way to touch and transform them. They practiced their religion faithfully, usually practiced much more than an ordinary life of prayer, and in many cases were active in some form of apostolate. Six of the Notre Dame students in the initial Pentecostal group were active in putting on "Antioch weekends," i.e., short, intense retreats designed to confront college students effectively with what it means to be a Christian.[21] Along with Father Charles Harris, C.S.C., Steve Clark and Ralph Martin were the original designers of the Antioch weekend; and during the eventful year 1966-1967, they were collaborating, without remuneration, in the student apostolate at Michigan State University.[22] Ralph Keifer, Kevin and Dorothy Ranaghan, and other prominent members of the group were (and still are) active promoters of the liturgical movement. The same thesis could easily be documented in other parts of the country also. Just as random examples, let me cite Mr. Robert Morris, a Cleveland lawyer who has worked a great deal with alcoholics, and Mr. Robert Balkam, executive secretary of the Gustave Weigel Society (for the promotion of ecumenism) in Washington, D.C. Many other people, without belonging to any particular organization, were nevertheless leading good Christian lives in a quiet, steady way before the Spirit came as a kind of fruit and reward, to bless and deepen what was already there.

The effect of the Spirit's coming [23] has been to give new depth

---

21. The name is inspired by Acts 11:26: "It was in Antioch that the disciples were first called 'Christians.'"
22. While there, in fact, they worked out an apostolic program which continued to be used by the student parish even after their departure.
23. Let me emphasize that I do not mean to imply that the Holy Spirit is wholly absent from a person's life prior to the Baptism in the Holy Spirit, but only that the latter is a new and more manifest coming. Cf. Acts 8:16.

and fire to their lives. I have already pointed out how many have been led to discover a new interiority in their life of prayer. But this does not mean that they have given up the apostolate or withdrawn into a self-centered spirituality neglectful of the needs of others. On the contrary, they have grown more sensitive and more strongly motivated in these areas than before. Their concern for others has a deeper, wiser and more persevering quality; they are not so easily disheartened by ingratitude or opposition. They have learned to base their apostolate on prayer, to seek divine light and help before taking a step, and to be attentive to the leadings of the Holy Spirit. Although many of them are now aghast at the thought of the "humanism" (which of course called itself Christian) that they used to profess, I believe they are more authentically and Christianly humane than before.

Many of them have come to live in an attitude of constant alertness to the spiritual needs of any chance person they meet. Conscious that God sometimes uses these casual encounters to impart some grace (as he did for the Ethiopian eunuch in Acts 8:26ff.), they are ever listening for the call of a hungry soul, however camouflaged it may be under trivial conversation,[24] and ever ready to declare, simply and gladly, the "reason for the hope that is in them" (I Pet. 3:15). Hitchhiking has become a specially privileged exercise of this apostolic spirit. Many of the younger people in the movement have to do a good deal of it, and they use the long periods of waiting that this entails to pray that God will send them a driver to whom they can speak about him. Often he does, sometimes with results that are as hilarious as they are salvific.

I have already mentioned that Steve Clark and Ralph Martin dedicated the year 1966-1967 to the student apostolate at Michigan State even before the Pentecostal movement began. Since then, others have joined them at Ann Arbor; meanwhile, similar groups have formed at Notre Dame and the University of Iowa. Still another group from the University of Portland went to Ann

24. *Loc. cit.*

Arbor for a year, and is now relocating at Oregon State. In all these cases, young men and women recently out of college, and in some instances with graduate degrees, have postponed jobs and careers in order to devote a year or a lifetime to the apostolate. They are doing it without remuneration, without even receiving room and board. They support themselves by odd jobs supplemented by occasional donations.

It is not only in the religious and apostolic dimensions that these people have been deepened; the whole of their life has been changed. Like other married couples in the group, Dorothy and Kevin found that their love for one another had grown, and been transfigured with new warmth and light. Its radiance has been visible to all who know them. The love of Christ, poured forth in their hearts by the Holy Spirit, has imbued and enhanced the human love that it found there.

Similarly, the joyous spirit that is natural to some members of the group has been beautifully enhanced by a new supernatural joy that the Spirit of Christ has brought. Ralph K. was always, so long as I have known him, a cheerful person; but when I met him on his visit to the Notre Dame campus in February 1967, even though I did not yet know anything about what had happened to him, I was struck by a new light of joy in his eyes that haunted me for weeks until I realized the explanation. Similarly quiet, gentle people have received a new Christian humility that adds depth and charm to their nature; cheerful, friendly characters have acquired a note of graciousness that is a flowering of Christ's love; those who have natural gifts of leadership have had these confirmed by many new gifts, such as firmness, tact and wisdom.

On the other hand, however, some people have been changed in directions opposite to the more obvious bents of their character. For example, people who are naturally extroverted are often made quieter through the action of the Holy Spirit, and more aware of the dimension of interiority and the value of silence. Perhaps even more often, those who have been introverted and reserved lose some of their concern with self and drop their inhibitions, as they discover the loveableness of others and the meaning and reality of Christian community. Liberals seem to become more conservative and conservatives more liberal; those who tend to be vacillating sometimes acquire a surprising new firmness, while those who were strong, perhaps to the point of harshness or rigidity, learn the meaning of gentleness. However, a person's natural temperament never seems to be reversed or radically altered. Rather, the Holy Spirit seems to make him more truly himself, by dissolving some of the artificial structures and deformations acquired by struggling in the competition of the jungle of life. Excessive traits are moderated and undeveloped aspects of the personality are strengthened; the man, however, remains truly and recognizably himself, and his characteristic traits are often sensibly enhanced by the supernatural.

Likewise, people's intellectual and cultural stances have not been destroyed. Liberals remain liberal and conservatives conservative, only they become more moderate in their positions, with an openness and understanding towards each other that was often lacking before. They are able to belong to the same community with a love and loyalty for one another that must stand as a minor miracle in the Church of today.[25] Dave Z. used to tell of a certain priest whose sermons he could not listen to. But after the two of them had been touched by the Holy Spirit,

25. I think that most people will agree that this is at least a favorable sign. I have heard, however, of one person who was scandalized at the report that liberals and conservatives in the academic community at Notre Dame had been brought into friendly and harmonious association with one another through the Pentecostal movement. It seemed to him a kind of inconsistency with one's basic principles! I can appreciate the zeal for truth and earnestness about intellectual viewpoints that cause a person to experience such a scandal; but I think he must be a person for whom only the intellectual life exists, who fails to realize that Christianity is not primarily a school of doctrine but a community of love. In such an outlook, men reduce everything to intellectual positions; and where two men differ radically in their positions, nothing remains for them to share in common. But thank God for not putting us into such a ghastly universe (it would be, I imagine, something like E. A. Abbot's *Flatland!*); and for the love of God, let us never put ourselves into it!

Dave found he could listen to this priest's sermons with real profit. Not everyone, however, who has received the Pentecostal experience had prepared for it by leading an admirable Christian life beforehand. Many declare plainly that they were nothing but "Sunday Christians" before the Spirit "hit" them. They were not interested in the Church or Christ or God. They were doing the bare minimum that seemed necessary to save their souls, while the interests that really absorbed their hearts lay elsewhere. They may have had love for their fellow man, and maybe not. But now in humble amazement they thank the Holy Spirit, who broke or shocked or burned away their lethargy, and made them know that God is more important than anything else, that He demands our whole heart, and that He can really be loved. Others speak of themselves as having been smug and complacent, until through the Holy Spirit God brought home to them the lesson of the church of Laodicea: "You say I am rich, I have prospered, and I need nothing; not knowing that you are wretched, pitiable, poor, blind and naked" (Apoc. 3:17).

DELIVERANCE

Others have been trapped in habits of serious sin which they had been unable to break until the Spirit set them free. Pentecostal literature for decades has been full of the stories of people of many denominations, or of no denomination, who have been snatched suddenly and dramatically from atheism, immorality, drunkenness, drug addiction, prostitution, and just about every disorder and degradation to which human nature is liable.[26] The Catholic Pentecostal movement, although its life span has been quite short, has already begun to accumulate its own repertoire of striking conversions. Most of them cannot be narrated here because of the personal factors involved; however, one instance may be cited.

26. Some of the most impressive of these are to be found in the story of David Wilkerson, *The Cross and the Switchblade*, edited by John Sherrill (New York: Spire Books, 1962) pp. 1964ff.

Pete was a young man of good Catholic upbringing, but had lost his faith by the time he reached college. Not only had he quit going to Church, he had ceased to believe in God. The students nicknamed him *Zeus,* because they said, if he doesn't believe in the Christian God, maybe he believes in a Roman one! A shy and introspective boy, he did not by any means find happiness in his disbelief. He had few friends, and his face was set in a constant cast of sadness. But he observed with his own eyes the remarkable change which the Holy Spirit brought about in two of his friends. He could not deny that something good had happened to them. Hence they were able to persuade him to attend a prayer meeting.

I was at that meeting, and I noticed him at once, because he was wearing the long hair of today's protesting college students. I said to myself, "If Zeus gets the Holy Spirit, for me the sign will be when he gets a haircut!" At the end of the meeting, Zeus was prayed over along with several others; but apparently this had no effect on him. Later, back at the dormitory, a few of the others were wondering what might have gone wrong. It occurred to one of them that in the New Testament the Holy Spirit is given only to those who have faith in Christ. So they went to Zeus and asked him, "Do you believe in Christ."

"Of course not," he answered. "That's what this whole thing is all about."

"Well, do you think you could make an act of faith in him?"

"I don't know."

"Would you be willing at least to give it a try?"

"I suppose I have nothing to lose." So there in the dorm at about 2:00 A.M., the others formulated a makeshift profession of faith which Zeus repeated after them. Then they prayed over him again, and this time the effects were dramatic. Zeus found himself overwhelmed with joy and love. For weeks thereafter he went about with such a smile on his face, it looked as though his cheeks might crack from the unaccustomed creasing. What is more important, he began again to pray and to attend Mass not only on Sundays but frequently during the week. In spite of his shyness, he was willing to stand up before groups of strangers and tell them of his experience.

Zeus became so dear to me personally that the time came when I no longer detested his long hair. It was too much a part of him. I thought that this was perhaps God's way of giving me the sign I had asked for, only in reverse; for it was undoubtedly a bigger miracle for me to change on that point than for Zeus. However, I got all that I asked for. At the end of the school year, the group held a picnic, at which Zeus showed up with his hair trimmed (it was Pentecost Sunday!).

In a number of cases, people have been released from psychological bonds such as scrupulosity, anxiety, and inhibitions, which, without necessarily implying any moral culpability on their part, nevertheless, did effectively impede them from serving God in complete and joyous freedom of spirit. The sensation of having been set free from some invisible bonds is one of the most frequently reported traits of the Pentecostal movement, although realized in the most varied circumstances. To give only the most innocuous example: several who had tried unsuccessfully to give up smoking found that after the baptism in the Spirit, the desire for cigarettes had simply left them. On an altogether different plane, one man confided that for months after he was prayed over, he had not experienced a single temptation to impurity.[27]

Finally, there have been several people whose life had approached the brink of disaster, when they were rescued by the action of the Spirit. One young woman had walked out onto a bridge in order to commit suicide, but lacked the courage to go through with it. She was bewildered and discouraged by inordinate emotions that put her into high spirits one day and into the abyss of gloom the next. The joy and peace that came to her with the

27. I trust no one will misunderstand my associating smoking and temptations to impurity with one another. The only thing they have in common is that they are both bonds from which many people struggle in vain to free themselves; from the moral point of view they are by no means on the same plane!

baptism in the Spirit did not eliminate her problem, but it did give her much more equilibrium than she had had before, with the result that the emotional hills and valleys were no longer so extreme. She began to use a little judgment and learn from experience, which had scarcely been the case before. She is still shy and awkward and somewhat unpredictable, as very likely she will always be; yet there is sufficient steadiness and normalcy for a person to deal with her rationally, and grounds to hope that she may lead a purposeful and useful human life. In many ways, I regard this salvaging of a lost human being one of the most beautiful works of the Spirit to which I have been a witness.

PEACE AND JOY

The effects of the baptism in the Holy Spirit vary with persons and circumstances. But two notes which seem to be universal, and are the surest signs of the baptism itself, are peace and joy. Whatever other graces a person has received, whatever deliverance he may have undergone, peace and joy always seem to accompany them. When a person speaks up at a prayer meeting to tell of what the Lord has done for him, these terms almost infallibly will come to his lips. And even if he does not speak of them, they are often plainly written in the expression on his face and in the tones of his voice.

Newcomers to the prayer meetings are commonly impressed above all by the joyousness of the people they meet there. Even if the tone of the meeting itself is somber, as occasionally happens, the people themselves are not. And their joy is radiant and contagious; it creates an atmosphere that often envelops and pervades those who come as visitors, and acts as a kindly invitation and encouragement to them. Bitter or hostile persons sometimes react with a vague sense of anger against the atmosphere, or shrink from it as an alien thing; but even their reaction is a testimony to its reality.

It frequently happens that a person has been suffering under deep grief, frustration or discouragement for a long time, and through the baptism in the Spirit is flooded with peace and joy, like day dawning suddenly after a black night. One woman had been coming to me for counsel because of some spiritual anguish of which she seemed unable to rid herself, and none of my suggestions or attempts at encouragement had more than a short term effect. One day I suggested that she attend a prayer meeting. This she was reluctant to do, for (unknown to me) she had visited one previously, and had been repelled by it. Nevertheless, she followed my recommendation. I gave her no hint of what to expect. The next day she returned, and even before she had closed the office door behind her, exclaimed, "Why didn't you tell me about the wonderful peace and joy that were going to come when they prayed over me?" In her case, these effects lasted about two months; and even when they finally disappeared, the anguish did not return. Ordinarily this peace and joy do not appear so abruptly. Often a person does not even advert to them until they have been present for several days or a week. Then, looking back over the time elapsed, he observes that the depressions, griefs or irritations to which he ordinarily would have been subject have not occurred. Instead, a quiet unobtrusive "lightsomeness" has pervaded his soul.

Carolyn is a young woman afflicted with an arthritic-like disease that causes almost constant, and sometimes intense, physical pain. She has endured it uncomplainingly for years with great fortitude. After having been prayed over, she went to the hospital for some treatments that were more painful than the disease. But her letters were full of joy; she remarked in one that the words of the Psalm kept echoing in her head, "This is the day that the Lord has made; let us be glad and rejoice in it" (Ps. 118:24). Several of her fellow patients in the hospital were so impressed by her spirit that they took new heart in their own sufferings, as one of them later told me gratefully.

There are of course, many kinds of peace and joy in human life; but those which are given by the Holy Spirit are quite unlike any other. The peace does not depend on exterior tranquility, and is not induced by psychological technique. Neither does it require some kind of heroic aloofness. It is an almost substantial thing that is received gently and effortlessly as a gift, and resides deep within, undisturbed by exterior conflicts. It is what Christ promised when he said, "My peace I leave with you, my peace I give to you; not as the world gives do I give to you" (Jn. 14:27). Likewise the joy is not aroused by singing and shouting, or any other group inter-action. It is not the wild intoxication of a person who has momentarily broken out of the inhibitions which will later close their cold jaws upon him once again, and lock him in a deeper depression. It is a strong, quiet joy that corresponds to another promise of Christ: "I will see you again, and your hearts will rejoice, and your joy no one will take from you" (Jn. 16:22). No man can take it away, because no man has given it.

This peace and joy seem to be not so much two distinct gifts as two aspects of the same thing: a peaceful joy and a joyous peace. The peace does not turn into torpor or numbness, because it is so joyous. The joy is not an elation, because it is permeated with peace. They are so delicate that sometimes a person does not even advert to their presence until after they have been present for days, but they are so sturdy that disappointment, contradiction or ridicule cannot dispel them.

Anyone involved in the Pentecostal movement is liable to find himself laughed at from time to time. The Holy Spirit doesn't ordinarily make people insensitive to hurt. In fact, this is what cuts short the enthusiasm of many people and causes them to separate from the movement. But again and again one meets those who, to their own amazement, have found that the glad serenity Christ has given them remains untroubled by things which normally would have disturbed them greatly.

ATTITUDES TOWARDS THE INSTITUTIONAL CHURCH

Because the Pentecostal movement spreads and expresses itself largely through prayer meetings, which have not been customary among Catholics for a long time,[28] people sometimes suppose

28. However, it should not be overlooked that the taste for prayer meetings, Bible vigils, and like began, at least so far as the United States is con-

that it is an anti-institutional movement, in which prayer meetings and other "esoteric" activities substitute for the liturgy and traditional devotions of the Church. I have observed that the exact opposite is true. The effect of the movement has been to give people a greater love and appreciation for all that is authentically traditional in the Church.

Among the earliest reports that reached South Bend about the happenings at Duquesne was the increased devotion to the Eucharist that had resulted from them. The same was quickly verified at Notre Dame, and has been confirmed by subsequent history. Nearly all those who take part in the prayer meetings also attend Mass daily or at least frequently. What is more, many have commented on how much more meaningful the Mass has become for them. One student remarked that he had come to love the long lists of little-known saints in the Roman canon, because the Eucharist meant so much to him that he was glad to summon all the angels and saints of heaven to join him in giving thanks for it.[29] Gerry R. says that, the night he received the baptism in the Spirit, his first instinct upon returning to the University was to go to the chapel to give thanks. There, he felt powerfully drawn towards the tabernacle, by a force that seemed almost physical. The presence of Christ on the altar seemed to dominate the entire chapel, and draw everything towards itself. In wonderment and rejoicing, he spent an hour or two in adoration before the Blessed Sacrament. Nothing of this sort had ever happened to him before.

Less often does anyone speak of the sacrament of Penance

---

cerned, early in the 1960's, and hence well before the Pentecostal movement. In fact, the people among whom the movement first took root in South Bend and Notre Dame had already been holding prayer meetings for one or two years before the first news arrived about the works of the Holy Spirit at Duquesne. On the other hand, interest in these meetings was waning, and some feel that they were on the point of extinction when the Pentecostal movement came to rejuvenate them.

29. It is my impression that he made this remark without any awareness whatsoever of the criticisms of these lists that are being made by promoters of liturgical reform.

in similar terms. However, several persons have mentioned that the Holy Spirit has brought them a new sense of sin, and with it an awareness of the value of frequent confession, which they had neglected before. And a very liberal young Catholic mother named Rita tells a hilarious story about a very conservative confessor she tried to avoid, but who kept turning up in the confessional unexpectedly, and giving her exactly the counsel she needed, until she finally determined to go to him regularly.

Several people have said they wished they could receive Confirmation all over again, now that they had so much more appreciation of the work of the Holy Spirit. It had meant little or nothing to them when they received it in youth.

A Benedictine priest relates that the most striking effect of the baptism in the Spirit on him was that it gave him an eager desire to sing the Divine Office. Previously, this had been more of a burden for him; but now he felt a great longing to praise God, and the office appeared as a beautiful way to do this. Other priests have reported that they too have found great joy in the recitation of the office as a result of the baptism in the Spirit.

Devotion to Mary has been greatly stimulated by the Pentecostal movement. Some people, who had always been devoted to her, have rejoiced to find that the Holy Spirit has made her dearer than ever before. Many, whose devotion has been perfunctory or lukewarm, have become much more earnest about it, to such a point that a couple have become real apostles of Our Lady. A few, who had always experienced a deep antipathy for Marian piety, now find that they can at least understand and accept it in others. Fritz and Rita M. tell how their prayer group, which began rather strongly, gradually dwindled until only one other couple continued with them. Finally, at one meeting, the four of them sat in silence for an hour, just "listening" to what God might wish to speak. Then they decided to cultivate devotion to Mary. From that point on, the group began to grow larger.

After a prayer meeting at which prayers had been said for the bishops of the Church, a visiting priest commented — wryly, "The Holy Spirit must be involved there somewhere. That was the first time I have heard anything good said about bishops in a long time!" I have heard similar remarks on several occasions, always in fun, of course, but with a serious point. Although attitudes towards the clergy, and in particular the hierarchy, vary from person to person, and also from group to group, I have noticed remarkably little of the anti-clericalism or the tendency to deride and defy the bishop that are often so strong among energetic Catholic lay groups today.

Since a very early age, it has been recognized that obedience to those who hold office in the Church is one of the surest signs that an inspiration comes from God rather than from some secret craving of self love. The Pentecostal movement has already been tested several times by this criterion. In January, 1969, the bishop of a certain diocese sent word to a prayer group meeting at a Carmelite retreat house that there was to be no glossolalia or laying on of hands at their meeting. This came as a severe blow; there was real fear that these restrictions might bring the meetings to an end and cast a cloud of suspicion over the entire movement. Nevertheless, the group obeyed, and instead of diminishing, they began to grow noticeably from that date onwards.[30]

Not a few of those involved in the movement had previously been bitter critics of conditions in the Church. Some were vehement advocates of radical reform; others were tempted to leave the Church altogether. I know of one couple whose friends are surprised to find them still in the Church today, and another couple whose efforts to "enliven" parish life had met with such discouraging rebuffs from the pastor that their faith in the Church, though strong, was severely tested. On all these people, the effect of Pentecost has been to restore their faith in the Church and awaken a new love for it. That some have remained in the Church, is directly attributable to the movement. Those who made criticisms and advocated reform still do so, but with less bitterness and more gentleness, patience and wisdom. No doubt, even in their fiercest moments, they had been animated by "zeal for the house of God"; nevertheless, it is a wonderful

---

30. The restrictions were lifted five months later.

thing when the Holy Spirit, without argument or exchange of ideas, but simply by his warm and loving breath, imparts the insight that enables a person to perceive and be grateful for the mysterious, fecund holiness which he creates in the Body of Christ despite its flaws, and to look upon the latter with understanding and compassion, rather than with the acrimony of a condemned judge.

Likewise several priests and nuns who had been on the point of abandoning their state have had their hopes restored by the Pentecostal movement, and have determined to continue to serve the Church in their calling. One priest, a member of a religious order, had come to the generalate with the precise purpose of announcing his intention to leave. He had to wait two or three days before he could see the superior; meanwhile, he observed such a change in the spirit of the men he knew there, as a result of the Pentecostal prayer meetings in which a number of them were taking part, that when he did finally see the superior, it was to announce that he had changed his mind and was not going to leave after all.[31] Sister M. L. is a nun whose religious life had lost its spirit and become a dead routine, and who had come to the point of not knowing whether she still believed in God. Contact with some Pentecostal Catholics, and their prayers over her, did not transform her into a model religious, but they did restore her basic faith once more, so that she could try again with some confidence and sense of purpose.

NO INSTANT SANCTITY

Before we close the subject of the effects of the Pentecostal movement, two critical points concerning the suddenness and the durability of these effects must be discussed.

---

31. The superior of this community told me that some other members of the house had been afraid that if the name *Pentecostal* got attached to their community, they would be regarded as "kooks," and lose vocations. But now, he can reply by pointing to at least one vocation that has been saved through Pentecost!

In the foregoing pages, we have seen many instances of changes brought about quite abruptly. Moral and psychological bonds which a person had been unable to break in years of struggle have been lifted from him when he received the baptism in the Spirit. Graces of prayer and an appreciation of Scripture quite incommensurable with anything in his previous experience have been given to him in a moment.

Let us not over-dramatize the matter. Most often the change occurs quietly, without any distinct awareness of it. Sometimes the fact that it has taken place is not even perceived until later. Also, when a given case is investigated, it often turns out that there has been more preparation than was evident at the moment. Looking back, one perceives that privileged moments of grace long ago had given him some foretaste of what was in store for him, or that suffering and anguish had been, in God's Providence, sapping the walls of Jericho and getting them ready to fall.

But when due allowance is made for such factors, it still remains true that for a considerable number of people, the baptism in the Spirit has been a mighty intervention of the power of God in their lives, giving them, gently and effortlessly, results for which they had labored and prayed without success, and placing them many steps farther ahead on the road from sin to sanctity than their previous progress would ever have entitled one to expect.

To avoid a possible misunderstanding, it should be pointed out that these are not cases of "instant sanctity," as some have supposed. I know of no one who claims to be, or who gives any evidence of having been, changed overnight into a saint. The graces in question are powerful aids toward sanctity, but they leave the recipient with many steps yet to take, in which he is subject to all the laws, perils and exigencies inherent in the spiritual combat.

Not rarely, a person seems to be delivered from one big fault or problem, but is left to struggle with many lesser ones. Or he is given a grace of prayer that is a source of strength and refreshment, and gives a new light and orientation to his view of life; yet he must laboriously work to bring the details of his day-to-day conduct into harmony with this grace. In particular, I have the impression that those who have received the grace of infused contemplation, without having gone through the purification which normally must precede it, are sometimes obliged afterwards to take the steps which they seem to have skipped over. Thus the baptism in the Spirit serves as an aid, stimulus and encouragement to the spiritual life, like the mighty works God did when he led his people out of Egypt and through the desert; but it does not exempt a person from the labor of subduing and tilling the land of Chanaan, which is the lot of all who have not yet entered into the Sabbath Rest of the People of God (Heb. 4:9).

DURABILITY OF THESE EFFECTS

Finally, we must take up the question, how long-lasting and durable are the effects of the Pentecostal movement?

In answer, a distinction must be made, I believe, between two classes of effects, some of which are essentially transitory, and others permanent, although the dividing line between the two is not clear cut.

The baptism in the Spirit frequently puts a person into a state of peace and joy, of intense and actual love of God and of all men, and of freedom from sin or sinful inclinations, which might be compared to the blessedness of the apostles on Mt. Tabor. This state never remains permanently, and there seems to be a sort of inverse ratio between its intensity and duration. It may have a first moment of extreme intensity which lasts only a few hours. With most people, there seems to be a state of lesser intensity which lasts perhaps a week or two. Seldom, I think, does it endure more than a couple of months, and when it does, it is only in the form of an unobtrusive peace and joy deep in the soul, that by no means make one impervious to trouble and temptation.

On the other hand, there are effects such as growth in prayer, apostolic zeal, the practice of love towards one's neighbor, etc. (It will be noticed that unlike the foregoing, these are all works dependent on the person's will.) These are the effects which seem to be by nature permanent in character,[32] and are the real fruits meant to be fostered by the more transitory graces of the baptism. It is with regard to them that the question must be asked, whether they are solid and enduring, or merely enthusiasms that soon vanish. The most comprehensive answer I know of to this question is contained in the parable of the sower:

> Some seeds fell along the path and the birds came and devoured them. Other seeds fell on rocky ground, where they had not much soil, and immediately they sprang up, since they had no depth of soil; but when the sun rose they were scorched, and since they had no root they withered away. Other seeds fell among thorns, and the thorns grew up and choked them. Other seeds fell on good soil and brought forth grain, some a hundred-fold, some sixty, some thirty. (Mt. 13:4-8)

Christ told this parable in order to give a picture of men's various reactions to the Gospel. In employing it here, I do not mean to suggest that a person's attitude toward the Pentecostal movement is the measure of his faith or holiness. I readily agree that there are sincere and devout Christians who are not attracted to this movement. Nevertheless, the parable does in a remarkable way provide us with apt classifications for the various fates of the Pentecostal fruits.

The first case mentioned in the parable would represent people who reject the Pentecostal movement outright, or who perhaps attend one or two prayer meetings to see what they are like, but do not really participate. With these we are not concerned here.

The people who have genuinely accepted the Pentecostal spirituality fall into the three other cases described in the parable.

---

32. The charisms also are, apparently, permanent in character. However, I am leaving them out of consideration here, because they are simply means of collaborating in the work of the Church, and are not properly *fruits* of the Spirit.

Some receive the baptism in the Spirit, including perhaps the gift of tongues and other gifts also, with great enthusiasm, but after a while (sometimes within a month or two) reject it. What has happened to them is difficult to say, for they are usually reluctant to speak of the matter themselves. Sometimes it appears that the derision to which they have been subjected was more than they could bear. Sometimes a person seems to have placed too much stock in emotionally experienced joy and love; when these subside, as they inevitably do, his enthusiasm does likewise. Sometimes the doubts about the reality of the whole experience, which commonly assail a person after the baptism in the Spirit has lost its freshness, are perhaps sufficient to corrode his faith in the movement.

There is another type of person whose acceptance of Pentecost has usually been much less enthusiastic than the former, and for those departure from it is also decisive. He does not so much reject it as he drifts away. Other matters absorb his interest: his studies, his work, social events, various activities in which he is involved. He finds that he has less and less time for the prayer meetings, or for the personal prayer and spiritual reading necessary to grow in the life of the Spirit. Eventually, it is evident that he no longer belongs to the movement in any real sense, even though he has not deliberately renounced it. The thorns have simply choked it out.

Do the two classes of people just described retain any lasting fruit from their Pentecostal experience? About this it is impossible to speak with any certitude. My impression is that they usually do not; but I suspect that there are cases in which some charismatic gift is left as a kind of sign and reminder to the individual of the grace God has shown him.

Thanks be to God, however, there are others whose life has received an abiding and fruitful orientation from their Pentecostal experience. It is now about three years since the beginnings of this movement among Catholics. Many of those who were among the first in it are still with it, and many others who have entered into it since then have also remained faithful. They have been faithful, not only to the "movement" as such — this would be a small thing — but to the grace they have received, and to the new life of intimate union with God and love of their brethren to which they have been introduced. Their early enthusiasm has matured in depth, strength and steadiness. They have kept up their life of prayer and the reading of Scripture, their apostolic endeavors have developed, their love has become seasoned with wisdom. No doubt one must be prepared for further defections, even of people who have developed well for a long time; however, in themselves the fruits of the Pentecostal movement appear to be deep, solid and firm, and give every reason to expect that they will endure and continue to develop.[33]

CONCLUSION

Such is the evidence, at least as far as it can be presented in a brief space, of the action of God in the Pentecostal Movement. (If anyone were to try to give a complete presentation of the evidence, not even the world itself could hold, I think, the books that would have to be written.)[34]

Each one will have to judge for himself whether the hand of God is here. In any case, it can be said definitely that this is not the product of some human method or idea. Either it is the work of the Spirit of God, or it is sheer delusion; but it is nothing in between, and a person is simply wasting his time to try to explain it as the effect of a new technique of group dynamics.

33. Whether a person perseveres and grows is not only a matter of his personal qualities, however. In many cases, it seems to depend largely on his being integrated into a community of people who share his vision and aspirations. It is very difficult for a person to maintain the life of the Spirit when he cannot share it with others and be supported by them. Hence more and more thought is being given in this movement to the matter of forming really Christian communities, and of integrating the Pentecostal fruits into the existing parochial and diocesan communities.

34. For many more details on this subject, however, cf. K. and D. Ranaghan, *Op. cit.*

My own strong conviction, based on well over two years of close attention to this movement, is that it is the work of the Spirit of God, ever ancient and ever new, who is doing a wonderful new work in our time, and yet a work that is in profound continuity with that which has been from the beginning.

Some ask, "Might this not be the product of illusion, the work of the devil?" I do not think it can be illusory because it has proved itself too durable: it withstands testing. Illusions can perch us on a rosy cloud for a few hours, maybe even for a day or two if they are really good ones. But it is never long before the abrasions of reality puncture the balloon, dissolve the cloud. The opposite has happened here; troubles and trials have confirmed the solidity of the work and brought it to maturity.

Likewise, it is not the work of the devil, because it is too good and wholesome. If it were his work, then Satan would be divided against himself, and how should his kingdom stand? If it is not the work of God, then I have never seen one of his works so good, so holy, so worthy of him as this.

Is it still too early to make a firm judgment about the Pentecostal movement? Must more evidence be awaited? It is certainly well to be cautious in such matters; but there comes a time when waiting for more evidence is tantamount to refusing to face the facts. In Christ's own time, those who were unwilling to believe kept asking for further signs (Jn. 6:30). Others must judge for themselves; as for myself, I have already seen enough evidence of God's work here that the rest of my life will not be time enough to praise him for it.

ERNEST L. FORTIN

4 Ecumenism - Where Do We Go From Here ?

Even if Vatican II had accomplished nothing else, it would deserve to be remembered as the Council that launched the Roman Catholic Church, belatedly but vigorously, on the path of ecumenism. It would be näive to think, however, that because ecumenism has become fashionable in both inner and outer Roman Catholic circles, an adequate solution to the problems that it raises is in sight. The true magnitude of those problems is only now becoming apparent to most of us and, as it does, the healthy but somewhat juvenile enthusiasm generated by the Council has tended to give way to a more sober approach to the question of Church unity as a whole. There is even a general feeling abroad that the ecumenical movement is foundering, at least momentarily. This appears to be especially true in Europe, for political and other reasons peculiar to the Western European countries and different in each one; but the noises that have been reaching us from various quarters suggest that a similar crisis is developing in this country as well. Struck by the same phenomenon, a columnist in the secular press recently went so far as to propose that what the movement most needed at the present time was "a pious kick in the pants."

The sources of the crisis, particularly as it affects college students, are manifold and run the gamut from confusion, impatience with Church practice and discipline, shallow ecumenical experimentation, latent or open hostility toward the institutional Church and, in a growing number of more extreme cases, the total loss of Christian identity. All of these symptoms, as nearly as I can make out, may be analyzed under two broad headings: rash or vulgar ecumenism and indifferentism.

By rash, vulgar, or unreflecting ecumenism I mean the kind of ecumenism that presupposes unity where it does not exist or acts as if it did even in cases where it is conspicuously absent. Vulgar ecumenism does not remove prejudice but hallows it by substituting a pan-ecumenical prejudice for an antiecumenical prejudice. It is essentially eclectic or opportunist and ignores the inner transformation that must take place within each one of us before an authentic communion of faith can be reconstructed from the *membra disjecta* of a divided Christendom. For that reason it is generally sterile and self-defeating, however much it may recommend itself by its apparent openmindedness. It does not achieve and often hinders genuine understanding by fostering a type of relativism that runs counter to the deeper and more serious intentions of the ecumenical movement. The practice of intercommunion, on which recent discussions have centered, is a case in point. I for one, speaking theologically and leaving practical or pastoral considerations aside for the moment, would be tempted to take a broader stand on the matter than some of our leading ecumenists; but it cannot be denied that the problem is not as easily settled as a certain brand of facile ecumenism would seem to imply.

By indifferentism I mean the relativization not only of the various forms of Christian faith but of the faith itself, provoked or hastened in many cases by the presumed inability of the Christian Churches to agree on the fundamentals of their common belief and predicated on the mistaken assumption that because Church unity is desirable and demanded, it must be actual or immediately accessible at all times. To the extent to which it seeks to articulate itself in terms of a philosophically coherent position, religious indifferentism jettisons the past in the name of an historical consciousness that is either totally exhausted by the radical newness of an indeterminate but glowing future. Indifferentism makes interfaith dialogue impossible by removing the common ground that constitutes the precondition of any real discussion. At best, it conduces to a vague "secular ecumenism" which solves the problem only by denying its existence.

Ecumenism itself has sometimes been blamed for both of those excesses. It would perhaps be difficult to deny that its practice has occasionally brought to light certain personal or theological weaknesses latently present in the would-be ecumenist,[1] but there is otherwise little evidence to support the contention that it poses a serious threat to anyone's faith. The real danger, as far as college students are concerned, does not stem from ecumenism as such but from crude misconceptions regarding its nature and, to an even greater degree, from broad cultural causes only incidentally related to it. Today's better students are generous, enthusiastic, intellectually alert, and often more sensitive than their predecessors to the great social needs of our time. They have few of the atavistic inhibitions of their elders. They travel more than they used to, and their frequent exposure to a large number of heterogeneous and at times exotic experiences helps to develop in them a certain worldly wisdom which might have seemed out of place in their opposite numbers of a short generation ago. But they generally lack the experience of profound attachments to profound things. Their tastes have been given little formation and it is rare to find among them an understanding of life and of themselves that is the result of thoughtful study of a prolonged meditation on any serious book, whether it be the Bible, Shakespeare, or even Dostoievski. Their ideas are the ideas they absorb with the air that they breathe or through their contact with the cultures and sub-cultures to which they happen to belong. All appearances to the contrary notwithstanding, these ideas, although passionately defended, do not as a rule strike deep roots in them, and anyone who is accustomed to dealing with such students on a daily basis knows from experience how fragile their most "unshakable" convictions, religious or otherwise, can be.[2]

1. As seems to have been the case with Charles Davis; cf. George H. Tavard, "Ecumenism and Religious Indifference," *Chicago Studies*, 1968, pp. 211-2.
2. The most perceptive article that I have read on the subject is that of Allan Bloom, "The Crisis of Liberal Education," in Robert A. Goldwin, ed., *Higher Education and Modern Democracy* (Chicago: Rand McNally, 1965), pp. 121-39.

If this diagnosis is correct, what is needed is not less ecumenical education but a more genuine ecumenical education, that is to say, an education that is not blind to the differences between the Churches but takes these differences seriously, an education that does not shortcircuit the process of Christian unity by weakening one's commitment to a cherished tradition but presupposes and enhances that commitment as the sole means of achieving a proper understanding of and respect for another person's commitment.

Genuine ecumenism is basically loyal and it looks for the same loyalty in others. It thus necessarily implies a painful tension between the desire for unity on the one hand and faithfulness to one's own heritage on the other. It can be sympathetic and fully open toward other Christians precisely because it does not succumb to the temptation of universal sympathy that is typical of the spurious ecumenism referred to earlier. Universal sympathy is problematic, if not altogether illusory, in so far as it requires that one bracket one's personal attachment to his faith and that he provisionally espouse another's attachment as his own. It is hard to see how such a posture could be more than a pretense. The problem with it from an ecumenical point of view is that it actually precludes any profound encounter with persons of a different religious persuasion. Since it operates on the principle of an histrionic rather than a serious identification with the other, it necessarily misses what is most important in him, the depth of his total commitment. It cannot be indulged in consistently without a subtle demotion and hence an implicit disrespect of all religious positions. Like Descartes' methodical doubt, to which it bears a definite epistemological affinity, it destroys the very object that it is striving to preserve without being able to guarantee its miraculous recovery. Upon close analysis, it reveals itself as more superficial than profound, more arrogant than humble, and more provincial than truly universal.

One hardly needs to add that the faithfulness required by true ecumenism seeks more than the simple preservation of one's heritage. It is ever ready to accept renewal or death to what is old in oneself as an essential condition of that faithfulness. In a word, it sees its tradition as a living tradition and implies above all faithfulness to the creative impulse to which it owes its origin or its greatness and which hopefully continues be operative in it.

At all events, the current debate about the pros and cons of ecumenism is bound to appear parochial against the larger background of modern thought and the breakdown of sociological Christianity. One cannot begin to discuss the problem without taking into account what Carl Braaten calls "the invisible partner" in the contemporary theological enterprise, modern secular man.[3] It is no mere coincidence that ecumenism should have come into existence at the end of the eighteenth century and the beginning of the nineteenth century, that is to say, at the very moment when the Christian Churches were compelled to face squarely for the first time the issue of their relevance to the modern world in the totality of its historical and social development. The sense of urgency created by this situation cannot be overemphasized. As matters stand, the search for Christian unity is not likely to be determined solely or perhaps even principally by the relationship of one Christian Church to another. The differences between various Christian groups all but pale into insignificance in a disenchanted, denumenized, and already largely post-ecumenical world or in a world which is seen as such by a new generation of enlightened, albeit confused, college students. As one prominent ecumenist put it recently, any argument about the merits or demerits of the ecumenical movement in the broad context of modern secularity will soon end up by sounding like a discussion of the principles of navigation on the deck of a sinking ship.

With this I come to the central question raised by the title of the present communication, the specific role of the college theologian in promoting ecumenism in our society. That question may be answered most simply in the light of the foregoing remarks by saying that the college teacher is in a unique position to endow

---

3. Carl E. Braaten, "Toward a Theology of Hope," *Theology Today*, July, 1967. Reprinted in Martin E. Marty and Dean G. Peerman, eds., *New Theology No. 5* (New York: MacMillan, 1968), p. 109.

the ecumenical movement with a sorely needed intellectual dimension. The experience of the past twenty-five years or more has
made it abundantly clear that the cause of Christian reunion will
not be sufficiently advanced simply by having Christians of
various stripes engage in common social action, improve their
relations with one another, or exchange impressions over tea.
Sooner or later people will have to come together, book in hand,
for the purpose of exploring jointly the intellectual and historical
roots of their traditional divisions. By and large such efforts have
hitherto been restricted to small and scattered groups of theologians and scholars. If, in accordance with the recommendations
of Vatican II's *Decree on Ecumenism,* the work of these scholars
is to bear fruit, its results will have to be extended beyond the
confines of narrow professional circles. The privileged breeding
ground of this renewed and intellectually competent ecumenism
could very well be the substantial number of interested students
currently enrolled in our colleges. Not that all of these students are
equally prepared for such endeavors or equally eager to participate
in them. Far from it. Indeed, a majority of them do not have a
sufficient grasp of their own religious tradition to engage in a
meaningful study of its ecumenical implications. But the few
who do, or are willing to acquire it, could accomplish much in
the long run to change the ecumenical picture at the level of the
grass-roots, which has yet to be attained.

The last five years or so have happily witnessed a number
of promising developments in that direction. To speak only of
Catholic colleges, the first significant step was to alter the perspective of the usual courses by taking a more positive stance
toward Protestant thought and by granting to it a more prominent
place in the presentation of Christian doctrine. But this was obviously not enough. Faced with widespread ignorance of other
Christian traditions on the part of most of their students, Catholic
colleges were soon prompted to add to their curriculum new
courses dealing thematically with Protestant and, in rarer instances, Orthodox theology, as well as with the nature and history
of the ecumenical movement. A third flank was turned shortly afterwards when, in a move that was considered bold at the time but

has since become commonplace, Catholic colleges began sharing faculty members and resources with non-Catholic schools or adding non-Catholic theologians to the staffs of their own departments. It is difficult to say at this point just how effective these measures have been. Although they augur well for the future, there is a legitimate concern that the sole presence of Protestants on Catholic campuses and Catholics on Protestant campuses could result in a mere juxtaposition rather than a thorough integration of ecumenical efforts.[4] To offset that possibility, new ways of bringing the two groups into closer cooperation are being sought. One modest but forward-looking experiment along these lines is the recently established Ecumenical Institute of Religious Studies at Assumption College, which, at the time of its inception in 1967, was the only program of its kind in this country or elsewhere. The Institute is remarkable in that it is itself a total product of ecumenicity. Founded at the request of the Worcester Area Council of Churches and the Roman Catholic Diocese of Worcester, it is ecumenical not only in scope but in its very structure, being administered and staffed by Protestants and Catholics alike and geared to the common needs of all Christian communities in the area. In this important respect it differs from other theological schools, which, although now open for the most part to persons of different faiths, are nevertheless organized along predominantly confessional or interdenominational lines; and it differs from professional schools of theology in secular universities, which have become considerably more ecumenical in their orientation than they once were, but which prescind from one's commitment of faith and ordinarily approach religion as an objective historical and cultural phenomenon.[5] It is likewise significant that instead

---

4. See also the pertinent remarks by Gerard S. Sloyan, "The New Role of the Study of Religion in Higher Education: What Does It Mean?" *Journal of Ecumenical Studies* VI, (Winter, 1969), p. 12.

5. On the subject of the difference between the teaching of religion in secular universities and in theological schools, cf. Thomas E. Ambrogi, "The Catholic University in an Ecumenical Age," *NCEA Bulletin* 42 (Nov., 1967), pp. 23-4.

of dealing frontally with the issue of Christian disunity the Institute has chosen to tackle the problem from a different angle by focusing on the common concerns arising out of the encounter of revealed religion with modern scientific and humanistic world views. The core of the Institute is a graduate program leading to an M.A. in Religious Studies, but through the various activities that it sponsors and through such courses as are open to qualified college students, it has already had a noticeable impact on the undergraduate population.

Here again, only time will enable us to assess the wisdom and the practicality of the formula. The partial but encouraging success with which the Institute has met so far is attributable in large measure to a variety of factors not always to be found in the same happy combination elsewhere, such a local population that is almost evenly divided between Protestants and Catholics, progressive leadership on both sides of the ecumenical divide, the relative proximity of a major theological center like Boston, and generous financial support from local foundations. In any case, its progress is being watched with a mixture of hope and skepticism by a number of people interested in duplicating the program or experimenting with some modification of it in other places.

One hardly dares to be optimistic about any program of studies these days, let alone a program of religious studies. Still, one cannot remain insensitive to the surge of new possibilities that these and similar developments have caused us to experience. It has been said with a good deal of penetration that modern thought is on the whole characterized by limited goals and high expectations. Having lived through the agonies of modern man's repeated failure to attain even these moderate goals, the time has perhaps come for us to raise our sights once again, even if the effort is to be accompanied by something less than absolute expectations.'

GERARD A. VANDERHAAR, O.P.

5 The Peace Movement, the Draft, the New Left and the College Theologian

Something big is happening in the world today. It's felt in a concentrated form in the student disorders on college campuses, but it's taking place outside the college setting, too. It's more than a generation revolt, it's more than war resistance, it's more than a racial struggle, although it is all of these things. In the world outside the university it shows itself in a drive for economic improvement, a thirst for political freedom, and an impatience with the ways of established authority. Lee Benson, writing in the *New Republic,* called it an "irrepressible world revolt."[1] It's grape pickers organizing in California, it's laymen and clergy instigating the removal of an Archbishop in Texas; it's French workers and students paralyzing a country; it's street riots against the government in Pakistan; it's Dutch priests demanding the freedom to marry, and it's protesters of all ages confronting the Chicago police. Many people are dissatisfied with the way things *are,* and are striking out at established social forms to try to make things better. They see personal dignity diminished by racial prejudice, by the military draft, by big-power imperialism, by confiscation of land for missile sites. And above all, they desire to participate in the decisions that shape their lives.

The universities are a focal point of this revolution. Not that the universities are microcosms of the larger society. They aren't; they're the temporary home of the intellectual elite. The university operates under a *system* of education and administration, and

1. *The New Republic,* Jan. 18, 1969, p. 17.

system means tradition and it means authority. The university brings together people whose intelligence has been sharpened by learning, and who possess at the same time the expanded awareness of an electronic age and the impatience of youth. Since most universities do not have physical resources of containment like the Soviet army, the Delaware national guard or the Chicago police force, and since most of them are still reluctant to summon these or similar agencies, the universities are places where the explosions are most often occurring. Berkeley in 1965 and Columbia in 1968 are the classic cases, but uprisings have also occurred at, for instance, the University of Nairobi (one recent winter) and the University of Rome (during President Nixon's visit in 1969). The tactics of confrontation are going to be around for a long time, and they are going to be seen with greater frequency and intensity on our college campuses including, after a while, those which had known nothing more lively than a school newspaper campaign against the cafeteria food or an indignant colloquium against *Humanae vitae*.

People at the heart of the campus movement today are not for anarchy, although sometimes they sound like they are. They and their spokesmen often cannot clearly articulate what alternatives they want for society, but they know they're against the way things are, and they're in favor of participation and of human dignity. They are present on most of our campuses, and their non-collegiate counterparts are alive and kicking out there in the world beyond the campus boundaries. These people, the movements they stir up, and the issues raised by these movements, are where the social action is in these times. And because of this they pose a challenge to the college theologian.

Michael Novak has written, "The mass media have both uncovered and promoted changes in public religious consciousness and have made the theologian aware — and a little shaken by the knowledge — that people are listening." [2] Theology is at

2. Michael Novak, "The New Relativism in American Theology," in *The Religious Situation* 1968 (Boston: Beacon Press, 1969).

the same time always old and always new. It is always old because it is based on revelation, on the Scriptures and on the works of other theologians down through the centuries. It is always new because it is bringing revelation to bear on the present human situation. At least it *should* do this. Theology, especially the brand practiced on a college campus, is what happens in the engagement between revelation and the current scene. Revelation is about man's relationship to God, and since this relationship grips man at the center of his personality, what theologians are really doing is examining the ultimate implications of current human problems when they bring revelation to bear on contemporary concerns. It is no surprise that this kind of theology is being widely read these days, and the contemporary theologian, aware of the issues and creatively interpreting them in the light of revelation, is listened to.

There is no lack of genuine theological interest on college campuses these days. Students are concerned about values; they want to understand whatever meaning life has. They are generally indifferent or critical toward the institutional church, but they have a hunger for deeper meanings and insights into life. Unfortunately, in most of our Catholic colleges, despite recent advances in updating curricula, students find these insights more often in literature courses, or psychology, or anthropology, or sometimes in philosophy, than they say they do in theology. Which means something is wrong, because theology has the potential to explore the ultimate values of human life more deeply than has any other academic discipline.

To meet the needs of these students a college theology teacher needs a combination of academic competence, personal involvement in, or at least awareness of contemporary issues, and a willingness to approach these issues in a non-traditional way.

There is really no substitute for academic competence. A teacher's first responsibility is to be a good teacher, and this involves continuing research in his field, openness to new techniques of communication, and the formation of an examined theological position for oneself. If the college theologian is not a good teacher, he has little chance of being theologically effective on the campus regardless of how strong an activist he is.

To be theologically effective on a campus is to reach one's students and to engage their interest in the theological material one is presenting. Fortunately, for most of us, good teachers are made, not born, and a person with the degree of knowledge attested to by his graduate degree can become a good undergraduate teacher through study, alertness, and willingness to grow. The good teacher will be respected by his colleagues and so have a firm position on the campus, and will find students generally receptive to the theology he is presenting to them.

Theological effectiveness also demands an awareness of contemporary issues. If theology is the meeting of revelation with the stuff of man's life, the theologian must know both ingredients. A theologian who repeats the formulas of the past without engaging them in the problems of the present is quickly tuned out by the students. The students themselves are involved with contemporary concerns — search for meaning and a set of values in life, the possibility of a higher level of living through drugs and sex; loneliness, the struggle for maturity; the weight of economic necessities; distorted parental and personal relationships — and they worry occasionally about the huge social problems of race, poverty and war. If the theology teacher is not going to simply restate past formulas, and so be deadening to his students, he will be alert to what is going on in the world around him. He will be curious, in fact, and will be always thinking about the meaning of revelation in these events and problems. The theology teacher may have valid reasons for not being actively involved in social movements, but he has no adequate excuse for being unaware of the issues, unless he is content with being a transmitter of theological history instead of a theologian. A college theology teacher ought to devote some of his study time to the daily newspaper, some journals of opinion and the college's student newspaper, the ordinary vehicles of knowledge about today's problems. He doesn't have to treat these issues in class explicitly, but he teaches theology in light of these issues, sometimes in fact he does bring them up, and he communicates to his students the feeling that he knows what is going on. The result is always greater student acceptance of the teacher's theological assessment of the problems that he does in fact deal with.

Involvement is not essential, but awareness is, and for effectiveness this awareness ought to be coupled with a willingness to approach contemporary issues in a way other than with the traditional answers of the past. To say that a teacher is willing to approach contemporary issues in a non-traditional way doesn't mean that he always will. A familar figure is the campus hot-shot, the teacher who is superficially popular because he is sensational. Willingness to be non-traditional does not mean courting fame by titillating the anti-establishment instincts of his students. But it does mean not being bound by past approaches when newer ones seem sounder. Because the Church has consistently taught that pre-marital sex is wrong, for instance, does not necessarily mean that the question is closed. The college theologian will be willing to look at the question in the light of contemporary psychologial and sociological developments, and reassess the problem. Because the Church in the United States for the past two hundred years has consistently supported America's wars does not automatically mean that the Vietnam war is just. The college theologian will be effective if he shows not only that he is aware of these issues, but that he is prepared to take new approaches to them, although he may not in fact do so.

The problem that frequently arises in Catholic schools at this point is the fear of reaction from authorities when a non-traditional position is taught in class. Except for those with exceptionally thick skins, most Catholic college theologians have at one time or another been haunted by the specter of the provincial superior or Mother General or the local bishop in the seclusion of a paneled office, receiving complaining letters about Father or Sister, and deciding that Father or Sister is imprudent and really ought to be told to be non-controversial, if not packed off immediately to meditate on the error of his or her ways at the community's version of the ecclesiastical penal farm. Fortunately, through the increasing professionalization of their status, theology teachers now have at their disposal ways of counteracting unjust authority pressures, such as the once-ignored AAUP, and the dawning awareness of the power of publicity. The Saint John's University (N.Y.) teacher's strike, and Father Dan Berrigan's trip to South America, won for the college theologian a new freedom to teach what he saw to be the truth, even when that truth is sometimes nontraditional.

A teacher's theological background, contemporary awareness, and non-traditional flexibility are given a sharper cutting edge by his actual involvement in the issues of our times. Students are naturally more respectful of a teacher who shows by his actions that he believes what he is teaching. If for no other reason than the sheer pragmatic desire to be more effective in the classroom, the college teacher should consider involvement. But there is a more compelling reason. The teacher is also a human being who lives in society, and in the light of the new social consciousness he sees that as a human being he has the responsibility to try to influence the course of events. The college theology teacher is more aware than most other Catholics of the teachings of Vatican II in this regard: "Profound and rapid changes make it particularly urgent that no one, ignoring the trend of events or drugged by laziness, content himself with a merely individualistic morality. Let everyone consider it his sacred obligation to count social necessities among the primary duties of modern man." [3] And "it grows increasingly true that the obligations of justice and love are fulfilled only if each person, contributing to the common good, according to his own abilities and the needs of others, also promotes and assists the public and private institutions dedicated to bettering the conditions of human life." [4] The Southern Christian Leadership Conference, sponsoring events like the Poor People's March is a "private institution dedicated to bettering the conditions of human life," so is the Fellowship of Reconciliation, and the Clergy and Laity Concerned About Vietnam. In the words of *Gaudium et Spes*

---

3. *Gaudium et spes*, no. 30, in Walter M. Abbott, ed., *The Documents of Vatican II* (New York: Association Press, 1966) p. 288.
4. *Ibid.*

all are urged to "promote and assist" the work of institutions like these. One can move from these words right out into a civil rights march or a peace rally, confident that he is acting under the mandate of the Church.

It is no longer unfashionable for a priest or a nun to be in the front lines in Roman collar or habit. Priests and nuns who seldom wear these uniforms any more may boldly put them on for such occasions. Selma made the involvement of clergymen and nuns respectable, and they have been in the forefront of the peace and civil rights movement ever since.

The question of activism, to be involved or not, must be settled by each individual theology teacher as a person, rather than as a teacher. The question of activism in these days of demonstrations provides a moment of truth for the theologian. He cannot be sure that taking part in a social movement is the most prudent and effective way one can act according to his social conscience and that therefore it is of objective obligation for everyone. A *social conscience* is objectively of obligation, according to Vatican II, but the means by which one acts according to it have to be decided by each individual. One can only be certain that in these times precedents are no sure guide. A college professor has a highly responsible position in the broader community, and his decision for or against active involvement should not be made lightly. It will be based on the seriousness of the issue, and care will be taken to evaluate the potential backlash his action, or lack of action, will produce. The person who goes against the mainstream — whether he demonstrates when this is unfashionable, or he does not demonstrate when it *is* fashionable — ought to have a carefully thought-out position on the issue. Much of the effectiveness of his stance is lost when a person cannot articulate and soundly defends his position, and this especially in a college teacher who is expected to be able to think.

All of these attitudes are significant for the three issues mentioned in the title of this chapter: the peace movement, the draft and the New Left.

A student who had been raised in India, the son of an American missionary, recently gave me a copy of an Indian church publication. In it was an article by a German Mennonite, containing this sentence: "Next to Hitler's war, the war in Vietnam (even if it ends tomorrow) is the most important social and theological issue of this century." The statement is a bit pretentious, because we still have almost a third of the century left. But even if the Vietnam war is not the second most important social and theological issue of the century next to Hitler's war it is still a very important issue for Americans. And if it's important for Americans, it's important for American theologians, because theology should address itself to the important issues. On a college campus these days the war is of nagging urgency, for the young men who must face the call to fight it as soon as they graduate, and it is also a problem for the girls who have influence on or are influenced by these same young men.

The war is either just or unjust. If it is just, we have an obligation to support it and to encourage others to support it, because it is such a serious matter. If the war is unjust we have an obligation to oppose it and to encourage others to oppose it, also because it is such a serious matter. The issue is there. We can't hide from it under the excuse that we don't know enough about it. The facts are abundant. More has been written about this war, about its causes and about the way it is being carried on, than about any other war in history. There is no valid excuse for the college teacher not having enough knowledge to make a judgment about this war.

The draft is a problem primarily because the Vietnam war is a problem. President Nixon has proposed that military conscription might be abolished when the war ends. However realistic he is in this suggestion, the clear problem with the draft today is the war. Quotas are high because the military machine needs to be kept at top strength to meet the needs of the war. Many college students fear and despise the draft precisely because of the war, because they might have to kill or be killed in it. Others are coming to see the draft as an instrument of social and personal repression. Students are frequently considering the possibility of conscientious objection, as they come to see that it is not only this war which is wrong and dirty and immoral, but *all* wars, and they are finding that they cannot in conscience serve in the army as instruments of war.

One of the functions most college teachers fulfill is that of occasional counselor of questioning students. On a campus which has male students there are bound to be requests for information on the draft and for help in making up one's mind regarding it. It is important that every such campus have available some form of draft counseling, people sufficiently informed of the issues that they can help students make a mature decision about the draft. It is also important that there be people with the necessary technical knowledge to help students fill out conscientious objector applications, or to provide information on the procedures for emigrating to Canada. A college theology teacher can make a valuable contribution to a campus by sparking the effort to set up a draft counseling service. On most campuses today several colleagues can be found who are willing to do enough reading to have a beginning familiarity with the problems.

The campus restlessness these days is not all due to the Vietnam war and the draft. Students are discerning and attacking abuses such as institutional racism, complicity between the university and the military, and the university's role as an economic power. Activists in these areas are linked with the war protesters and the Black Power advocates under the label "The New Left." The New Left is not an organization, but a scattered and uncoordinated group of people who share certain basic criticisms of contemporary life, a common style, and a similar impatience with traditional institutions. Kenneth Keniston in *The Young Radicals* described the few basic assumptions of the Movement: "First, it is assumed most major decisions in American society are ultimately determined by the industrial-military combine...Traditional liberalism has failed not only in its foreign policies, but also in its inability to give power and dignity to the poor, the deprived, and the disadvantaged." [5] Those of the New Left ex-

5. Kenneth Keniston, *The Young Radicals*, New York, Harcourt, Brace and World, 1968, p. 17.

plicitly reject the attitudes of the "Old Left," the liberal movement of the 1930's and 40's, which they feel is not nearly radical enough and which has become tired and anyway is responsible for the present social systems in this country. They also reject communism, because they see that it can become just as fixed and oppressive as the present system closer to home that they're fighting. They feel that new social and political institutions must be created, institutions which should be local and decentralized; they should aim at enabling all men and women to participate in making the decisions that affect their own lives.[6]

There are two issues confronted by the New Left which could fruitfully occupy the college theology teacher's attention. One is the black-white conflict, which is going to be the most critical problem in American society for the next decade. As black people become aware of their dignity and grow in it a severe split is occurring which must be healed if the society is to survive. *Gaudium et spes* has said that "the promotion of unity belongs to the innermost nature of the Church." [7] The theologian can bring to the black-white split the ideal of unity, and the entire thrust of revelation toward bringing this unity about.

The second problem is violence as a means of bringing about desired social change. The non-violence of Ghandi and Martin Luther King is not the tactic of the New Left. It is paradoxical that the same Movement which protests the institutional violence in Vietnam often advocates individual violence in pursuit of a better society at home or in Latin America. The theologian can with mutual profit — to himself and the Movement — address the problem of revolution and violence in the contemporary world.

The efforts of a college theology teacher in areas suggested by the peace movement, the draft and the New Left, departing from active demonstration, taking to the streets and occupying buildings, should include the whole range of academically professional activities. The teacher can take advantage of his opportunities for

6. *Ibid.*
7. *Gaudium et spes,* no. 42; Abbott, S.J., p. 241.

writing and speaking in order to grapple with the issues. He can engineer panels, symposia and debates, and see that vital speakers on the issues be brought to the campus. Within his own department he can press for taking the significant issues in already existing courses, or for new courses on war or race, for instance, to be adopted. He can be alert in his own classes for opportunities to make applications to these issues within the tolerable range of the professional ethic of responsibility to his primary subject matter.

Occasionally one longs for the days when college campuses were serene citadels of learning and when most Americans were convinced that conquer we must for our cause it is just. This country has come to a rude and painful awakening in the decade of the 1960's. While it is more comfortable to be drowsy, I for one am glad to be a college theology teacher in this decade. The challenges are here, but so are the resources. We have much to do, and the time is short.

WILLIAM J. KELLY, S.J.

6 Student Power and the Theology Professor

The fact that this topic was selected for this volume as a "current problem" for the college theologian suggests that there is some connection between student power, as a concept and as a phenomenon, and theology, as it is taught and studied in the contemporary college.[1]

But the connection between student power and theology is a presumption. It may yield to the facts in a given college. It may yield to the facts that may come to light in the course of this chapter. However, for the present, the connection between student power and theology will be taken as a working hypothesis and an attempt at verification will be made. It is generally inferred that theology departments and theology professors (teachers in the Church) are expected to have an attitude toward student power that is positive. They are expected to promote it, at least as far as it signifies active participation in the direction of the department and the institution. They are supposed to be able to relate it to the total theological enterprise. Part of the task of this chapter will be to determine if this is feasible, and, if feasible, what specific theological activity might be indicated.

Student power is really neither a new notion nor a new phenomenon. Its history is known and will, in all probability, be written one day. The variety of its expressions, organized or loose knit,

---

1. Cf. Resolutions for *The College Society*, Chicago, Illinois, April, 1969, annual National Convention. Note that it is *participation* that is uppermost in this notion of student power.

planned or spontaneous, peaceful or violent, is, likewise, not new. But, because student unrest is occurring in many places throughout the world, and because the unrest is usually accompanied by claims for an increase of student influence and power, it may be classed as something relatively new to our decade. There is something that *is really* new, and that is the effort that the various disciplines within the colleges and universities are making to subject the concept and the phenomenon of student power to a depth analysis. For, no matter whether one is favorable or unfavorable to student power, all experience a need to account for it.

On the face of it, it seems that a definition and/or description of student power belongs more properly to the social sciences. Some sociologists and intellectual historians are attending to this description. Our purpose will be to determine whether or not theology has a real stake in the general consideration of student power and whether this stake is substantial or coincidental. Our procedure will be as follows: the phenomenon of student power will be discussed; the concept of student power will be analyzed and a definition attempted; finally, the relationship of the phenomenon and the concept of student power with theology will be presented. This latter part of the chapter will be divided into two parts, a theoretical presentation of the relationship, and an empirical presentation of the discussion at Marquette University. The empirical part is based on a survey carried out at Marquette relative to the student's awareness of the phenomenon, familiarity with the concept, and the connection with theology.

1. The Phenomenon of Student Power.

Student power looks like it is here to stay. From Beirut to Brandeis to Berkeley, student unrest and student claims to power are substantially parts of the daily news, considered worth reporting to the world. *Time* reported all this under the rubric "Upsetting Old Patterns,"

> On the campuses, groups of radical students sought nothing less than the destruction of the university. Columbia nearly fell

to them last spring, and San Francisco State College was still reeling under their attacks as the old year closed. Despite the Administration's halting steps toward peace, massive antiwar demonstrations still took place in parks and arenas, men still burned their draft cards, priests and pedagogues still faced trial for attempting to subvert the Selective Service process.

In the U.S., as elsewhere in the world, there was an undeniable legitimacy to many of the dissenters' causes. When they clamored for greater participation in academic decision making or more meaningful curricula or better job opportunities in the ghettos, colleges and corporations and city halls generally proved willing to meet their demands, at least half way. Indeed, one of the most remarkable aspects of a remarkable year was the resilience of American society to such wide-ranging attacks on so many hitherto sacrosanct institutions.[2]

Although student movements have upset old patterns before in history, and episodes of the exercise of student power occurred in university circles as far back as the middle ages, it seems that the nineteenth century is the parent of the present kind of student movement, with its desire for social change and its sense of power to effect change. In the nineteenth century, the "age of ideology," large numbers of students, the middle class, were present in the university centers of Europe. In pursuit of intellectual culture, their critical faculties were being developed at the same time that they were coming into an awareness of their relationship to man and society.[3] Lewis S. Feuer calls attention to patterns in the Russian student movement of 1873-1877. These Russian students were convinced that it was their mission as "intellectuals" to bring "social consciousness to the people." In their own self-consciousness, "students in student movements, have been the bearers of

2. "Upsetting Old Patterns," *Time*, January 3, 1969, p. 10.
3. Cf. Henry D. Aiken, *The Age of Ideology* (New York, Toronto: The American Library, Mentor Books, 1956). See Chapter I, "Philosophy and Ideology in the 19th Century."

a higher ethic than the surrounding society." [4] Feuer seems to suggest that students are a real class in society, but some of today's elders do not seem willing to give them this much status.[5] Frederico Mancini, reporting on the Italian Student Movement,[6] points out that real power in the universities lies in the chair professors and students are considered tolerated guests. He refers to a Brooks Report [7] for a more complete explanation of the Italian university system. But he claims that the Italian students, largely representative of the middle class (petty bourgeois), do not manifest what Marx called the "bedurfnis der Gesellschaft." They are not truly Marxist, though they still venerate H. Marcuse as a prophet of the Left. Their main interest seems to be to change the power structure, wherever it exists. Mancini dismisses the charge of neo-Fascism also.[8] And, though the university system is

4. Lewis S. Feuer, "Conflict of Generations," *The Saturday Review*, January 18, 1969, pp. 53-55; 66-68. In another book, Mr. Feuer judges that "liberal civilization begins when the age of ideology is over." But he suggests in this *Saturday Review* article that student movements may be too tied to the ideologies of the previous age, and thus inherit all their weaknesses. Such students would not be acceptable heralds of the liberal civilization. Mancini (see Footnote 6) judges the Italian Student Movement as more akin to the real liberals of the Enlightenment, and not so tied to the ideologies of Marxism or Fascism, and hence more reputable leaders of a new Liberal movement. Cf. Lewis S. Feuer, *Psychoanalysis and Ethics*, (Springfield, Illinois: Charles C. Thomas, Publisher, 1955), p. 128.

5. W. H. Ferry, "Students and Society," *A Center Occasional Paper*, (Santa Barbara, California: Published by the Center for the Study of Democratic Institutions, 1967), p. 2, refers to "a self-proclaimed class, the young."

6. Frederico Mancini, "The Italian Student Movement," *AAUP Bulletin*, 54 (1968), pp. 427-432.

7. *Ibid.*, p. 428. The Brooks Report, 1967, was published by the Organization for Economic Cooperation and Development. Mancini says that there is quite a bit written on student movements, but that the best is Rossana Rossanda, *L'anno degli studenti* (De Donato, Bari, 1968).

8. *Ibid.*, p. 432. This charge was made by Andrew M. Greeley in his syndicated column, *The Catholic Herald Citizen*, 99 (January 1969), p. 10. A similar warning is raised in an editorial of *America*, "Campus

"short-sighted," dominated by a "power crazy oligarchy" and though student "protest, subversive and violent is legitimate in Italy," the Student Movement is not really concerned with the conditions described nor really interested in changing them. Their consuming interest is

"... not so much the socialization of the means of production, to which they pay little more than lip service, as the elimination of the present, or rather, of any structure of power." [9]

Closer to home, the student movement in the USA is getting its share of attention from the analysts. A recent Gallup poll showed that it was a number-one topic of conversation.[10] But the Cox Commission report made an effort to analyze the student movement in depth for the American scene.

In this report, the main lines of the phenomenon of student power are drawn — participation and confrontation. The underlying causes of the student unrest were tabulated. These all seem to be constants in the student movement in the USA.

Though decidedly better off in quality of student life than their counterparts in France or in Italy, the students in the USA have in common with their brothers a deep and stirring concern. Student concern for racial justice, concern for peace (especially in the Vietnam conflict), concern for a sick society, and concern for the unconcerned faculty.[11] Accompanying these deep causes of unrest is the realization of the present lack of power among

Near Fascism," *America*, March 29, 1969, pp. 350-351.

9. *Ibid.*, p. 431 of the Mancini article.

10. George C. Gallup, "College Rebellion Embitters, etc." (Princeton, New Jersey: Institute of Public Opinion, 1969), as quoted in *The Milwaukee Sentinel*, March 3, 1969. Another indication of the current interest in this problem is the fact that there was a panel on May 2, 1969 at the annual meeting of the AAUP. Cf. "Annual Meeting Confronts Challenge and Change Issues," *Academe*, (March, 1969), announcing the 55th annual meeting.

11. *Crisis at Columbia, The Cox Commission Report* (New York: Random House, Vintage Books, 1968).

students to do anything about eliminating these evils. Moreover, there is the open accusation or the hidden unspoken charge that those who do have the power, the "Establishment" (parents, educators, politicians, police, clergy) are guilty of not having applied it to the weaknesses of contemporary society. Hence they desire a relocation of power, preferably totally in themselves, or failing that, at least a better balance in their favor than that which they have experienced up until now.

According to the Cox Commission report, students of today seem to exhibit a higher level of social conscience than students of the immediately preceding generations.[12] Students of today take ideals seriously and seek to save society from its sickness. In the paternalistic and authoritarian university, students are seeking to be brought *into the decision making,* not only in regard to university and student affairs, but in all matters which they claim affect them as students and as persons. Racial injustice and the war in Vietnam are the major inconsistencies of contemporary society. The university is an accomplice in the perpetuation of these inconsistencies. The students, then, seek to harness the resources of the university and direct them against these ills, and the omnipresent urban ills of poverty and lack of equal opportunity. But the present power structure, authoritarian and paternalistic, and guilty of collaboration in these present injustices, offers them only talk. And conventional discourse tends to produce in the most idealistic the most frustration. Hence, direct action, confrontation, gradually replace efforts at participation. Then sit-ins, and other forms of protest (more or less violent), are applied on occasion of the manifestation of institutional weakness.

At Marquette University, history repeated itself; and the phenomenon of a student movement *Respond,* and its exercise of student power, along with the reasons underlying the move-

12. *Ibid.,* p. 35. According to Feuer (cf. footnote 4) there is a striking similarity of these causes of unrest among the Russian Students of the late 19th Century, before the revolution was taken out of their hands.

ment and its exercise of power were nearly identical with what occurred elsewhere in the world and in the country. Although the empirical part of this paper will provide a more detailed and a more accurate analysis, some of the obvious points of similarity can be mentioned here. The student movement *Respond* formed largely against the backdrop of the broader civil rights issues and racial justice. Organizations already operative in the university structure (e.g., YCS, and Students United for Racial Equality) yielded to the newer, spontaneous, unstructured "movement" *Respond.* The role of SDS in this particular manifestation seems to have been minimal. The MU student, as his counterpart in Italy and elsewhere in the US, was touched in his conscience over racial injustice, the war in Vietnam, and the general inequality in the urban life (ghetto vs. suburbia). Though initially working within unspoken but generally acceptable limits of dissent, a small group become more and more militant as they apparently became more and more frustrated at the slowness of the general student body, the faculty, and the administration to act. Disruption was soon considered by a few to be an acceptable means of reaching the goal of *Respond,* since the goal was judged praiseworthy, and a conscientious duty. Other factors contributed in a lesser way to the student unrest. The students lost confidence in obtaining a real participation in a common enterprise. There was a feeling that they were being financially exploited for the profit of the university and that the faculty were too busy with their academic careers to devote much time, energy, and attention to talking with students.[13]

The theology professor at MU is very much at home in

13. These factors no doubt were present, but the survey which will be summarized in part three of this paper will let the Marquette students speak for themselves. The Commission and the general Marquette experience are general enough, and seem to have been the same as reported in the study at the Center for the Study of Democratic Institutions. Cf. Jeffrey Elman, "Democracy, Students, and the University," *Students and Society,* A Center Occasional Paper (Santa Barbara, California, 1967), p. 15.

certain areas of this student movement and in the general causes
of student unrest. Inasmuch as they touch upon social consciousness, there is a similar quickening within contemporary theology
of the emphasis on community and responsibility. Inasmuch as
the student movement appeals to the idealists, the theologian would
be interested in this audience. As for the issues of civil rights,
concern for the poor, waging the peace — all of these are in the
mind of the contemporary Christian theologian. For he judges,
and rightly so, that the religious and theological traditions have
much to offer on these issues. It is not surprising, therefore, that
the theology professor feels challenged to get involved and share
the student concern. Nor is it surprising to find some theology professors even attempting to awaken the same concern in segments
of the student population that do not yet reflect the concern of
the others.

But it is also true that the movement does not need the theologian, not at MU or anywhere else for that matter. Nor will
the movement wait for him. Much of it is going on without his
support or the support of Christian theology as such. It may
be true now, as it was true in the nineteenth-century Russian student movement, that a residual Christian doctrine of hope was
alive and at the source of the student action. But it seems to be
equally probable that much of the activity present is carried on
without reference to religious faith, modern or contemporary. This
is not so true in the MU movement, which at least initially was
guided by some very ardent and convinced Christians; but it became evident that the disruption and the confrontation could be
carried out by ardor unrelated to Christian fervor and devotion.

2. The Concept of Student Power.

Student power has been labeled a "loaded term" [14] redolent
of competing interests or power blocs. Charles Hartmann, Dean
of students at Georgetown, disclaims any legitimacy to the term

14. Charles Hartmann, "Student Power Should Be Constructive," *Georgetown Today*, 1 (1969), pp. 10-11.

so conceived. He suggests rather that student power is based on an obligation "as teachers and learners — as colleagues in the academic fraternity — to demonstrate their concern for the health of the community. The university cannot be described in terms of competing power groups but in terms of a community with common aims." In this community "student power can and should be a constructive force, free of divisive manipulation and role playing." Student power is based on the "legitimacy of students sharing in university affairs in the fullest sense. In this context student power is meshed into an institution with a new sense of community rather than a system of separate domains and vetoes. This concept of shared power does not argue that a university is a democracy based upon 'one man, one vote' with all entitled to an equal claim to power." It may be said that this tells more what student power should and should not be from the viewpoint of a university administrator, and obviously one that will appeal to many university administrators, faculty, loyal parents, and alumni today.

The following defines the same from another point of view, that of Jack Cummins, Instructor in the Theology Department at MU and member of the *Respond* Steering Committee: "Student power very simply means that students have decision making powers in areas in which they are competent," [15] and "most power resides with the administration" since "faculty and students have been too apathetic to assert their *proper role* in a university." Cummins argues there is no reason why the delineation of power and responsibility cannot be done in a rational way. "However, if the power is not given up by the administration, then there is every justification for protesting the abusive usurpation of power on their part." Cummins adds that the student responsibility is to redirect or to effect a change in the stance of the "university toward the community at large." [16] What becomes obvious is that there

15. Jack Cummins, "Perspectives," *The Marquette Internationale* (Formerly *Nota Bene*), (Milwaukee, Wisconsin: private circulation for the Marquette University International Students, October, 1968), p. 1.
16. *Ibid.*, the italics are mine.

are many definitions of student power, or at least that the words carry certain levels of meaning depending upon who is using them. Lewis Feuer, in defining what a student movement is, gives elements of a possible definition of student power.

Student movements are born of vague, undefined, emotions which seek for some issue, some cause to which to attach themselves. A complex of urges — altruism, idealism, revolt, self-sacrifice, for a strategic avenue of expression.[17]

The student movement usually finds another movement in the social order and attaches itself to this as a "carrier" movement. Feuer proceeds with his definition:

We may define student movement as a congregation of students inspired by aims which they try to explicate in political ideology, and moved by an emotional rebellion in which there is always present a disillusionment with and rejection of the values of the older generation.[18]

In this attempt at a definition of a student movement, it seems that Feuer defines *power* in the political ideology, though this is not perfectly clear. At least it may be said that the political context is his central interest, and he does not develop the "aims" that inspire the student. One of Feuer's critics, Irving Horowitz, also is concerned with the political level of meaning in the term student power:

It is clear that this generation has the time and the affluence to see itself as a social subclass having permanent political and social aims, even though the state of being a student is transitional.[19]

17. Lewis S. Feuer, "Conflict of Generations," *The Saturday Review* (January 18, 1969), p. 55.
18. *Ibid.*
19. Irving Louis Horowitz, "Young Radicals and Their Professorial 'Crit-

Horowitz defines student power in terms that are political and ideological, but is, in contrast to the critics of the New Left and the student radicals, more than ready to admit the moral concern underlying the political action. For Horowitz, the "question of control is eminently moral." [20]

To acknowledge underlying "aims" of student power as Feuer does, and to admit the dimension of moral concern as Horowitz does, opens up other levels of meaning for student power. Cummins is also concerned with the political significance in the term. He includes this in commenting on the control that he wants students to have through the exercise of their student maturity and competence. This control is exercised through decision making, relatively autonomous in areas specifically touching student affairs. The type of control that is uppermost in this thinking is participatory; for the students are conceived as acting in concert with other competent sources of direction in the university. But Cummins is ready to identify the power source behind the control as love, or Christian charity. This replacement of love for aims or moral concern brings the term student power more directly into the Christian student's quality of life, and, therefore into the sphere of interest of the theology professor.[21]

In a paper, advertised as a product of the *Respond* Movement at Marquette University, the attempt is made to discuss the concept of student power so that both parties of the dialog, students and administration, might share the same level of meaning. This paper enters into the concept and defines it with still another level of meaning, suggesting that student power is best understood as

tics,'" *Commonweal*, LXXXIX (January 31, 1969), pp. 552-556. Horowitz responds especially to critics of the New Left, who chided the New Left for being a *moralizing* force rather than a *political* force.
20. *Ibid.*
21. Jack Cummins, "Perspectives," *Internationale*, (Milwaukee, Wisconsin: 1968, A Private Circulation for the International Students of Marquette University). "The problem of determining basic priorities is even more imperative in a Catholic University, *because love would of necessity be the foremost priority* and not money." (Italics mine).

signifying authority, more specifically charismatic authority.[22] The author of the paper bemoaned the fact that the lack of conceptual clarity made the dialog between the administrators of the university and the students impossible, and that it was this fact, more than anything else, that brought about the confrontation.

It would seem that, in an intellectual community like a university, the communication of meaning could be achieved more easily, more efficiently, and less painfully by attempts at conceptual clarification, than by direct action confrontation.[23]

The author suggests that a simple translation of the word *power* into *authority* might be the initial stage of clarification, but takes the occasion to instruct his readers as to the precise meaning of authority. In the context, authority itself is defined as "having power for a specific purpose and within specified limits." Each authority is limited by the purpose for which it exists. The power for a specific purpose is further defined as a power for "determinative decision making" within its own area of specific competence. Certain known tensions in the levels of meaning of authority appear immediately. There is a tension between juridical (or legal, official) authority and personal or communitarian authority (derived from the scholar's common life and purpose).[24] Legal authority or official authority is seen as that which pertains to administrative competence, and this is immediately translated into an authority of service — service to the community of scholars.

---

22. Harry B. Zerner, "Student Power: An Attempt to Define the Term With Conceptual Clarity," (Milwaukee, Wisconsin: *Ad usum privatum*, 1968).
23. *Ibid.*, p. 1.
24. *Ibid.* Father Zerner is using concepts here that are derived from ecclesial theology. He is making the application to the university. But one of the weaknesses of this application is the fact that the community of scholars (and this includes the students) is really no longer united by sharing the same purpose; at least they contest the interpretation of the purpose or end of the university. This is one of the sicknesses spoken of in the collection referred to earlier: "Students and Society," p. 15. See note no. 5 of this paper for the complete reference.

This service presumes competence. If there is no demonstrable competence, then the authority is lost. And so a further tension in the meaning of authority appears, that of official authority and authority of competence. This latter tension is most felt by students when the university's official authority is conceived of as an extension of parental authority — an illegitimate extension which is the origin of "paternalism" and the cause of the prolongation of student immaturity.

Student power, or student authority, in this context means that students are prepared to confront administrators with the limitations of their authority and competence, and are prepared to uphold their own rights and authority for decision making and self-determination within the area of their own sphere of competence.[25]

Though obviously borrowed from reflections on ecclesial authority, the translation of *power* into *authority* would be applicable in any university community; for this substitution of authority fits logically into the general interest of democratization of the university institution.

But in a university that is Christian, other levels of meaning are in the term *student power,* for other levels of meaning are in the term *authority.* In its political and democratic level of meaning, student power can be guided by the principle of enlightened self-interest, but in a Christian university a more challenging principle is at work.

But it is also possible in a Christian university to operate within the context of prophetic or charismatic principles, i.e.,

25. *Ibid.,* p. 4. Various spheres of student competence are: (a) areas of private life (e.g., housing, off campus actions); (b) natural rights due process in disciplinary actions); (c) student rights (those derived from the contractual relationship); (d) student rights (those derived from the expectations the student has from the advertised commitment of the University).

principles not of legitimate self-interest but of selfless service.[26]

With this added dimension of meaning, student power or authority would signify a prophetic message to the other members of the university. The precise function of this charism is compared with the function of "soul power," that is, the power to overcome evil with good by uncompromising love and unselfish service. A Christian university, itself dedicated to this ideal of moral excellence, can and should rejoice that its students signify this in their concept of student power.[27]

This new level of meaning in student power is not as helpful as it looks at first sight; for it is based on an unresolved definition of authority in the Church. Granted that "infallible teachers" and "impeccable administrators" are "incredible," the same is true of student authority if, as the elders suspect, the student authority assumes similar claim to infallibility and impeccability. Granted that student power, when translated into authority inspired by charismatic principles of charity and selfless and uncompromising love, is more meaningful and offers the Christian university community dialogical possibility, the problem remains: who can discern the validity of this charismatic power of students? This is a deeper and more involved question than any argument over the exact limits of areas of competence. The warning of the *America* editorial, reflecting the thought of Dr. Tibor Szamuely, may not be lightly dismissed. No matter how one describes student

26. *Ibid.*, p. 6.
27. Cf. James Hitchcock, "Catholic Universities: Repeat Performance?" *Commonweal*, LXXXIX (January 31, 1969), pp. 556-559. In this article Mr. Hitchcock sounds a warning to Catholic universities and to theology departments in particular, to the effect that they can ill afford to indulge within present university structures a moral effort that would succeed only at the expense of something only recently and painfully gained, namely, academic excellence and integrity. The presumption of moral concern is in the Catholic university's favor; if this presumption is erroneous in some cases, then other remedies should be looked for and not the surrender of academic goals. A special appeal is made to students to consider this carefully.

power in terms of love, and self-lessness, the danger of power or authority that exists for its own sake is ever present.[28]

This warning sounded and taken to heart, it is nevertheless true that the level of meaning in the term *student power* that is deeper than the political and is related to the charism of love and service in the Christian community is the level of meaning that rightfully brings in the theology professor. For if the commitment to intellectual and moral excellence is real, and if theology is at home in reflection upon the faith-experience, then the theology professor can aid the task of the discernment of power and authority and can guide the students to this kind of necessary theological reflection. Theology professors and departments lay no claim to total discernment of the Spirit. But they do claim to reflect on the experience of Spirit-in-community. They do claim to reflect on the style of life demanded by the presence of the Spirit-of-Christ in the community. The question of authority in the Church does pertain to the theological enterprise. If the notion of student power is going to be translated into authority, then the theologian can guide the committed Christian student to reflect on the deeper meaning of this authority. The theology professor can guide the student to conduct the translation on both the level of scholarly reflection and that of practically living-out the conclusions demanded by this level of meaning.

The third part of this chapter will present further reflections on the contribution that theology can make to the concept of student power. The hypothesis that was accepted in the introduction —— that student power and theology are related — is not yet verified. But the verification process at this point has

_____

28. "Campus Near-Fascism," *America* (March 29, 1969), pp. 350-351. *America* editorializes on a warning of Dr. Tibor Szamuely: "The New Left does not understand power" and real totalitarians know that "it is not ideology but the jackboot that conquers"; and concludes with a warning of its own, "the tragedy for many idealists is that they may be stampeded into serving causes far less human than the abuses they condemn."

greater probability than it had at the beginning for the translation of power into authority is an acceptable theological and political translation, and it can be confirmed as consistent with Christian sources.

3. The Relationship Between Student Power And Theology: The Paradox of Christian Power.

A. *The Theological Reflection.*

It is clear from the preceding material that the phenomenon and the concept of student power pertain largely to political action. The direct concern of student power is the possession of power for the guidance of the institutions by the students themselves, either totally or at least with a greater share of the decision-making function than previously allotted to them. But when student power also signifies "soul power" and assimilates the charismatic principle of selfless service, then theological reflection is very much in order, for these are part of the Christian experience. It is the theologian's task to reflect upon this experience.

> Theology may be defined as the study which, through participation in and reflection upon a religious faith, seeks to express the content of this faith in the clearest and most coherent language available.[29]

As is indicated in the general theme of this volume, theologians do participate in the Christian faith, do speak from this faith. And though they have individual styles as they consider the problems with which they are confronted, they are, in a sense, spokesmen for the community and are "charged with a special responsibility within it." [30]

29. John MacQuarrie, *Principles of Christian Theology,* (New York: Charles Scribner's Sons, 1966), p. 1.
30. *Ibid.,* p. 2.

The concept of student power now carries in its definition a level of meaning drawn from the Christian experience and spoken of in terms of the Christian experience. Hence it is the task of the theologian to reflect upon this experience and to seek to express its content in the clearest and most coherent language available. Here is the precise stake of the theology professor in the student movement and the exercise of student power. Herein is the verification of the hypothesis stated in the introduction of this chapter. But here is the theology professor's embarrassment also. For the relationship of the Christian experience and the world of politics and power, including student power, is set in some of the most baffling paradoxes. The notions of power and authority, both inside and outside the Christian community, are not as yet clearly managed by the theologians nor uniformly interpreted by the exegetes. They are not at first sight promising analogues for a clear and coherent theological analysis of student power.[31]

A question I posed above asked whether the stake of theo-

31. On Sunday, April 20, 1969, Quentin Quesnell, S.J., delivered a Lecture at Marquette University, Brooks Memorial Union, entitled *The Authority for Authority*. The following is an excerpt from some pre-notes. It illustrates the many unresolved questions facing theologians on the nature and exercise of authority.

"The lecture is an attempt to answer the further question: Not only, what is authority, or, who has it, but, why should there be authority in the Church at all, and, where does it come from? If Church authority is said to be grounded in Scripture, what gives Scripture, a document from centuries past, decisive authority for the life of the Church today? The lecture will try to trace the ultimate roots of authority to see if any enduring principle can be uncovered which will be valid even in time of change and doubt . . . in still other words, the lecture will explore the theological question of the ultimate foundations of authority, especially how to apply these effectively in making concrete decisions in a time of transition. What makes authority authoritative? What does it rest on theologically? Suggested and mythical justification for authority will be rejected; suggested and inadequate justifications will be expanded; sociological and anthropological justifications will be theologically ordered and transformed."

logy in the student power movement is substantial or coincidental. A tentative answer can be suggested at this point to the effect that it is both substantial and coincidental. It is substantial because substantive Christian attitudes are involved. It is coincidental because there is literally a falling together of political involvement and Christian commitment.[32] Of the many problems for the theologian, both theoretical and practical, two are singled out for comment, the Christian attitude toward power and the notion of shared charismatic authority. The two concepts are not unrelated. The Christian has always been concerned with power, but perhaps never more than today. Franz Böckle, professor of moral theology at the University of Bonn, says that "Christians are constantly reproached with the fact that in two thousand years they have not yet succeeded in carrying out their noble social principles." [33] The Second Vatican Council's Constitution, "The Church in the Modern World" (Gaudium et spes), calls Christians to a new awareness of their relationship to society. "The Church is considered an institution of social criticism and Christians are being called to the new awareness of the responsibility of the members to become politically involved and thus ensure real social progress." [34] From this emerges the new theme of "political theology." Theology professors must take it upon themselves to place this language of politics and power, involvement and concern in the context of the total Christian paradox.

John McKenzie, S.J., in his book The Power and the Wisdom tries to show what political power is in the mind of the New Testament writers. In the "render to Caesar" (Lk. 20:20-26)

---

32. This falling together of religious commitment and political interest is indicated in the results of the interview schedule that forms the last part of this paper.
33. The Social Message of the Gospels, Volume 35 of Concilium: Theology in the Age of Renewal, ed., Franz Böckle, (New York; Glen Rock, New New Jersey: The Paulist Press, 1968), p. 1.
34. Faith and the World of Politics, Volume 36 of Concilium: Theology in the Age of Renewal, ed., Johannes B. Metz, (New York; Glen Rock, New Jersey: The Paulist Press, 1968), Preface.

passage, McKenzie says that no serious political philosophy was intended.

A political philosophy based on this statement would be rather skimpy. Jesus says nothing about the roots of political power, its legitimacy, its competence. He takes political power as a fact of life and offers nothing except submission to the fact. He places no limitation on the exercise of political power except the sovereignty of God. This is a vital limitation but he does not define it.[35]

Commenting on Rom. 13:1-7, McKenzie shows that Paul is only reflecting the Old Testament conviction that all power is from God. But power as such is morally neutral. "No nation and person can have any power which is not committed to it by God; but the exercise of the power is not thereby authenticated." [36]

There is only one power in the universe and that is the power of God. This is a power to judge and to save. God exercises his power through agents. Nature is such an agent . . . Men and nations are likewise such agents; unlike nature, they are moral agents. But when they act as agents of God's power to save or to judge, they are morally neutral in so far as they are agents; it makes no difference whether they are good or bad, for God can use either . . . . (Jn. 19:11) . . . it is the same power in either case, and it is not diminished by its misuse.[37]

It seems that in Father McKenzie's analysis, there is as much a case for Christian passivity in the face of political power as for Christian initiative. Perhaps more accurately, neither political withdrawal, nor political engagement is endorsed by these New Testament passages. What McKenzie does suggest is this: no

35. John McKenzie, S.J., *The Power and the Wisdom*, (Milwaukee, Wisconsin: The Bruce Publishing Company, 1968), p. 237.
36. *Ibid.*, p. 239.
37. *Ibid.*, pp. 240-241.

matter what attitude is taken toward political power, the "Christian event is not itself violent, and its effects are not felt through vulgar power." A "revolution is always an excessive response." [38] Theologians would do well then to point up the constant need to understand that the New Testament is not a specific guide to proper moral conduct in student movements and exercises of student power. At the risk of complicating the theological task, theologians should point up other aspects of the paradox of power as exemplified in II Corinthians, "My favor is enough for you, for only where there is weakness is perfect strength (*dynamis*) developed," (II Cor. 12:9) and ". . . for it is when I am weak that I am strong (*dynaotos*)" (II Cor. 12:10). That *power* can be a synonym for Christian authority is assured from the briefest glance at a concordance. As a matter of fact, *power* and *authority* are frequently used together. The power of God's grace establishes authority in the weakest and most miserable of human persons. However, *grace, power,* and *authority* taken as synonymous, must be used for judging and for saving. When student power is baptized with this reality, then it does take on this level of meaning and does become a new concept and a new phenomenon. For this kind of power is not ambiguous.[39] This kind of power is a charisma and it is distributed throughout the community of believers. Theologians can point out to the total community that claim to this charisma is not unwarranted and that the total community should expect some claim to this called for in gatherings of Christian students. But theologians have the parallel responsibility of pointing out to Christian students that the discernment of the possession of the charism and the proper exercise of it in service to the community and to humanity is not automatically authenticated.

Power is part of man's world. It is an altogether essential factor in the building up of the human community. It belongs to man's

---

38. *Ibid.,* p. 242.
39. Lionel Rubinoff, *The Pornography of Power,* (Chicago and Toronto: Quadrangle Books, Burns and MacEachern, Ltd., 1968), reviewed in *Ecumenist* 7 (1969), 30-31.

own self-making. Yet the ambiguity of this power is awful. Hidden in the quest for power are sources of destructiveness and violence. In his book Rubinoff tries to examine these sources of evil in human life.[40]

But this warning carries over into the consideration of shared power and authority in the *ekklesia,* the second problem singled out for special consideration.

It goes without saying that all baptized Christians share the authority and the power that is the grace of Christ's saving and judging presence. They share this in an active sense, not a grace to be guarded, but to be exercised and extended to humanity. When student power is meaningfully translated into this grace-filled life, and when power is translated into authority, then the theologian bears the responsibility of helping the Christian student understand the mystery of the sharing of authority in the Church, part of the Mystery of the Church itself.[41]

By the sacred sign of Baptism, a man is incorporated into Christ. He becomes another Christ, an extension into the present and into the future — into time and into history. By Baptism a man is joined to the assembly of the people of God and identifies his life activity with that of the head of the body, Jesus Christ. It is by the Christian community, the Church, that the Leader of the people of God continues to act in history, continues to fuse the historical and eschatological elements of mediating God's intention and activity to all of mankind.

God's intention and activity include that of the exercise of his power — to save and to judge. This exercise of power, then,

40. *Ibid.,* p. 30.
41. William J. Kelly, S.J., "Reflections on the Status of a Theology of the Layman," *Theological Studies,* 28 (1967), p. 718. "There is but one mysterious authority of the transcendent God, made incarnate in his only-begotten Son, Jesus Christ, of whose person the *ekklesia* is an extension; the *ekklesia* possesses the Spirit, which guarantees the divine authority and is its source in our time. Consequently, the laical element of the *ekklesia,* in possessing the Spirit, possesses the Divine authority."

belongs to all in the community. All share in the prophetic role of saving and judging and all have some share in the charismatic principle. The Christian student, aware of this grace and this prophetic power, should not be viewed with alarm if, like Ezekiel, he acts as a sentinel sent by God to safeguard the children of God (Ezek. 9:8-12). The more committed the Christian student is, the more likely he is to be concerned with the proper exercise of his student power.[42]

It is ardently hoped that a mature awareness on the part of the Christian student will be accompanied by an equal authority of competence. The student's own vigorous critical rejection of incompetence of other levels of authority as this touches his student life should be turned as vigorously against his own incompetence when it is manifested. For the grace of prophecy signified in the charism of Christian student power is not an authority of competence. Nor is it an authority of office, from above; it must be discerned. And an excellent beginning of the discernment is in the preparation of the total competence of the student subject of this Christian power. The effective exercise of the full saving and judging activity of the people of God (and through this mediation to all of humanity), depends also in good measure upon an authority of competence. Such power as derived from competence is best achieved for Christian students in dialog with their peers in student organizations,[43] and with other levels of authority in the university. There is no doubt then, that *student power* with its Christian dimension of meaning is an object of interest and concern to the theology professor.

Defined as personal competence and responsibility for decision making in their proper role in the university, inspired by aims which they try to explicate in a structural political ideology, accompanied by an awareness of their fundamental Christian office, supported by a sincere and finely honed critical power that can

---

42. In general, the survey bears this out at the Marquette University scene.
43. William J. Kelly, S.J., "The Response of the Woman Religious to the Demand for Christian Leadership," *Review for Religious*, 25 (1966), 814-867.

reject all that is false in older and present generations, exercised in relative autonomy in their special student "class," — this is a student power that theology professors as teachers in the Church can endorse and promote.

B. *Empirical Study of the Relationship Between Student Power and Theology.*

It was immediately obvious at the outset of the writing of this chapter that here in the USA as elsewhere in the world of higher education, the exercise of student power occurs with or without reference to theology and the ideas and attitudes of the various theology or religion departments within universities.

At Marquette, there was a confrontation that brought student power into focus. This was the *Respond* movement of May 1968. For all practical purposes, this movement was inspired by and directed by some persons involved in the theological enterprise. Though not an official Departmental effort, the influence of theology was felt in the persons involved. Most of the members of the theology faculty were in sympathy with this application of student power as it was closely connected with the ideals of the promotion of racial justice. Eugene Shaw, S.J., was requested to prepare a survey of student opinion on the *Respond* movement and related activities. Some specific questions were prepared to get at the actual student concepts of student power. Furthermore, an attempt was made to determine if the students themselves connected involvement in student power related to their theological doctrines.

An empirical study of the Marquette experience was fixed upon as most suitable for the consideration of other Christian universities and it is with this conviction that the results of the empirical study are included following this chapter.[44]

---

44. Copies of the Interview Schedule are available on request at Marquette University. A more complete work on the Schedule, with other correlations, is planned for a separate publication. These may be requested from Eugene Shaw, S.J., Fordham University, Bronx, N.Y. 10458.

EUGENE F. SHAW, S.J.

7 Student Power at Marquette University : An Empirical Analysis

At the request of Fr. William Kelly, who wished to have some empirical data on the subject, a survey on student power was conducted on the Marquette campus early in February of 1969 among 539 students in the day division of the University. These completed interviews constitute more than 90 per cent of the systematically drawn sample of 598 from the then current official list of the undergraduate and graduate student population of Marquette.[1] This survey was a class project of the "Research Methods" course in the Department of Sociology and Anthropology. Under the supervision of the instructor, members of the class served as interviewers and prepared the data for computer analysis.

The research instrument is appended to this chapter. Its items include indicators attempting to measure students' attitude toward student power, the factors determining student role in the exercise of that power, student preference for specified degrees and varieties of participation in university affairs, and their involvement in, and verdict on, the *Respond* Movement. The major test, or explanatory, variables incorporated into the analysis include sex, age, class status, school affiliation, student satisfaction with Marquette, self-assessment on political orientation, and theological and religious dimensions of student power.

To the extent that the data have been analyzed thus far, this report will focus on these last named and stipulated correlates of

---

1. Systematic sampling is a type of probability sampling. Cf. Frederick F. Stephan and Philip J. McCarthy, *Sampling Opinions* (New York: John Wiley and Sons), pp. 207-209.

power, especially as they relate to the 1968 spring demonstrations on the campus. A more comprehensive study of the data is being prepared. The final report will review the major sources of errors inherent in a project of this sort and the controls used to reduce their contamination of the data. For the present we may point out that there is sufficient evidence to guarantee the overall reliability and validity of the results.

An Overview of the Study

Before we concentrate on the campus demonstrations and the hypothesized theological and religious correlates of student attitude toward, and participation in, the *Respond* Movement, a brief look at the larger study, along with a description of the sample's composition, seems advisable. These pertinent excerpts will provide a better framework for assessing the findings of that subanalysis which is the focal interest of this report.

The sample is quite representative of the undergraduate population in its composition by sex, age, class status and college affiliation [2]: 62 per cent are males, 41 per cent were born after 1948, 43 per cent are lower-classmen, and 47 per cent are enrolled in the College of Liberal Arts; 86 per cent acknowledge that they were raised in the Catholic faith, 69 per cent say they participate in religious services regularly (at least "about once a week"), while 37 per cent claim religion plays a great part in their life. On campus issues, 5 per cent of the sample view themselves as politically radical or even militant. Both radicalism and conservatism are more prevalent among the male than among the female students. The women prefer to regard themselves as moderates, though at least their verbal responses to other items in the survey would suggest that they are more liberal, if not more radical, than their male counterparts. The under-20 age group has the fewest con-

2. The graduate students are underrepresented in the sample. They account for 31 per cent ($N = 18$) of the non-completed interviews ($N = 59$). No sex, school or age bias resulted from the failure to obtain interviews from the entire sample.

servatives. Other age categories distribute themselves about equally among the liberal, moderate and conservative classifications. It was interesting to note that 85 per cent of the respondents agree that Marquette is a good place to go to school — and this, despite the questionnaire's initial focusing on three possible sources of student discontent: alleged faculty disinterest in the students, administrative mistreatment of them, and implication of the impersonal character of a large university. Only a small percentage (4%) pick student membership on the board of trustees as the most favored form of student participation in university affairs, but an even smaller percentage (1%) want no voice at all. Opinion is fairly evenly divided among the three other proffered options: student control of nonacademic matters, student consultation regarding curriculm and examinations, and student representation on policy-shaping academic committees; this last has a slight edge over the other two for the entire sample and is the preferred feminine choice.

The respondents would concede to the administrators the most power in making major university policies, but would like to see it shared with the faculty and, to a lesser extent, with the students themselves. More than three-fourths of the sample want something more than a consultative voice for students, though this role for students in university affairs becomes increasingly more popular among the undergraduate classes as they approach graduation. The majority claiming "some power," however, remains steady throughout the four years. There is almost unanimous agreement among the respondents concerning one's right to self-determination, but some ambivalence exists regarding the means of assuring its exercise. Recourse to violence finds support among 46 per cent of those interviewed, although many of these are also included, by necessity, among the 71 per cent agreeing that improvements should come about by democratic methods and through limited action within the present social structures.

Student power is overwhelmingly regarded as something valuable, good, brave and timely. For the respondents the concept refers, moreover, to something that is clean, wise, mature, admirable and rational. They see it, decisively, as something usual and promising, though decidedly rash and aggressive. On other scales there is less agreement. More students view student power as shortsighted rather than farsighted, ethical rather than pragmatic, severe rather than lenient — though neither polarity in any of these three dichotomous sets receives a majority vote. More specifically, the students look upon student power as a means of asserting their human dignity and as a check on possible administrative injustices, but they express some hesitation in resorting to violence to counteract alleged administrative complacency and faculty indifference regarding their problems or to attain a "democratic voice" in university affairs, even though a large majority are of the opinion that university officials tend to govern by force and not by consent of the university community.

The "type of student leadership" appears to be the paramount factor in a student's decision to participate in the exercise of student power. This is closely followed by the legitimacy of the proposed means employed and the social importance of the issue. Of the six named factors, theological implications of the issue ranks fifth in importance, somewhat behind faculty support of the issue, with only 24 per cent considering such implications to "matter a great deal." The majority reject the notion that mere opposition to authority would have appreciable influence on their decision.

Most students accept the idea of a Christian revolutionary movement in contemporary society and profess to see the relevancy of the study of theology in their lives, but are somewhat reluctant to accord a militant leadership role to the Church or to find support for student militancy in the deliberations of the Vatican Council.

The *Respond* Movement

Of this sample, 68 per cent were enrolled at Marquette during the 1968 demonstrations on campus. Almost three-fourths of these think the *Respond* Movement was at least "somewhat successful"; more males than females demur from such a positive characterization of the Movement (27% to 15%). Perceived success of the Movement is associated with how one views student power in general. Those considering it timely, admirable, valuable, far-sighted, optimistic and promising attribute success to it more often than do those who regard it in quite the opposite way, though "success" is the majority verdict of all categories on these attribute dimensions of student power. The greatest percentage difference in granting success to the Movement occurs on the hopeless-promising-dichotomy — 55 per cent to 76 per cent. A similarly large discrepancy in perceived success of the demonstrations is apparent between those who were sympathetic and those unsympathetic toward them and even actively opposed to the Movement: 88 per cent of the former and 68 per cent of the latter hold the outcome of the *Respond* demonstrations was successful. There is also a closer association of perceived success with perceived improvement of student-faculty relations as a result of the demonstrations than with similar perception of improvement in relations among students or between students and university administrators. The students are divided, however, in their support of the Movement; 10 per cent actively participated in the demonstrations (proportionately twice as many women as men, 17% to 8%), and 6 per cent actively opposed them and the Movement itself (proportionately more men than women, 8% to 1%). More than one-eighth of the sample claim they were disinterested and in no way involved in the demonstrations, either in support of or in opposition to the Movement.

Active supporters and organizers of the demonstrations are found principally among those least satisfied with Marquette. By far the strongest correlation with *Respond* support among the three specific items measuring discontent is that dealing with inconsiderateness of administrative personnel toward students (21% of those who disagreed vs. 3% of those who agreed with the statement that "In their contacts with the administrative personnel, students are treated with the consideration due a human being.") Indeed, proportionately four times as many disagreers as agreers with the statement claim they helped to organize the Movement. The nature of involvement in the demonstrations is, of course, strongly associated with political self-tagging: the conservatives were largely unsympathetic and the liberals were overwhelmingly sympathetic to the Movement. But while 21 per cent of the self-styled liberals (and 84% of the self-proclaimed radicals and militants; since the sample contains only 13 who so regard themselves, they are not analyzed separately) either helped to organize or actively participated in the Movement, only 11 per cent of the conservatives worked to oppose the Movement. Almost one-fourth of the conservatives declare they were disinterested and in no way involved, far outdistancing the rest of the student body in apathy on this matter.

On particular ideological orientations that distinguish the more conservative from the more liberal groups, the students are wondrously consistent: the nature of their involvement in the demonstrations was for the most part congruent with their beliefs regarding: (1) the necessity of orderly and rational change within the present social and political structures. Eighteen per cent who disagree with this stated necessity actively participated in the demonstrations and an additional 44 per cent were interested sympathizers, while 2 per cent opposed the Movement — in contrast with those who strongly agree with the need for orderly change: 11 per cent of these actively joined forces against Respond and 24 per cent sympathized with it. None in this category of status-quo supporters in the sample apparently was active in the *Respond* Movement, but almost one-fourth of them held themselves aloof from the entire proceedings; (2) the nature of student power. Twelve per cent who agree that its essential purpose is "to show the authorities that students exist as human beings who want an opportunity to decide their own future" actively joined the *Respond* Movement, with 45 per cent more being sympathetic and interested in it and only 3 per cent actively opposing it. The role pattern is reversed for those who disagree with the statement that tries to encapsulate the essential purpose of student power: 10 per cent of these actively opposed the Movement, 54 per cent were unsympathetic to it, and only 4 per cent joined the Movement; (3) the Church, religion, and theology. A rather strong statistical relationship exists between the expressed desire that the Church be a power structure working for radical change and the student's role in the demonstrations, as Table 1 clearly indicates. Fifteen per cent of those who want the Church to work for change made positive contributions to the Movement, and an additional 42 per cent were sympathetic to its goals, in contrast to those who are unfavorable to the idea of a militant Church: only 35 per cent were at least sympathetic to the Movement, among whom were found only a few participants in the demonstrations.

There is not only greater favorable reaction to the *Respond* Movement but also less variability in the role adoptions among those who essentially agree that student militancy for necessary change is in keeping with the spirit of the Vatican Council than among those who tend to disagree. The latter's indecisiveness may also account for the large percentage among those who, according to Table 2, claim to have been disinterested in the entire affair.

The correlation, reported in Table 3, between participation in the demonstrations and admitted importance of religion in one's life tends to be curvilinear. But those who admit religion plays a large part and those who say it has only a small or no effect at all were more inclined to make a positive contribution to the *Respond* Movement than were those who assign to religion a role of only moderate importance, though those for whom religion plays a large part contributed most of the organizers to the Movement. The moderately "religious," on the other hand, were more apt to organize the opposition to *Respond*. The disinterested were most likely to be found among those for whom religion assumes little or no importance.

The possible impact of one's theological studies on the nature of his or her activities during the demonstrations is less clear. Those agreeing that "study of theology advances one's quest for meaning in one's life" were likely to organize the *Respond* Movement, while those disagreeing with the statement were more apt to be the core of the opposition. But Table 4 also shows a greater percentage of those who deny the influence of theological studies than of those who affirm its influence actively participated in the *Respond* Movement.

The theological orientation of the Movement may perhaps be suggested by the analysis in Table 5. Most of the organizers of *Respond* found in the sample are those who claim that the theological implications of an issue is crucial or matters a great deal in determining the student's role in the exercise of student power on campus. Sympathy with and interest in the *Respond* Movement, moreover, decreases as the claimed effect of theological implications on the use of power diminishes.

The seriousness and the earnestness of the students involved in the demonstrations might be derived from an inspection of the series of analyses found in Table 6. Of the several listed factors, in addition to theological implication of an issue, stipulated as determining a student's role in the exercise of power, the social importance or urgency of the issue, the type of student leadership and the legitimacy of the means employed are more closely associated with positive student contributions to the demonstrations than are the prospect of successfully opposing university authorities or even faculty support of the issue. The respondents believe that the demonstrations tended to improve student-faculty and student-administrators relations rather than worsen them, and the former more than the latter, though the majority profess to see no change in these relations.

The theology department contributed the most militant students and the most militant faculty members to the Movement, according to the respondents, who conceded, however, that neither were "actually too militant." Thirty-two percent of the sample named students from the theology department as the most militant on campus during the demonstrations; a third of these respondents considered theology students very militant. Of those naming non-theology students most militant, only 18 per cent thought them to be really militant. Sixty per cent of the sample, both males (57%) and females (63%), present on campus during the demonstrations volunteered the theology department as the most militant faculty group on campus. This tendency to associate the greatest militancy with the theology faculty is apparent among students of all schools and colleges in the university. It is most pronounced among the journalism-speech students (69%) and liberal arts students (66%) and least pronounced, but still sizable and the modal category, among the engineering students (47%). Selection of the theology faculty for militant honors is not associated with political ideology or class status, but progressively a greater percentage volunteer the theology faculty as class status varies from sophomore to senior standing (57% to 65%). The graduate students, by ranking highest in refusals to name a department, deny thereby the theology faculty a majority but not the modal vote.

It may be of interest to add that those naming theology faculty members as the most militant were less likely than others to see student-faculty relations deteriorate "because of the demonstrations." In contrast, student and faculty members of the theology department get only a small percentage of the "most militant" vote of the newcomers to the campus. This discrepancy among the two groups, those present and those not present during the period of the demonstrations, gives added weight to the suspicion that the high visibility of members of the theology faculty during the demonstrations accounts for that department being the most frequently volunteered by the respondents as the most militant.

More than one-fourth of the newly arrived students on campus, when asked to recall their reaction to the demonstrations at the time they heard about them, either claim they couldn't remember or do not admit to hearing about them before enrolling at Marquette. Of those that did hear about them, the more typical reaction is reported as favorable rather than not. In this subsample of 170 students, a clear majority of 63 per cent would at least be sympathetic to such demonstrations as occurred on campus during the spring of 1968. These recent campus arrivals perceive student-faculty relations to be quite good, but student-administrators relationships quite strained and even, in the estimate of one-fifth of them, very bad.

Conclusions

Further work needs to be done before an adequate empirical test is had of the hypothesized relationship between theological considerations and the exercise of student power. Multivariate analysis is required to tease out the independent of interactive impact of theological studies and religious conviction — to assess the explanatory and predictive ability of each commitment, disci-

plinary and doctrinal, regarding the variation in student use of
power — and to check for spuriousness (merely statistical and
not really functional associations). Partialling analysis is called
for also to distinguish more precisely among political and theological implications of the *Respond* Movement. Such analyses are
now being programmed and their results will be included in the
final report. The analysis carried out to date, however, suggests
that theological correlates of student power and of demonstrations
on at least one Christian campus cannot be cavalierly dismissed as
inconsequential or non-existent.

APPENDIX

CORRELATES OF STUDENT PARTICIPATION IN THE **RESPOND** MOVEMENT, MARQUETTE UNIVERSITY CAMPUS, SPRING 1968

TABLE 1. Type of Involvement in the Demonstrations, by Attitude Toward a Radical Church [1]

Radical Church:	For	Against
Helped to Organize the Movement	3%	1%
Actively Participated in Movement	12	4
Sympathetic and Interested in Movement	42	30
Unsympathetic but Interested in Movement	29	45
Actively Opposed the Movement	3	4
Helped Organize Opposition to Movement	1	2
Disinterested and Uninvolved	10	14
(Number of cases) [2]	100%	100%
	(169)	(182)

1. The statement eliciting degree of agreement or disagreement was actually worded in a negative way: "The Church should *not* be a power structure working for radical change."
2. Fourteen responses were "Undecided" or "Don't know" on item about the Church.

TABLE 2. Type of Involvement in the Demonstrations, by Image of Vatican Council as Supporting Student Militancy [1]

Council Supports Militancy:	Agree	Disagree
Helped to Organize the Movement	3%	1%
Actively Participated in Movement	14	3
Sympathetic and Interested in Movement	48	30
Unsympathetic but Interested in Movement	27	43
Actively Opposed the Movement	2	6
Helped Organize Opposition to Movement	1	2
Disinterested and Uninvolved	5	15
	100%	100%
(Number of cases) [2]	(160)	(165)

1. Item was phrased in the interview schedule as follows: "It is in the spirit of the Second Vatican Council for a student to be a militant crusader for necessary change in the world today."
2. Twenty-five responses were "Undecided," fifteen were "Don't know" on item about the Vatican Council.

TABLE 3. Type of Involvement in the Demonstrations, by Importance of Religion [1]

Religion Plays:	Small or No Part	Moderate Part	Large Part
Helped to Organize the Movement	5%	1%	0%
Actively Participated in Movement	9	5	11
Sympathetic and Interested in Movement	38	37	37
Unsympathetic but Interested in Movement	36	37	31
Actively Opposed the Movement	3	4	3
Helped Organize Opposition to Movement	1	3	1
Disinterested and Uninvolved	8	13	17
	100%	100%	100%
(Number of cases)	(128)	(153)	(84)

1. Item was phrased in the interview schedule as follows: "What part does religion play in your life?"

TABLE 4. Type of Involvement in the Demonstrations, by Attitude Toward Theological Studies [1]

Study of Theology Helps:	Agree	Disagree
Actively Participated in Movement	2%	1%
Helped to Organize the Movement	7	11
Sympathetic and Interested in Movement	40	33
Unsympathetic but Interested in Movement	36	33
Actively Opposed the Movement	3	6
Helped Organize Opposition to Movement	1	3
Disinterested and Uninvolved	11	13
	100%	100%
(Number of cases) [2]	(257)	(93)

1. Item was phrased in the interview schedule as follows: "A study of theology advances one's quest for meaning in one's life."
2. Fifteen responses were "Undecided" or "Don't know" on item about the study of theology.

TABLE 5. Type of Involvement in the Demonstrations, by Saliency of Theological Importance of Theological Implications

Helped to Organize the Movement
Actively Participated in Movement
Sympathetic and Interested in Movement
Unsympathetic but Interested in Movement
Actively Opposed the Movement
Helped Organize Opposition to Movement
Disinterested and Uninvolved

(Number of cases)

TABLE 6. TYPE OF INVOLVEMENT IN THE DEMONSTRATIONS,

Respond Movement:		Social Importance, Urgency of Issue				Legitimate Means in Its Exercise		
	4	3	2	$(1-0)^2$	4	3	2	$(1-0)^2$
Helped Organize It	5%	1%	0%	0%	2%	2%	1%	0%
Participated in It	17	7	1	0	7	10	5	8
Sympathetic to It	40	41	35	16	40	38	43	8
Unsympathetic to It	30	35	41	37	36	34	35	38
Opposed It	3	3	3	10	5	3	1	8
Organized Opposition	0	1	3	5	1	3	0	4
Uninvolved	5	12	17	32	9	10	15	34
N =	103	148	95	19	115	158	68	24
(Number of cases:)		(365)				(365)		

Implications of Issue in Determining Student's Role in Exercise of Student Power

Crucial	Great	Some	Slight	No
8%	5%	0%	2%	0%
8	5	11	6	8
42	46	39	38	25
30	33	39	37	30
4	0	2	5	8
4	3	0	1	3
4	8	9	11	26
100%	100%	100%	100%	100%
(26)	(63)	(124)	(87)	(65)

Y EFFECT OF SIX FACTORS ON STUDENT'S EXERCISE OF POWER [1]

	Type of Student Leadership				Faculty Support of the Issue				Success in Opposing Univ. Authorities			
4	3	2	(1-0)[2]	4	3	2	1-0	(4)[2]	3	2	1-0
1%	2%	2%	4%	2%	2%	2%	1%	6%	0%	2%	2%
6	11	10	0	7	7	8	10	6	4	11	8
7	40	36	25	41	39	37	36	41	39	41	35
7	32	36	46	31	36	36	36	29	40	32	36
6	2	2	4	5	2	4	4	0	2	1	5
1	2	2	0	2	2	2	0	6	4	1	1
2	11	12	21	12	12	11	13	12	11	12	13
9	144	58	24	42	117	123	83	17	54	94	200
		(365)				(365)				(365)	

1. All columns total 100 per cent.
2. Parentheses around column heading indicate percentages for that column are quite unreliable because of small N. 4 — Crucial; 3 — Matters a Great Deal; 2 — Matters Somewhat; 1-0 — Matters Slightly or Not at All.

III The Theologians in the Church

JOHN H. WESTERHOFF

8 Where, How, and Why You Think is What You Think

College teaching is under intense and unusually adverse critical examination. A new generation seeks the radical reform of education. Our best students want to change the curriculum, eliminate examinations and grades, affect the methods by which they are taught, and vote on faculty appointments. Perhaps the most significant segment of our society, the New Generation, demands that we make learning relevant. Most of us believe we are already doing that. The result is obvious — an increasing estrangement.

Teachers respond differently to the New Generation. I enthusiastically affirm their demands. I take seriously their concerns, realizing that I am an immigrant to a new age. Often I have pondered that phrase, "a new age." I recall a young intern's confession that the medical oath no longer made sense. He had promised to preserve life at all cost. But he had an elderly patient whose life he was preserving in a vegetable state at a financial and emotional cost the family could not afford. He knew that he could continue to do that for some time. He was confronted with a new question: Should he do so? Something had changed. Now he could play God and no one, least of all his teachers, had helped him to decide what he should do.

We do face a new time. For the first time in history youth are able to teach adults the issues and questions, which must be addressed. The New Generation is aware of our new age, its demands and possibilities. But I wonder what role we teachers are paying in their struggle for meaning and purpose? Why do our best students cry for relevant, meaningful learning experiences when we believe that we are providing them? Perhaps we have as much to learn from them as they do from us. Perhaps we are the ones who must change. The adding machine was just a bigger abacus, but the computer is not just a better adding machine. The book was a bigger scroll, but television is not a different kind of book. The gun was a bigger bow and arrow, but the atom bomb is not a larger gun. Technology gives man destructive and constructive possibilities beyond the imagination of science fiction writers. New communications systems are making our world into a small global village. Atomic energy, biological and germ warfare have placed our future in man's feeble and finite hands.

Fifteen years ago Margaret Mead made the case for changing education to fit changing times:

> When we look realistically at the world in which we are living today and become aware of what the actual problems of learning are, our conception of education changes radically. Although the educational system remains basically unchanged, we are no longer dealing primarily with the vertical transmission of the tried and true by the old, mature, and experienced teacher to the young, immature and inexperienced pupil. This was the system of education developed in a stable slowly changing culture. In a world of rapid change, vertical transmission of knowledge alone no longer serves the purposes of education.[1]

We didn't seem to hear her. Now we are forced to do so. We face a challenging generation of students. No longer is a teacher believed to be an authority or the college a center of learning and knowledge. There is a new breed invading our once hallowed halls of ivy. They are brighter, less compromising and more committed to justice than our students in the past. They are grappling for a fresh understanding of the intellectual enterprise. They rely more on insight and induction than deductive logic. Consciousness re-

---

1. Mead, Margaret. *Harvard Business Review*, 1953.

places analytical reason as their basic category of inquiry. Experience has become primary and reflection secondary. Participation and action are their medium of thought. Feeling is raised to the height of thinking. All of this is difficult for those of us over thirty to understand, but understand we must.

In our day it made sense to ask someone, "What do you teach?" If he answered, "Theology," we knew all we needed to know. That question has become meaningless. Today students seek to ask, "Where do you think?" "How do you think?" and "Why do you think?" Those questions are much more difficult to answer, but more crucial. Harvey Cox in his book *On Not Leaving It To The Snake,* wrote:

> *What* we think is determined far more than we realize by *where* we think ... and *why* we think (the *aim* of theological inquiry). I argue that the purpose of theology is to serve the prophetic community. For this reason the place of theology is that jagged edge where the faithful company grapples with the swiftest currents of the age. Any "theology" which occurs somewhere else or for some other reason scarcely deserves the name.[2]

> (The theologian) must try to stand with one foot in the discordant history of Israel, old and new, and with the other foot in the convulsive habitat of the frankly profane man of our late twentieth century. This teetery platform provides our *place. We* stand there trying to hear and to help our comrades in the cadre of prophets, as together we discern the traces and sometimes drink the wines of the coming new era.[3]

Where we think is what we think. How we think is what we think. Why we think is what we think. The where, how, and why

2. Harvey Cox, *On Not Leaving It To The Snake* (New York: Macmillan, 1967), p. 14.
3. *Ibid.,* p. 2.

questions are the crucial questions for those of us who teach theology in colleges today. To take these questions seriously is to become part of a radical reform movement in our colleges, a move few of us are prepared to make. In September 1968, Krister Stendahl, the new Dean of the Harvard Divinity School, had prepared a convocation address on the role of a theological school in our age. Two days before convocation, a group of concerned students offered symbolic sanctuary to an AWOL Marine in the divinity school chapel. The next day the military police entered the chapel and led the Marine away. Stendahl rewrote his address.[4]

In a quiet Swedish accent, the Dean noted the long, glorious period in theological studies, with its emphasis on the recovery of a Christian tradition that was coming to an end. He pointed to signs of creativity that were emerging in theology. He acknowledged that theologians were seeking new ways to speak about God and his will for his world — a new idiom, instead of stretching the old to fit new situations. Quoting the slogan, "The world writes the agenda for the Church," Dean Stendahl said. "For theology this means we cannot first have the perfect theological system and then apply it. There must be two-way traffic." He continued by quoting the apostle Paul, who,

> In discussing the problem of marriage and divorce in the church of Corinth . . . started with a simple case. And on that he said there was a clear word from the Lord that there should be no divorce . . . . But then, says Paul, of course there are special cases. And in his second case, the case where one was a Christian and the other wasn't, Paul in his first letter to the Corinthians, chapter 7, says, "On this one I have no word from the Lord."

"It seems," continued the Dean, "that Paul was the last preacher in Christendom who had the guts to admit that simple fact. He could, of course, have done what we will all do and what

4. Krister Stendahl, "Convocation Address," *Harvard Divinity Bulletin,* Vol. 2, No. 1, Fall 1968.

the Church has been doing for centuries. He could have said that it follows from the word of the Lord quite clearly that, in this case, it is so and so — which is a much nicer way and feels, at least, like a much safer way to handle new situations.

But faced with a situation that apparently Jesus had not thought about — or at least there was no word from Jesus about it — Paul instead says, "On this one I really have no word from the Lord, but I'll try my best and I trust that the Spirit will help me!" [5]

The Dean's candid confession that the university is now confronted with new moral questions, for which there are no clear pronouncements, was significant. Even more so was his implication that the university community had the obligation to determine their moral responsibility together. Theological studies were no longer to be confined to classroom lectures by professors — students, faculty, workmen and townsfolk were to act and reflect together on the issues that confronted them.

He ended his address by announcing that the faculty had decided to devote its third Colloquium (the first was the Roman Catholic-Protestant in 1963 and the second was the Jewish-Christian in 1966) to the topic of the Moral Responsibility of the University. He made it clear that they intended to examine the specific issues facing Harvard University. They would invite the governing boards, the administration, the students, the faculty, the university police, and the health services personnel and those who worked for building and grounds, to join in the colloquium, to be planned by a student-faculty committee.

It occurred to me that the implications of his remarks were more radical than he intended. Not only was he implying that classrooms might cease to be the primary place of teaching, but a new way of acting and reflecting was to replace a body of material as the content of courses. It seems to me that his remarks made the case that just as the business of citizens and

5. *Ibid.*, pp. 3-6.

statesmen is not political theory but politics, the business of the
people of God and theologians is not doctrine, but theological
thinking — not so much content, as the process of reflection and
discourse related to human life and action.
Gordon Kaufman writes in his recently published *Systematic
Theology,*

> Theological work is not merely the uncritical rehearsal of
> tradition. It is rather in each new instance a creative act seek-
> ing to deal with the most problematic dimensions of human
> existence.[6]

And toward the end of his book he concludes,

> Christian existence remains life in this world, participating
> in ordinary creaturely work, but to the end that the Creator's
> will be done and his Kingdom come.[7]

I would suggest that teaching theology is enabling people to
think about daily existence in ways that will equip them and inspire them to do just that. To teach theology is to help persons
learn to think theologically. And anyone who would learn to
think theologically needs to be fully immersed in the world. He
needs to begin there. Herbert Thelen told it "like it is" in his book
Education and the Human Quest.

> We have made hard and fast divisions between thinking and
> doing, creating and applying, planning and acting, preparing
> and fulfilling .... These divisions have made modern life
> purposeless. For as long as we maintain the division we shall
> never have to find an organizing principle to integrate the parts.
> The organizing principle we have thus succeeded in avoiding
> is purpose.[8]

6. Gordon Kaufman, *Systematic Theology* (New York: Scribners, 1968), p.
viii.
7. *Ibid.,* p. 479.
8. Thelen, Herbert, *Education and The Human Quest* (Evanston: Harper
and Row, 1960), p. 215.

The purpose of teching theology is to enable men to think theologically which is to help them learn a process. When we make the purpose of theological teaching primarily a matter of communicating doctrine — the content of faith as formed by other men's intellect — we make a division in men's lives. To think theologically is a process of bringing the essence of faith into colloquy with the existential realities of the moment so that a person may respond as a thinking-feeling person in action.

The organizing structure for teaching theology, then, must shift to life issues and concerns. This means offering more courses on problems such as "White Racism" and "Racial Justice" and fewer on subjects such as "The Thought of Early Christian Fathers." It is not a question of reflecting or not reflecting on the thoughts of the early Fathers. But we cannot afford to always begin with their thoughts and then attempt to relate them. More often we must begin in our teaching with a problem and then see if there is any wisdom in the Fathers to help us solve it.

Students and teachers need to move out of their classrooms where lectures on dogma lull students to sleep, and into bar rooms, jails, ghetto schools and urban slums, to join picket lines and demonstrate at the doors of draft boards. More teachers of theology need to join the action, i.e., become involved with the New Generation in their quest for humanness. More teachers and students need to have common experiences as they participate in the struggle to become whole persons. It is through this mutual reflection on their action that theology will be learned. The theology classrooms of the future will be the streets and theology teachers will have to get out and walk them.

But there must also be two-way traffic. I am therefore not suggesting that we dispense entirely with courses on tradition or on the historical approach to theology taught in classrooms. If we were to eliminate all such courses we would suffer an immense loss. What is at stake is man's historical consciousness itself. If we are genuinely to learn from history and tradition — and that we must do — we must allow history and tradition to have their own integrity. We must attempt to avoid imposing on the past our own problems and issues. We need to allow the formulations of the past to teach us something about reformulating the problems and issues of the present. Through such an endeavor we may sensitize ourselves to dimensions of experience that otherwise would not be possible. A student and his teachers ought to devote some of their time to this kind of work; otherwise we will be the prisoners of our own present experience.

What may appear the one-sided emphasis of my remarks is meant to be a necessary corrective. But what I would like to do is shift the emphasis from teaching content to teaching process; from teachers telling pupils the truth to teachers and students helping each other to discover the truth; from reflection on the past with a hope of action to action in the present with reflection on that experience; from passive classrooms to active community involvement.

Gerhard von Rad, in *The Theology of the Old Testament,* suggests that God educates by interfering in the lives of men. In the Old Testament, the people of God live from event to event. All God's teaching is related to their history. That is why, he writes, it is difficult to find a systematized set of concepts in the Scriptures. Rather than theological content, one finds stories of events and the insight men gained from them. As von Rad points out, this does not make for inconsistency, but rather a consistent attitude of continuous listening and readiness to consider and change. Each age must do its own thinking in the light of its memory.

There is both an existential and a theoretical side to theology. Both are an important part of teaching, but for too long colleges have ignored first-hand existential experience in theological thinking. In order for persons to learn to think theologically we must provide opportunities for students and teachers to share in a common experience of that process.

All examples pose limitations, but I recall an experience at an upper management program at the Harvard Business School which may be helpful. In the past, the business school offered corporation executives a course in business ethics, taught by a theologian. Each day he crossed the Charles River, armed with a prepared lecture for his note-taking students. After answering a few questions, he would return to his library office at the divinity school and prepare his next piece of wisdom for his expectant students. For both students and teacher, the course began and ended in that classroom, although that was not the intention of either. The teacher obviously expected his students to apply their newly acquired knowledge to their work. But it never seemed to happen.

One day, the Dean of the Business School came to the conclusion that the aim of the course was valid, but the method for reaching it was wrong. No more would theologians be brought in to teach a course; no more would those business men be offered a course in business ethics. Instead, a few theologians would be invited to participate fully in a case-centered program. Theologians would room with businessmen, eat with them, study and recreate with them. They would join their daily attempts to find solutions to their most pressing corporation cases. They would become businessmen and learn to think about corporation problems. At the same time, the corporation executives would become theologians and learn to think theologically about their problems. They would help each other learn, not by telling each other what to believe or do, but by striving together to solve mutual problems. The first few meetings were a struggle. Each group was overly conscious of the other. The theologians struggled to be "good businessmen," according to their often erroneous perceptions of what they meant. The businessmen tried to be "good theologians," according to their equally erroneous perceptions of what that implied. Then it happened. They were discussing the cases of the Auburn Shoe Manufacturing Company.

Permit me to over-simplify the case for the sake of my point. There were two executives, a personnel manager and a vice president. It appeared that the personnel manager was very much concerned about the company's employees. You couldn't help but like him. He was a "nice guy" and seemed to treat every employee in what might be called a "Christian way." The vice president, on the other hand, was the "bad guy." It was difficult to like him. He came off as the typical cut-throat businessman. A policy conflict emerged between these two executives. The chasm between them was too great to be resolved. One of them had to be released. That decision was up to us.

In discussing the case, the business executives tried very hard to be ethical. They had almost convinced each other that the vice president had to go when one of the theologians said, "I don't know a great deal about running a business, but it seems to me that the shoe manufacturing business is highly competitive and there is a very slim profit margin. Auburn has no other industry to employ these people. The company is their life. If the company gets into economic difficulty and has to close or move, the whole community will be brought to the brink of disaster. Only if the company makes a profit and stays in business will those people have food and clothes and a roof over their heads. I don't like the vice president any better than you do. But under these peculiar circumstances, I think he is the one showing the most love for these people by the apparent ruthlessness with which he handles them. Perhaps in this situation, the personnel manager should be released."

Such an engagement with real life questions provides the necessary experience that a student needs to learn the process of theological thinking. Teaching theology in this manner enables a student to learn a process of thinking that integrates the Christian revelation and tradition with today's concerns. He can then apply that process to any life-issue or concern. Studying theology then helps him to make enlightened responses in faith to the demands of a rapid and radically changing world. It enables him to become a self-conscious Christian.

In this sense, theological thinking is analogous to political reflection — that is, the musing of men about those forces that influence and determine our lives individually and socially. Such thinking is not doctrinaire, abstract, or irrelevant to our daily needs. To be concerned with learning, to think theologically is to be concerned with where we think, why we think, and how we think. What is most important is that we stop talking about life situations and get involved. Learning takes place in the midst of action.

Too often we forget that the way we teach is what we teach. When our aim is the communication of information and ideas and concepts, we can teach through assigned readings and classroom lectures, supplemented by questions for discussion. But when our objective is a process of thinking about important issues and concerns, then such methods are not only inadequate, they are destructive. Live situations provide a better content for theological reflection than dogmatics, historical theology, and biblical studies. Perhaps a theological teacher's role is to bring persons together so as to explore common issues and concerns.

Not long ago I sat on the floor of a cold room in a slum of an American city and watched this happen. A single 60 watt bulb hung from a cracking ceiling, dimly lighting the room. I had joined a group of college students — a few were committed Catholics and Protestants, some confessed atheists, two were Jews, and the rest agnostics — who had chosen to live as a community, sharing work, food, money, and worldly possession in this black ghetto row house. That night, they put their books aside and discussed a community concern. They were angered by the attitude of a private hospital near their slum home. During the past year, a number of black poor had died while being transferred, before treatment, to a city hospital across town. The moral concern, political acumen, and prophetic character of this group was profound. They all came from affluent suburban homes to study at a large university, but they were unwilling to live in the isolation of a college campus. A young Roman Catholic instructor in religion at the university had chosen to live with them. Together they engaged in a process of action and reflection, of theological thinking, that was more relevant than most college theology classes and closer to quality education than their other courses in the university. Here is the side of teaching theology the New Generation is concerned about and I have been attempting to defend.

Surely what we need is a plurality of offerings and teaching styles if a college theology department is to take theology and the New Generation seriously. I would like to suggest four examples of learning opportunities which might be offered by college teachers which would be relevant to today's educational demands.

Picture a theology teacher running the following announcement in the college newspaper: *"God, Man and Society* — during the course of several informal conversations, I plan to explore the thesis that the structure of the society in which a man lives determines his understanding of man's nature and his beliefs about ultimate reality. Anyone interested is invited to sherry and supper at my apartment on Thursday evening. RSVP." That evening, a small group might share their perceptions about the question, talk about how they would test it, discuss aspects of the question that interest them, and decide how they might share their learning. The group would be organized on the principle that a person learns what he wants, when he wants, in the way he wants. The teacher would coordinate their learning experiences, as well as feed in his own. In a sense, everyone would be teachers and students.

A second opportunity would be more radical. Instead of beginning with a teacher's concern, this model begins with a teacher's awareness of an issue in the college community. The teacher would attempt to bring together, in a community seminar, those most interested in the issue. The group might include faculty members, students, administrators, and others from the community. The group would be as inclusive as possible. The teacher would be an enabler. The course might include reading, movies, TV shows, field trips, projects, interviews, or exposures. Such a group might address the issue of public education, beginning with the question, "What makes a public school public?" Perhaps the assumption that there is a clear distinction between public and private ventures in education, a boundary marked by differences in finances and control, is invalid. Some parochial and private schools help to educate responsible and mature human beings, while others nurture ignorant bigots. In either case, perhaps parochial schools should be included within the perimeter of our concern for quality education. Though seemingly "private," their impact is public. All that happens in all schools, private or public, is finally the business of the public. What does this imply for our action in the community? Other questions explored might be: What is education? Is education synonymous with schooling? Isn't education the sum of all those ways men recognize and accept their relationship to one another? Is the end of education to shape the public? What kind of public are we forming? For whom are the schools? Who should control them? What are the criteria for judging centralized and de-centralized schools? Their goal would be organized action directed toward education in their community.

A third option might be more like a laboratory experience. Once again, the aim would be to enable people to think theologically, but it would do this through active participation in a significant task. A teacher might take his students and together act on behalf of a cause. Their concern could be any national or local issues such as peace, poverty, or racism. They might unite with existing groups in the community, join a local political party, live in a slum residence, work with a welfare mothers' group, with a gang, or in a ghetto church. Students and teacher would learn through participation, by doing and reflecting together. They would learn by an intense involvement in decision-making and community action programs. They would be found in demonstrations and on picket lines or in coffee houses reflecting on their actions and planning for the future.

These three learning models would break out of the college walls and bring otherwise estranged groups together for mutual growth. All three learning contexts are equally important and should probably occur concurrently. They should be understood as an integral part of the academic life of both students and teachers. All three should be considered offerings of the college theology department.

A fourth context for learning provides a necessary check and balance on these other three. There will always be the need for a few teachers to work in libraries and lecture halls. They will be the researchers and critics for the community of faith, the spe-

cialists and resource persons. They will explore the tradition and
share its insights with students in more traditional classroom
teaching situations. All four learning and teaching models are
significant and all four are necessary for a contemporary college
and its theology department. If this last context is the only one
your theology department offers it is dead. If that context is the
only one your college legitimates then its future is dim.

The lecture remains valuable as a means of setting out a
sustained piece of reflection. While it is a crime that so often
there is no point of contact between these ideas and everyday life, we also need opportunities to relate experiences to
each other with concepts of increasing generality until we can
put the parts together into a meaningful and coherent whole. We
need opportunities to look at life as a connective systematic whole.
This is the justification for books, lectures and the like in which
an attempt is made to work out a theoretical position, and not
only reflect on immediate experience. Theory without immediate
experience is completely dead; but (to paraphrase Kant) immediate experience without broad-ranging theory is blind and
ultimately meaningless.

In the past we have had too uniform a pedagogical procedure.
This needs correction. I want to encourage those aspects of education we have neglected in most college theology classes. I want
to emphasize the existential side of the theological task. If I
have seemingly failed to recognize the value of what is, I have
done it in behalf of what is not, with the hope that a new balance
might be achieved.

In any case let me affirm my belief that education is not the
preparation of people for participating in the life of society at
a later date. Learning is an end in itself which enables a person
to participate completely, responsibly, and meaningfully in life
now.

The task of teaching theology is to help people make sense out
of life, to make clear the options, and to enable people to decide
how they should respond, i.e., what they should be and do. What
is usually called teaching theology often turns out only to be
long tirades on yesterday's pieties and the puzzles of antiquarian

thought rather than a confrontation with the issues which face
the man of faith in a world of change.

We cannot prepare students for life by witholding them from
it. I doubt if we can teach them theology — a life-participating discipline — by restricting them to the confines of a college and its
classrooms. People learn through experience. But there is little
real life experience in the typical teacher-centered college classroom. The natural tendency in a classroom is to teach a subject,
which usually means requiring a student to use his brain for the
storage and retrieval of information about something. But learning is more than this, and learning to think theologically is very
difficult under such circumstances. At best, teachers in classrooms
give a description of the process and then advise students to go
out and apply it. Is it any wonder that our graduates do not reflect
on life theologically after they graduate?

I would also like to assert that theology is not a discipline
reserved for specialists called theologians. Theology belongs to the
whole people of God. Christianity is an intellectual faith, a faith
that asks man to use his mind, but it is not a faith for a few intellectuals. It is a faith that seeks understanding, that enables man
to respond with thought and feeling. Teaching theology in college
ought to enable a graduate to do just that.

The Church is a celebrating, learning, and witnessing community of faith. It is a community with a memory of God's action and
the resulting response of his people, a community with an awareness of God's activity in the present, which calls his people to
join in his history-making, and a community with a hope of God's
future kingdom building with its opportunities for a participating
response by his people, according to their ability to read the signs
of the times.

Teaching within such a community is not so much telling the
facts of that history, as developing in men of faith an historical
consciousness, not so much communicating the conclusions reached
in past times, with their resulting doctrines, as enabling men to
think theologically today about issues and events confronting
them; not so much giving men a set of prepared right and wrong
actions, as enabling them to use their heads and act morally

wherever they find themselves. The Church is a community of faith that has learned to think theologically as it celebrates its perception of life.

One night not long ago I found myself in the living room of a suburban home near a small college campus. A young priest, wearing sports clothes, had invited a few faculty members and students to join him, some adults, and teenagers from the community. The adults and teenagers met regularly to celebrate their common faith and life in the world. In the dining room, a long table was set with loaves of bread and bottles of wine, as well as fruit and cheese. The house had a festive atmosphere. Large colorful paper flowers and birds hung from the ceiling. I was greeted with a bag decorated on the outside with large dayglow colors which read, "We Care." Opening the bag, I found a large red and yellow sheet of tissue paper with a hole in the middle and a variety of other things. We each picked a partner to dress in the paper costume. We read our partner part of an E. E. Cummings poem found in the bag: "I love you most beautiful darling, more than anything on earth, and I like you better than anything in the sky." We fed each other a Hershey kiss. Together, we stuffed a balloon with confetti, blew it up, tossed it into the air, punctured it with a pin. As the confetti fell over us, we blew party horns. The daily news programs, blaring from the two television sets in the room, were turned down as someone began to strum a guitar. Everyone joined in the folk song, "Turn, Turn, Turn," as we made our way to the table.

We each greeted our neighbor at the table with the ancient kiss of peace. Everyone had a part in the reading of Scripture and the brief simple English prayers. We prayed the Lord's Prayer. But following, "thy will be done on earth as in heaven," reports from the day's newspaper were read, and we each made our confessions of apathy in the light of need. An offering of money and fair housing pledge cards were made. Each person made a personal affirmation of what he believed. We affirmed our understanding of the Christian faith as: "Where there is life, there is death, but where there is death there is hope." We acknowledged that with such a perception of life we could affirm the negative

aspects of our history as the birth pangs of our new age. Our
priest, who taught religion at the college, broke the bread and
blessed it. He poured the wine and blessed it. Each person served
his neighbor. We joined hands and sang with joy. We concluded
with Jesus' words to Simon Peter, "Simon, Son of John, do you
love me more than all else?" We answered with Peter's words,
"Yes, Lord, you know that I love you," and our host responded
with Jesus' words, "Then feed my sheep." As we shared bread
and cheese and wine and fruit, we talked about what we believed
each must do individually and corporately about racism in the
community and the places where we studied and worked. Two
hours later, after making definite resolves for action, we sang, "We
Shall Overcome," and with the kiss of peace, departed into the
night.

Education isn't synonymous with schooling, defined as formal
instruction carried out in classrooms. People learn what they live,
while they live, and where they live. And teaching, as always,
remains an art, an art that takes shape wherever the life of a
student intersects the life of a teacher.

Elia Kazan, distinguished author and director, spoke of his
education at Williams College thirty years ago, saying,

> I didn't pick up any information here. I left with my bag empty
> of facts and formula. But I had known five or six men . . .
> who changed my life. And that's not a figure of speech. I
> took away no answers, but they did start a process within me
> that can only be described as an awakening.

Do you remember Peter Abelard pursuing poor William of
Champeaux from hall to hall, questioning his teacher's wisdom?
The divinity students at Harvard published the *Peter Abelard Review* as a means of conversing with their professors about teaching.[9] In commenting about a young instructor called upon to
teach a new course, they wrote,

---

9. *Peter Abelard Review*. Michael Beudreaux and Glenn Johnson, editors,
Harvard Divinity School, Cambridge, Massachusetts.

A less imaginative teacher might have lectured his students to death all semester. But he . . . turned the situation to his own advantage by handing the course to his students. Stepping down from the professional podium, he sat down with his students and helped them teach the material to each other. . . . Most important of all, many students agreed that giving their own course was better than listening to a semester of lectures no matter who the lecturer was.

What students took away from the course, they continued, was not a thick notebook full of someone else's ideas. Instead they came away with a firsthand knowledge of what they knew and what they didn't know. More important, they came away with an experience of working with a man who saw his subject not only as an academic discipline but as an opportunity for self education.

They commented negatively on another faculty member, who claimed in the catalogue that his course in theology was a course in learning to think, but instead presented a series of rigorously organized lectures. The students wrote, "Though he intended to teach his students how to think, he seemed to be trying to teach them what to think." In praise and appreciation for another professor, they write, "He didn't give this course and students didn't take it . . . it was not something you had or got, but something you did." This particular course was considered an educational success because students were encouraged to think theologically for themselves, rather than having someone else's thoughts pushed on them. It was a process a student experienced by being stimulated to think about his experiences. I would like to suggest that that's what education is all about. The challenge of the New Generation is to those of us who call ourselves teachers.

In 1836, Mark Hopkins said in his inaugural address as president of Williams College:

We are to regard the mind not as a piece of iron to be laid upon the anvil and hammered into shape, nor as a block of

marble in which we are to find the statue by removing the
rubbish, nor as a receptacle into which knowledge may be
poured, but as a flame that is to be fed as an active being
that might be strengthened to think and to feel — to dare (and)
to do.

That's what teaching theology is about. To do so today calls
for more than a conventional reform movement, which would
provide a new curriculum or redesign the content of courses, or
increase the use of new teaching methods or new educational media.
What we need is a radical reform movement, that moves the place
of teaching outside the college walls and does away with lectures
in the classroom so that students and teachers might move together into the streets where experience, participation, and action
can become the medium of thought.

A New Generation with a vision of a new world stands within
our gates asking that we join them in their quest.

The question remains, will we care enough about what they
think to turn our attention as teachers of theology to where they
think, how they think and why they think? To those that do,
God, I believe, has willed the destiny of our world and of
humanity itself.

JOHN KELLEY, S.M.

9 Academic Freedom and the Catholic College Theologian

The substantive question of Academic Freedom for the Catholic College Professor I shall address under four points: first, the rash of actual problems which concern these issues; secondly, the history of the draft statement of the American Association of University Professors on academic freedom in Church-related institutions; thirdly, the presumptions upon which we can define the question; and fourthly, some basic distinctions from which we can suggest how working relations might be developed within the Catholic university community.

Part I: Problems at Particular Universities

A rash of problems relating to academic freedom have arisen in the last four years. These situations stemmed from questions of a philosophical and/or theological nature but they were accompanied by other problems of a pastoral nature. The concrete situations were complicated on the one hand by administrations resistant to change, and on the other by a growing professionalism among faculty — expressed through formation of local chapters of AAUP, as well as by the existence of unions in several instances. I shall describe only the more prominent cases, in order to locate the issues.

(1) In 1966 the case of a priest-instructor in the Department of Classics at St. Mary's College in Minnesota dramatized the problem. The instructor withdrew from the priesthood, married and was subsequently discharged from the College. The case was brought to the attention of the AAUP. This Association studied

the issue in terms of its statements on academic freedom and finally declared that this College should be placed on the list of censured administrations. (*AAUP Bulletin,* Spring, 1968, 37-42; Summer 1968, 174. Subsequent references to this source will indicate merely the season and year and page.)

(2) About this same time St. John's University, N.Y. drew considerable attention to itself. In a situation with which we are all familiar, I merely recall for you that the administration encountered difficulties with a faculty that felt that it should have more weight in the decision-making of the University. The formation of an AAUP Chapter had taken place as early as 1948, but became effective only from 1963. The formation of the Chapter and the concurrent organization of a faculty union prepared the way for subsequent confrontation of faculty and administration.

In 1966 the situation rapidly eroded. In the sequel the University was censured "for the extraordinarily serious violations of academic freedom and tenure," and lost both prestige and faculty members. In the long run what had been requested by the faculty was granted in whole or in part (Spring '66, 12-19; Autumn '68, 325-361).

(3) The University of Dayton drew widespread attention when, in 1966, one of its lay instructors charged several other lay instructors with heresy. The case was studied by a University committee appointed by the President. Then a second committee appointed by the local ordinary restudied the situation. The issues which eventually emerged dealt with the magisterium, birth control, the nature of original sin and purgatory.

In February, 1967, the committee of the local ordinary published its conclusions in a brief statement (2/13). Within the week the Chairman of the Board of Trustees (who was also the Marianist Provincial) issued a statement. Finally in April, 1967, after much consultation, the President released the "Statement Relative to the Controversy Touching Academic Freedom and the Church's Magisterium." Most of the faculty responded positively, but in the aftermath several professors withdrew voluntarily.

To avoid continued exacerbation of the administrative and academic issues, the President called for a full study of the matter of academic freedom at the University. The seven-man Ad Hoc Committee for the Study of Academic Freedom released its findings in July, 1967. Subsequently he commissioned a special study of purposes of this University. On March 15, 1968, the results of this study on the purposes were circulated among the faculty for additional study and for a new formulation of university purposes. During the fall semester of 1968 the draft of this statement was worked over by seminars open to all faculty (and students, for that matter); a draft of this statement was referred to the Board of Trustees early in 1969. At last report the results were in the hands of the Trustees.

Meanwhile a full storm was brewing over the matter of the termination of services of several professors, two of them in the Department of History and one in the Department of Theological Studies. As the agitation became more acute in one instance, investigators were invited in from the American Association of Colleges and from the AAUP to advise the President. In their evaluations both investigating groups expressed desire for improvements in the mechanics of the University, especially in the matter of the selection and rotation of departmental chairmen, but both expressed satisfaction in the manner in which the dismissals had been handled.

A special issue of "unionism" entered the picture at this point. Several professors had been instrumental in the organization of a nucleus of a union. The professors mentioned were among the organizers. One of these organizers withdrew in the summer of 1968 without fanfare, the other claimed that the University was firing him because of his union activities; in addition he claimed that the administration had done him an injustice by refusing to state publicly the reasons for the non-renewal of contract. Many students and some faculty moved at first to support him, especially in a dramatic confrontation on December 16, 1968.

The AAUP offered the recommendation that if the professor requested it, a public hearing should be given him. In the meantime the local AFL-CIO censured the University for its "union-busting" tactics and threatened a civil suit. The American Civil Liberties Union also indicated that it was investigating the situation.

On March 8, a special meeting of the AFT met with the President, some members of administration, faculty and students to discuss possible alternatives. The AFT is currently weighing the possibility of a court suit.

Central to this issue has been the question of tenure, the University officials being reluctant to contract on a permanent basis with a doubtful performer.

(4) At Catholic University in Washington the experiences were no less exasperating. Although all the particulars are at variance, the same kinds of tensions exist. In 1967 the Administration had first been confronted when it had dismissed one theology professor for his position on birth control. Outraged at the arbitrary manner in which this and a number of other decisions had been made, a large scale faculty and student support of the professor elicited reconsideration and reenstatement. The reenstatement was made public but privately a number of the Trustees were unhappy with the action.

In the summer of 1968, on the occasion of the publication of the encyclical *Humanae vitae,* the issue flared again in a manner well known to us. (For a review of the facts, cf. the *Catholic University Alumni Bulletin,* Fall, 10-12.) The encyclical was released on Monday, July 29. By Tuesday evening some 87 names of academic personalities had been placed on the famous statement of dissent. In the weeks to follow the list was to grow to 300 published in the *National Catholic Reporter* (8-14-68, 8) and reportedly the number is well over 600 professional academicians in the United States.

Outside of Catholic University but within the Washington Archdiocese, 39 priests were disciplined in one fashion or another. Despite several attempts to establish machinery of reconciliation, no negotiations have been effective. It may be important to state here that these priests are not in the category of university instructors and have not enjoyed any of the protective devices of academic professional associations. The case of the 39 remains unsettled as of this writing. There are not even many signs of hopes for mediation for them at this time.

On the Catholic University campus, within six weeks the

situation had evolved to the point where all seemed agreed on "due academic process" (*NCR*, 9-11-68, 1). In a meeting of September 5, 1968, the members of the Board of Trustees (23 of the 29 members being present) in a marathon session called on the twenty faculty members to refrain from engaging in activities "inconsistent with the pronouncements of the ordinary teaching authority established in the Church." With the collaboration of the Academic Senate and the Rector, a five man committee of peers, including one outside theologian, was given the task of studying whether the twenty should be formally charged and placed under investigation for irresponsible academic procedures. The Committee's formal report was released on April 13, 1969. The unanimous recommendation of this Committee was to exonerate the professors and to drop all consideration of formal investigation. (Incidentally Catholic University does not at present have a faculty union).

(5) More recently we have heard of the terminal contract given to a woman instructor at Boston College (March 3, 1969), the demonstrations of the students there, and her eventually receiving tenure.

(6) Before leaving these specific cases it must be stated that there is a growing problem of special anguish: that of the priest who is leaving the ministry and/or the priesthood, who is in the process of laicization and/or marriage, and who wishes to continue teaching theology. (Of course the same problem, *mutatis mutandis,* exists for Brothers and Sisters who are leaving.)

The response of the institutions thus far has been all too predictable, with some degree of relief expressed over the fact that such persons go some other place to continue their profession.

In order to obtain dispensations and to have their situations regularized, priests have been required to meet a number of restrictive requirements, such as moving 500 miles and promising not to disclose their past. In conversation with an officer of the National Association for Pastoral Renewal, I learned that thus far there is probably only one case where such a priest has been permitted to continue to teach within the same institution.

In at least two instances, large Catholic universities have refused to hire men whose situations were canonically rectified, apparently on the ground of "scandal." On the positive side, about ten bishops have given some indications of sympathy and willingness to work out arrangements for such men. What is not clear in all this, is how the pastoral intentions of the Christian community are to be related to the specifically academic character of Church-related institutions. What is clear is that some professional grouping will be necessary to assure the individual scholar due process in safeguarding his academic freedom.

Part II: History of the AAUP Position

Allow me to summarize the actions of the AAUP on the question of academic freedom and theology:

The history of this question begins in 1915; in that year the Association published its "Declaration on Principles on Academic Freedom and Tenure," pleading for openness and declaring that church-related institutions should be "differentiated only by the natural influence of their respective historic antecedents and traditions" (quoted in the 1965 Committee Report). The second effort was in 1925, in a document entitled "Conference Statement on Academic Freedom and Tenure." This statement was a joint statement from the AAC (American Association of Colleges) and the AAUP. In 1940, again in conjuction with the AAC, the AAUP endorsed what has become their classic statement, the "Statement on Academic Freedom and Tenure." This is commonly referred to as "the 1940 Statement."

All subsequent statements relate to the 1940 Statement as their base. The key clause in the 1940 Statement which touches our topic is called the "religious limitation clause" and reads as follows:

Limitations of academic freedom because of religious or other aims of the institution should be clearly stated in writing at the time of the appointment. (The entire document has been reprinted in Autumn 68, 385-388.)

This joint document has been updated several times within the Association by the following developments: in 1958 the "Statement on Procedural Standards in Faculty Dismissal Proceedings"; "Standards for Notice and Non-reappointment"; "A Statement on Extramural Utterances"; and in 1964 "Standards for Non-reappointment." Pursuant to a resolution of the 1965 Annual Meeting, the Association appointed a Special Committee to study the 1940 Statement and to update it by making it "more explicit."

In 1966 the "Report of the Special Committee on Academic Freedom in Church-Related Colleges and Universities" was made and the "Statement on Academic Freedom in Church-Related Colleges and Universities" was presented as a "draft statement" (Winter 67, 369-371). It remains in the category of a draft statement and the Association would welcome discussion, criticism or support of the statement.

In 1967 the College Theology Society gave its endorsement to the 1940 Statement. Endorsements of the Statement at that time came to a total of 62 professional groups; of these, three are Catholic professional societies. This means that all of these professional groups have supported the entire document, with its "religious statement clause." In all honesty it must be said that this clause is central to the controversy over academic freedom in church-related institutions.

In July 1967, a group of Catholic administrators developed the "Statement on the Nature of the Contemporary Catholic University," and in the Winter of 1968 the AAUP Bulletin printed the 1968 Recommended Institutional Regulations on Academic Freedom and Tenure (448-452). This document lists four pages of norms for the institution to observe in the termination of services of its faculty. In February 1969, study was initiated by a joint committee of the AAC and the AAUP to review the 1940 Statement. Although the conclusions of this study are not yet available, these associations are concerned about the rapid rise of complaints concerning administrative neglect of tenure (there was a 35% rise in 1967 over 1968 in the number of complaints under study, a 50% increase in the incidence of complaints requiring investigation and study, and a rapid increase in the six months following, i.e. up to October '68. (*Academe*, Oct. '68; 2: 4, 2).

Part III: Presumptions

Certain presumptions must undergird our discussion, if it is to be fruitful. I shall enumerate what I consider to be basic presumptions.

First, I presume that we are talking about teaching the academic discipline of theology within the sociological context of "the Catholic university." I therefore put aside questions about Catholics teaching theology at secular campuses, or the matter of other-than-Catholics teaching theology at other-than-Catholic institutions. On the other hand I do not exclude consideration of non-Catholics teaching in Catholic institutions. Many Catholic institutions now hire non-Catholic professors, e.g., at the University of Dayton, Protestant and Jewish scholars are teaching in Theological Studies. Whatever norms for academic freedom are drawn up should be normative for them as well as for Catholic instructors.

Secondly, I am presuming that the Catholic university is both desirable and possible in our pluralist society. I personally believe this, although there are such eminent persons as John Cogley who incline in the opposite direction. My intuition here is that the Catholic university which is truly "catholic" offers greater freedom rather than less. I feel this is so because the university which is able to bring a tradition of faith to its insights brings more light, as well as a different kind of light, to the various disciplines which are taught. We might think of the professor of a secular subject, biology for the sake of an example, bringing the light of his own theological intuitions to bear upon a question of life. This freedom is surely greater where the sociological context assures this freedom rather than inhibiting it. Each of us has felt moments in his life when the social context has encouraged him to reflect his most personal thoughts of faith on such questions.

We must realistically observe that all freedoms are relative, exercised within functional systems which either support the exercise of this freedom or constrain it; but in any case the system forms the ambiance within which the freedom is to be exercised. Without the system, there is no guarantee of the possibility of the exercise of this freedom.

Thirdly, I presume that we are all agreed that theology must be treated as any other academic discipline, with the same demands being placed upon the formation of the instructors and upon the presentation of the material. Excellence of the academic aspects of theology must parallel the excellence of all other disciplines, or there is no justification for instruction in this area. Excellence and competence are the criteria.

Another issue, however, intrudes itself at this point: the matter of the roles which are played by instructor and institution. There must be as little confusion as possible over pastoral roles and magisterial roles, even though in the concrete these two overlap one another.

My final presumption is one which merits some questioning and I shall try to indicate the direction in which this questioning might be pursued. I presume that a Catholic university constitutes a Christian community, indeed a very special kind, but a Christian community nonetheless. Now every Christian community must identify itself and its areas of ministry. The Christian community within the Catholic university must identify its ministries and identify the interrelations of these ministries with non-ministerial functions.

In other words the pastoral function of the Catholic professor of theology (indeed of every professor of every discipline) must be clearly delineated from the professorial function. The ministry of such persons must be clearly identified in their own minds as well as in the institutional goals or sets of values. The professor who accepts a contract makes this contract with the entire institution and its declared goals. He must relate his performance to these goals.

What seems to me to be at the heart of the question here is that we are at a moment in history in which the basic understandings of community, university and ministry are being rethought.

Ministry itself is being radically reassessed. The Catholic instructor must have some clear notions of his ministries and how these apply to the teaching of his discipline whether this be theology or not. One of the troubling aspects here is that the clienteles of students and parents have need for some similar understanding (at least in a general way) of what the instructor is expected to do, and the fashion in which he may be expected to do it. The anti-intellectual attitude of many parents will constitute an irritant when the instructor attempts to open questions to truly intellectual presentation and discussion. In those circumstances where the students and parents are going to react emotionally and negatively, the instructor must ask himself what his responsibilities are and how he is going to meet these several responsibilities. He cannot act responsibly if he disregards the culture or the psychology of his students. They are culturally conditioned persons who can properly be called "disciples." An axiom of art might be kept in mind: whatever is received is received in the disposition of the recipient.[1] What has become clear to me in this study is that the Catholic institution is having problems which are concerned with behavior as often as they are with academic freedom.

I am being all too brief on this point but I wish to insist that if the Catholic university community has any reason for existence, then its *raison d'etre* relates to the ministry this community has. This ministry of the university community extends itself first to its own constituents, but ultimately performs service for the larger community (the "Church") and the secular community.

Part IV: Five Distinctions as Premises

There is a tension between the academic and pastoral goals of the Catholic university community. We teachers suffer from the strong temptation, suffered with all professors, to view these questions purely from one point of view, according to our disposition, often times according to our profession as teachers. The

---

1. *Quidquid recipitur in modo recipientis recipitur.*

preoccupation of professors is more with need for academic freedom in professional research and teaching, than with any question of immediate pastoral impact. The preoccupation of responsible professional groups such as the AAUP is also on academic freedom. On the other hand if we approach the question from the viewpoint of our Christian identification and religious commitment, rather than from that of our professional identification and commitment, we may find that the problem is much larger and more complex. The professional interest coexists with the pastoral interest. The two coexist within the one Christian community. There is naturally a tension between such concomitant interests, and sometimes the tension becomes great and even painful. I shall try to offer here five basic distinctions which may hopefully reduce the distance betwen these two interests.

First, I think that there is growing acceptance of the notion that professors are not primarily — in their function as professors — agents of evangelism. As professors they have their own competence, their own specificity and consequently their own proper functions. To teach, to counsel in academic matters, to evaluate, to criticize, to research, to write. The professor considered as professor (that is to say, considered in only one aspect of his performance) has no ministerial function. He is contracted to perform within the profession, not to develop the sodality. As a Christian, on the other hand, he must be prepared to distinguish the various hats he must wear and know at what point his Christian commitment calls for a Christian ministry.

Secondly, then, we must move toward a clearer definition of Christian ministry. What seems to me to be basic here is that we must go through very fundamental questioning of the theology of ministry, "servant-hood," following the leads given us by the Council. The ministry of the Christian teacher of the secular subject in the secular institution may be easier to define than the ministry of the professor in theology; and the ministry of the individual may be easier to define than the ministry of the Christian community to the secular community. Nonetheless there is need for such defining. Another way of putting this is to say that the university community has a priority of goals proper to it and that these goals specify it from all other communities. The most specific goal of the university community is learning. Knowledge — wisdom — intellectual perspective — these words characterize what is most proper to a university as such. By contrast the Christian community is specified in another way: the community of faith is specified by other objectives, most specifically to minister to all through proclamation of the good news. In other words the specific character of the Christian community is to proclaim the gospel, and subsequently to worship together, to become a sharing of life, to witness to the power of God working in it and through it.

The Christian *koinonia* is not ultimately specified by the academic. The Christian university as Christian is specifically evangelistic. It includes teaching under larger perspectives of magisterium, perspectives that include the teaching of the gospel, as well as all those elements of culture which enable men to perceive and to live the gospel. I suggest that the distinction might be put in this way: the academic community exists to reduce the mysteries of ignorance, or positively to bring together the entire body of knowledge, whether of science or of faith. By contrast the Christian community exists to vivify the mystery — to share lived truth — in such a way that all men are enamored of it and desire to share in its vital creativity.

Our *third distinction*: the Catholic university community has a duality of goals which places it in an habitual tension.

In more traditional language the Catholic university has as its specific and proximate goal the object of learning. It has however a further goal, an ultimate finality, in its relation to the service of the kingdom of God, either directly in the service of the Church or indirectly in its service to the world community. Permit me to reflect here that a simple-minded approach to this complex reality will fail to grasp the duality of the existence of the Catholic university community. An either-or mentality will not grasp what I am grappling with: there is no question of dichotomy here, but rather of the intimate and vital symbiotic relationship of this complex reality, the Catholic university, to its larger totality, the Christian community (the Church), and to the world community.

There are tensions built into such communities, tensions first of priorities, and tensions of means. I suggest that the Catholic university is called in a special way to live with these tensions and thus to become a paradigm for other special interest communities. But the very atmosphere in which we live is sometimes charged with anti-system, anti-institution, anti-community dispositions. This is understandable, and to some degree even necessary. We should accept the fact that living community grows through some conflict. But as we go, we run the risk of becoming atomistic, destructive people. Our ministration must not be destructive of administration. Among our Christian goals we must develop working relations with others which relationships grant us rather more freedom than less, because the relationships are mutual and because they are developed within an ambiance of trust.

Fourthly, the university is a moral person and must develop symbiotic relations. As the individual person exists within a social context and there establishes a multiplicity of relationships, the quality of which determine whether he is healthy or not, so too does the moral person of the Catholic university exist within a complex situation, within which it must establish its relationships to the larger Church and to the world community. It must serve all three: its own legitimate vitality, the Church, the world. It has a ministry to each. It may not neglect any of the three. It is important to see these relationships symbiotically. They do not benefit one party unilaterally. The relationships are mutual. They feed vitality into all those who are plugged into the synergism. The university within a vibrant cultural ambiance will grow and develop within it; the ecologist would say that the plant grows in good earth under water and sun. The environment in turn will be fed by it. The alternative is to coexist within inimical elements which stir hostile reaction; these will be expressed in tactics of disruption and destructive conflict.

We have been considering some basic apprehensions of the reality of the Catholic university and the teacher of theology. As a *fifth* distinction, I should like to suggest that the situation is today infinitely more complex after Vatican II than it was before the Council. Since 1965 our situation has been made much more demanding by the development of cultural and anthropological theology. This means that one aspect of our problem of academic freedom is the changing character of truth. Truth is being assessed in more biblical and existential understanding. This means that there is a new epistemological dimension to our communications.

The university entered a new phase of being when it saw itself in relationship to a pluralist world environment. But it is in this ambiance that it lives, off of which it feeds, and into which it pushes its own life. The complexity of our culture demands much more of theology than it has ever done before. It demands of us that we understand our profession better, the teaching of our discipline in its interrelatedness, and it expects that we shall serve larger interests than the ivory tower. It demands of us that we specify our ministry and relate it to the needs of the Church and world.

Conclusions

It should be clear that I am supporting academic freedom in the teaching of theology. I am aware that there is great stress upon many individuals who find that the system by which they are employed is repressive and stifling, if not unjust. My suggestions in the conclusions must not obfuscate my real support of academic freedom. We cannot have vigorous and exciting programs in theology if the instructor is unfree. On the other hand our problem requires us to face multiple responsibilities — only if we live the several responsibilities can we claim the right to academic freedom.

For the sake of pinpointing the discussion which this chapter may evoke, I should like to set forth the radical conclusions to which my thoughts seem to be leading:

(1) Within the cultural ambiguity which encompasses today's university, the sense of pluralism is high; there is therefore greater need for tolerance of various forms of expressing truth; consequently there is need for both greater freedom and for greater responsibility.

(2) It seems to me that the Catholic university has a great need to identify its functions, or more largely, to identify its own corporate personality and to elicit from its components a consensus about the character of the Catholic university community.

(3) Such identification must include an identification of the pastoral role of the Church-related institution which has an academic role as its specific *raison d'etre*.

(4) In specifying its academic role, and reasserting its need for academic freedom for its professorial personnel, it must retain consciousness of its role of Christian service (ministry) to all of its own components as well as to the communities to which it relates.

The Catholic university can be freer than an institution without theological commitment; it cannot act responsibly if it denies its theological commitment. If it is sure of its own identity and is well-oriented to service of the various communities to which it relates, it can have greater academic freedom and live its loyalties to the Church at a deeper level.

I do not like to think about alternatives to what I have suggested. It seems to me that the alternatives are to close down the Catholic institutions and thus to bring the university systems one step closer to one monolithic system which cannot but produce one-dimensional men.

COSMAS RUBENCAMP, C.F.X.

10 Religion as a Humanistic Study :
The Holbrook Thesis

In its thirteenth national convention (1967), the College Theology Society endorsed the statement on "Religion As an Academic
Discipline" by the Commission on Religion in Higher Education
of the Association of American Colleges.[1] Thus, the CTS placed
itself on record as supporting an approach to religion study "designed to promote understanding of an important human concern
rather than confessional commitment." It endorsed the academic
study of religion considered as "an almost universal experience
of mankind throughout history" and as a "major cultural phenomenon." In the perspective of this document religion is "the study
of man's ultimate values and their translation into human actions." [2]
The motion in favor of the endorsement of the AAC statement
carried without generating much, if any, opposition. The decision
did, however, mark quite a definite stage in the evolution of the
self-understanding of the Society, which at its next convention
changed its name from the Society of Catholic College Teachers
of Sacred Doctrine, to the College Theology Society. One of the
factors leading to this development was indicated in late 1967
in an unrelated article by Thomas E. Ambrogi, who maintained
that the burgeoning of the academic study of religion in state
as well as private universities could not "help but have a profound effect on the shape and mission of theology in the American

---

1. Copies are obtainable from the AAC, 1818 R Street, N.W., Washington,
   D.C. 20009.
2. All preceding quotations are from the cited statement.

Catholic university." [3] This effect has in fact taken the form of an identity crisis for both the liberal arts religion department and the seminary and divinity school.

Without getting into the problems of the professional and preprofessional schools and departments, we will consider here the situation of the liberal arts setting for religion study in the Catholic college and university. Most Catholic, as well as many Protestant, departments of religion exist, as a matter of fact, because of the pastoral responsibilities of the sponsoring Church to protect and deepen the faith-commitment of its student-members. Unfortunately, however, the academic respectability of such programs, which in Catholic colleges at least were generally diluted versions of the tractate curriculum of the seminary, was certainly questionable. In Ambrogi's words:

> Our method was primarily evangelical or catechetical, and our purpose was essentially to hand on the "tradition" — every last word of it, so that we might produce adult Catholics well informed about their faith. [4]

Professors have, of course, achieved tenure in departments like these, departments which are now beginning to see their function from another perspective: that same perspective from which their colleagues in other liberal arts departments work, and from which their fellow religion professors on state and private secular campuses work.

Now, departments of religion find themselves having to insist that the pastoral aims of the sponsoring Church must be served by the chaplains or other forms of ministry to the students and faculty. The pastoral responsibility of the sponsoring Church is being more frequently considered as distinct from the educational responsibility of the department.

Religion departments are becoming preoccupied with the pheno-

3. "The Catholic University in an Ecumenical Age," *NCEA Bulletin* (November, 1967) p. 22.
4. *Art. cit.*, p. 25.

menon noted recently by Paul VI in an address to a group of pilgrims:

> The events which follow one another in our times, the currents of thought which inform the modern mentality, the political and social movements which agitate our world, the subjects which today are of greater interest to the religious field . . . all converge . . . to a central question, which prevails over the consciousness of contemporary thought, and it is *the question of man*.[5]

One of the most discussed formulations of this orientation of academic religion study has been Professor Clyde A. Holbrook's work in the Princeton Study Series, *Religion, a Humanistic Field*.[6] The purpose of this chapter is not to provide another review of the book, but rather to discuss its central thesis, especially in reference to the situation of professors of religious studies in Roman Catholic institutions of liberal arts education — and among this group, Holbrook's study does not appear to have been widely noticed.[7]

The "humanism" central to Holbrook's thesis is a new humanism, wider than the Renaissance humanism which limited its focus to *homo occidentalis et christianus*. It involves seeing the university as responsible for exploring and evaluating the significance of man's experience as man, in all of the cultures which have served as the context and product of this experience. As described recently by the then-president of the American Academy of Religion:

> Humanism is . . . a fundamental perspective that focuses its

5. "On the Church's Defense of Man," September 4, 1968 (Washington, D.C.: U.S. Catholic Conference, 1969). Emphasis mine.
6. Englewood Cliffs, N.J.: Prentice-Hall, 1963.
7. One major exception: Mark Heath has reviewed it in *The Catholic Educational Review*, LXIII (January, 1965) pp. 47-49; he, however, discusses it mainly in the light of its relevance to secular colleges and universities.

interest upon man in his individual and collective life. From
this perspective, man is important, his life is significant, and
his ultimate well-being of primary value.... Humanism...
displays confidence in — or at least reliance on — man's capacity to confront human life and cope with its problems....
Humanism... depends upon rational analysis of human experience, all human experience.[8]

On this last point, Holbrook himself is even more concrete:

> Experience and reactions range from awe in the presence of
> the underlying mystery of existence itself to ecstatic parti-
> cipation in the intrinsically enjoyable, from tragedy to comedy,
> from contemplation of nature to the introspective probing of
> the psyche, from the creation of art forms which reflect the
> varying moods and insights of man to the development of
> rigorously logical structures of thought, ingenious play with
> languages and sound to the celebration of crucial experiences
> of human life.[9]

The *religious* experience, those who advocate the humanistic
approach insist, *is* just such a human experience. Humanism, as
the rational analysis of the total human experience, cannot restrict
itself to the empirical experience of the phenomenal; the human
experience of the noumenal is also potentially the object of humanistic study, for the humanities, as a broad field, embrace the
exploration of the significance of the vast areas of all of man's
productivity as spirit in the world — i.e., as characterized by a
capacity for, and a drive towards, self-transcendence. It is as
spirit that religious experience is possible for man, and it is as
spirit that he can analyze and explore the significance of this
experience.

8. John F. Priest, "Humanism, Skepticism and Pessimism in Israel," *Journal of the American Academy of Religion*, XXXVI (December, 1968) pp. 312-14.
9. *Op. cit.*, p. 41.

Thus, we come more specifically to the question of this analysis and evaluation — the question of "religion" as a humanistic field. As used by Holbrook, "religion" refers to the "study and scholarship which takes as its province certain activities and beliefs commonly known as religious." [10] He is no more willing to attempt to define "religion" than, as he puts it, biologists are willing to give an a priori definition of "life." It is a broader, more inclusive term than "theology," which he sees as one of a variety of academic approaches to the study of the religious experience of man. Holbrook's most comprehensive statement of the concept puts it this way:

> Religion embraces the study of those forms of conviction, belief and behavior and those systems of thought in which men express their concerned responses to whatever they hold to be worthy of lasting and universal commitment. [11]

Note that Holbrook *does* include *systems of thought* in his description of his field. Thus we come to the question very pertinent to the Catholic college and university — the question of the place of theology within the broad field of religion study. Does the humanistic study of religion preclude the study and teaching of *theology,* properly speaking? Holbrook puts his own position on this issue unambiguously:

> In spite of a certain illiberalism which remains suspicious of the term itself, theology properly belongs to the field of religion . . . . It cannot be regarded as alien to the domain of the humanities unless they be conceived with such narrowness as to deny entrance to any form of thought which takes seriously the existence of a supernatural realm. [12]

10. *Ibid.,* p. 28.
11. *Ibid.,* p. 36.
12. *Ibid.,* p. 30.

Theology is, of course, as Holbrook admits, often suspect in the liberal arts context. In a review of the book we are considering the great religion scholar Nels S. F. Ferré raises this question:

> Why is it that the religion which is mostly acculturation, although least needed, is most warmly received; while the religion which, using both the creative and critical reason, finds a faith directly relevant for education, the religion for culture rather than merely of culture, usually meets academic closed doors? [13]

However we might want to respond to the question, Holbrook certainly sees theology as an integral part of religion in the university setting. Theology in this sense is the intellectual analysis, the organization, and the deepening of man's *understanding* of his own religious experience; it is not, however, directly concerned with *imparting* this experience (and this is the crucial point made by those who defend theology as a humanistic enterprise).

Systematic theology will, of course, probably remain the center of focus more in the professional schools than in the liberal arts departments, but this is not to exclude it from being an integral part of the humanistic approach of these departments. In the latter case, however, college theology is a different undertaking from seminary and professional school theology. Holbrook, for example, describes it as less "a way of speaking to the Church about itself or its relationship to the world than as a way of understanding the traditional problems of theology in relative independence of the Church's concerns and employing the resultant insights for a critique of the Churches and culture." [14] In the process of making this clearer, Holbrook distinguishes three "modes of theologizing":

(1) The "open-ended" approach: no proposition or system is viewed as divinely authoritative, and all systems and propositions are subject to correction by subsequent insight;

---

13. *Journal of Higher Education*, XXXV (October, 1964) p. 414.
14. *Op. cit.*, p. 163.

(2) The "synthesizing mode": an attempt to systematize man's total historical religious experience according to some organizational principle (not excluding the possibility of other valid syntheses);

(3) The approach which stems from a presupposition of revealed truths forming the substructure of a deduced system.[15]

It should be noted that Holbrook would allow even the third approach the possibility of being authentically humanistic, provided, however, that theology were *not* viewed as a "queen of the sciences," for as Ronald Gregor Smith has pointed out succinctly, "Theology cannot consist of pronouncements, but must rather hope to provide a contribution to the dialogue about our common human predicament." [16]

In a real sense, humanistic theology is a process of man's defining himself. It might, in fact, be said that man's theological self-definition is his most profound definition of himself. But he undertakes this process of ultimate self-definition from a particular standpoint; he begins where he is. Theologizing, in other words, takes place within a tradition and, even more specifically, within the community which is identified by its tradition — the faith-community. The practice of psychotherapy has long since demonstrated that we cannot know who we are unless we know where we came from. If we are to achieve any sort of self-understanding as spirits in the world, we can only do so by situating ourselves within our context — in this case, the context of the Judeo-Christian faith-community in search of understanding. For the Christian, as H. Richard Niebuhr has pointed out, is "one who counts himself as belonging to that community of men for whom Jesus Christ — his life, words, deeds and destiny — is of supreme importance as the key to the understanding of themselves and their world, the main source of their knowledge of God and man." [17] Thus, theology can be seen as Christian faith seeking deeper understanding of the human situation in its ultimacy. While we will take up below the question of the commit-

15. *Ibid.*, pp. 163-64.
16. *Secular Christianity* (New York: Harper and Row, 1968) p. 8.
17. *Christ and Culture* (New York: Harper and Row, 1951) p. 11.

ment of the teacher from this perspective, let it be said here that
most theology teachers would probably agree that without commitment on their part to their faith-community there would be little
possibility of the depth of understanding which personal commitment is likely to achieve as the result of its seeking.

In summary, the goal of the humanistic study of theology
is to become a *man* or a *woman* — to live a life of intellectual
and human integrity, to assume mature responsibility for the
world and society. This sort of goal is not the outcome of unexamined faith, for the unexamined faith-commitment, like the
unexamined life, is not worth the living. Thus, humanistic theology
is very much a *questioning process.*

Holbrook describes the objectives of the humanistic study
of religion in general as: "to acquaint the student with the perennial
questions which men have raised and have attempted to answer
concerning their meaning and destiny as these are reflected in
systems of thought, cultic acts, and characteristic attitudes and
beliefs." [18] Christian theology attempts to grapple with these
questions in the context of the Christian experience. Thus it aims
at contributing to the deeper penetration of the implications of
the *human* experience as such. And, though it may have been
introduced onto most Catholic campuses for other than humanistic
reasons, Christian theology deserves its place there when it aims
at analyzing a human experience — man's religious experience.

The Catholic institution of higher education is faced with
the challenge to demonstrate that it can theologize in a humanistically respectable way. To do this, it will have to explore and
expound, in an ecumenically open fashion, Christian experience,
Christian gropings with ultimate questions, Christian answers to
human needs. As Ambrogi states it:

> Its task will be scholarly inquiry into all the profound depths
> and nuances of the Christian revelation in its meaning for
> modern man, and this in conscious and sustained dialogue with

18. *Op. cit.,* p. 71.

all the theological traditions of the divided Christian Churches. It will have to demonstrate that the more Catholic theology becomes ecumenically catholic, the more authentically Christian it becomes.[19]

In this process, Catholic theology can only benefit from a more explicit understanding of its relationship to religion as a whole.[20] Theology runs less a danger of parochialism, and takes more seriously its responsibility for achieving a theology of religions, as it is consciously done within the larger context of man's total religious experience.[21]

Obviously, there are problems in achieving this sort of approach to college theology. The first one stems from the need for the college department to be in an independent relationship to the hierarchical *magisterium,* at least to the extent of not being considered an arm of the specifically pastoral concerns of the Church. The statement which issued from the meeting in July 1967 of the educators belonging to the North American region of the International Federation of Catholic Universities put this bluntly:

> To perform its teaching and research functions effectively, the Catholic university must have a true autonomy and academic freedom in the face of authority of whatever kind, lay or clerical, external to the academic community itself.[22]

19. *Art. cit.,* p. 26.
20. This was the experience of Tillich at Chicago in his joint seminar with Mircea Eliade; cf. his "The Significance of the History of Religions for the Systematic Theologian," in *The Future of Religions,* edited by Jerald C. Brauer (New York: Harper and Row, 1966) pp. 80-94.
21. Cf., for instance, Heinz Robert Schlette, *Towards a Theology of Religions* (New York: Herder and Herder, 1966), as developed further by Antonio R. Gualtieri, "Descriptive and Evaluative Formulae for Comparative Religion," *Theological Studies,* XXIX (March, 1968) pp. 52-71.
22. "The Catholic University of Today," *America,* CXVII (August 12, 1967) pp. 154-56.

A second problem area, calling for more discussion, is the question of the faith-commitment of both students and professors. Those who would accept Holbrook's thesis conceive of their task as that of deepening in their students an awareness and understanding of one aspect of human experience — the religious experience. Their task is not that of persuading their students to adopt a specific set of beliefs or a specific code of conduct (just as a professor of political science cannot aim to persuade his students to belong to a particular political party or espouse particular political policies). The AAC statement referred to above puts the ideal in this way:

> Man's religions are closely intertwined with human history and with the gamut of human thought and action. Sooner or later, the study of religion demands of the student a personal experience of the questioning, of the search for relationships and for ultimate answers, which is the sense of the religious. Hopefully, in this process he will come to understand the religious dimension of the human mind and thus become free to choose intelligently for himself values which can provide a basic orientation for his life. Scholarly study of religion, which is essentially the study of man's ultimate values and their translation into human action, can and should lead the student to a disciplined examination of his own values.

The interiorization of values is definitely an objective of humanistic academy study in *all* areas; Holbrook sees this as a responsibility of the religion department as well. It must, however, be discharged humanistically, which involves the opportunity,

> . . . provided somewhere in the religion curriculum, for the student to come to grips with his own life-posture, to identify to the best of his ability what he believes in the light of increased knowledge and evaluative techniques developed by the study of religious concepts and practice. So long as the student deals with his own deepest concerns and not those which he believes to be agreeable to the instructor, and so

long as the instructor's aim is that of assisting the student to clarify and enrich *his own beliefs,* the purposes of liberal education are being served.[23]

This sort of objective, however, has to be clearly distinguished, to the fullest extent possible, from the aim of *indoctrination,* and so the question arises: does the humanistic approach demand such objectivity as to exclude reference to the professor's own religious commitment? And does commitment on the part of the professor lay him open to the charge of indoctrination? Discussing the problem in connection with the issue of independence and freedom, the Federation of Regional Accrediting Commissions has given this opinion:

> Intellectual freedom does not rule out commitment; rather it makes it possible and personal. Freedom does not require neutrality on the part of the individual nor the educational institution — certainly not towards the task of inquiry and learning, nor toward the value systems which may guide them as persons or as schools.

> Hence institutions may hold to a particular . . . religious philosophy as may individual faculty members or students. But to be true to what they profess academically, individuals and institutions must remain intellectually free and allow others the same freedom to pursue truth and to distinguish the pursuit of it from a commitment to it.[24]

Though the indoctrination question is complicated by the reality-factor of the professor's own faith-commitment, which will influence students, this does not *ipso facto* constitute an impediment to the humanistic study of theology, as long as the professor insists on the students' using their own critical faculties and exer-

23. *Op. cit.,* p. 84.
24. "Institutional Integrity," The Federation of Regional Accrediting Commissions, Policy Paper 66.4 (October, 1966).

cising their own responsibility in making a religious commitment. Negatively, he must avoid not only the obviously deceitful brand of brainwashing — withholding information, exposing the student to only one point of view, controlling discussion, and so forth — but also the more subtle ways of convincing by the force with which one viewpoint is advanced, while its contrary is alluded to only in passing. In any case, he should not fear doing what any responsible professor would do to communicate to his students an awareness of the importance of the perspective of his field of study on the general culture, and an enthusiastic interest in the study of the field — these aims are educating, not indoctrinating.

Frequently still to be overcome in this connection is the attitude on the part of the pastoral Church and some parents and administrators that, as Holbrook puts it, the goal of college theology is:

> ... to persuade the student to adopt certain attitudes favorable to those held by the instructor or to a particular religious tradition. The manner, content and purpose of teaching accordingly are expected to be quite different in character from other courses in the curriculum. Since it is assumed that the purpose of teaching religion is to produce religious persons, it is also easily assumed that there can be no other purpose for offering work in the field.[25]

The problem is exacerbated by statements of bishops and other churchmen concerning the role of the Catholic college and of college theology as a pastoral one. The Catholic college normally makes it clear that one of its objectives is the inculcation of Christian values — an objective certainly not incompatible with the proper goal of a liberal arts college — but a delicate situation can arise when the religion department is expected to assume the key, and perhaps exclusive, role here, thus becoming quasi-chaplains to the student body.

25. *Op. cit.*, p. 24.

Finally, presuming the acceptability or even desirability of the humanistic approach in the liberal arts context of religion and theology, it is possible to fall into the trap of giving mere lip-service to the thesis that our current programs are in fact humanistic in the sense described here. Courses which are by design courses in Christian theology, for example, must constantly and rather consciously reflect the fact that the students are participating in the Christian community's rational and systematic reflection upon its human experience, which it finds revelatory of some of the dimensions of Ultimate Reality itself. With the aid of the light shed by the parallel reflections of other religious traditions, the students hopefully will be better able to adopt a coherent interpretation of the meaning of life. In the words of the IFCU study group statement cited above, "the theological faculty must engage directly in exploring the depths of the Christian tradition and *the total religious heritage of the world,* in order to come to the best possible understanding of religion and revelation, *of man in all his varied relationships to God."* [26] At the very least, it should contribute to the ability of our students to *hear* questions and not to *fear* them — perhaps the most important capacity we can help them develop.

---

26. "The Catholic University of Today," p. 155. Emphasis mine.

ROGER BALDUCELLI, O.S.F.S.

11 A Phenomenological Approach to Religion

My task is to make a short presentation of an approach to the academic study of religion which for the sake of convenience has been named phenomenological.[1] The word "phenomenological" is itself a presentation of this approach, but there is in it too much of that indeterminate determinacy the phenomenologists speak of to make a modest accumulation of words necessary.[2]

In any intellectual inquiry one may distinguish a point of departure constituted by questions occasioned by accessible data,

1. Students of phenomenology will have to decide whether the approach here presented merits the label used to describe it. The point is debatable, especially in view of the fact that there is no orthodoxy in phenomenology. Under the circumstances the use of the phenomenological label may not have to be experienced as a severe breach of propriety. On the other hand the reference to phenomenology is not meant to commend respect for the approach. The whole project is still very much on the move, and can profit from exposure to the frownings of critics more than from indulgence or admiration. I may report, however, that the classroom has been a critical testing ground for the approach, and that the reports coming in are not unfavorable.
2. Students of religion partial to a phenomenological approach may profit by some titles that have proved useful in one way or another. It is difficult to speak with authority in this matter, but my conviction is that things begin to happen phenomenologically only after the student of religion has succeeded in intuiting the phenomenological viewpoint, and finds himself comfortable in it. This entails effort, for the phenomenological viewpoint does not coincide with any of the viewpoints that are likely to be familiar to those among us who have "taught" religion. This initial difficulty needs to be overcome by a study of the phenomenological movement which provides the experience of the genesis of meaning out of which alone meaning can arise. See for this H. Spiegel-

an anticipated point of arrival constituted by the answers to these
questions, and a set of precepts designed to guide the inquirer from
the one point to the other — questions, answers and method. A
phenomenological inquiry into religion can be described according
to this scheme. The crucial decision concerns the questions to be
raised with regard to religion. This is the decision that determines

berg, *The Phenomenological Movement: A Historical Introduction* (2nd
ed.; The Hague: M. Nijhoff, 1965) 2 vols.

The phenomenology of religion proper has not received as much attention
as the religious phenomenon seems to deserve by its sheer magnitude.
Husserl regarded the problem of God as the fundamental philosophical
problem, but never in his long philosophical career did he apply himself to the study of this problem. See L. Dupré, "Husserl's Thought on
God and Faith," *Philosophy and Phenomenological Research*, 29 (1968)
pp. 201-215.

Of the four original collaborators of the *Jahrbuch für Philosophie und
phänomenologische Forschung* only Max Scheler inclined toward the
phenomenology of religion. See H. Spiegelberg, *op. cit.*, Vol 1, pp.
262-265. During the so-called Catholic period Scheler produced *Vom
Ewigen im Menschen* now available as *On the Eternal in Man*, trans.
B. Noble (London: SCM Press, 1960). See also H. Hafkesbrink, "The
Meaning of Objectivism and Realism in Max Scheler's Philosophy of
Religion: A Contribution to the Understanding of Max Scheler's Catholic
Period," *Philosophy and Phenomenological Research*, 2 (1941-42) pp.
292-308.

The best known phenomenological study of religion is without a doubt R.
Otto, *The Idea of the Holy*, trans. J. W. Harvey (New York: Galaxy
Books, 1958; first published 1923). See R. F. Davidson, *Rudolf Otto's
Interpretation of Religion* (Princeton: Princeton University Press, 1947);
C. A. Bennett, "Religion and the Idea of the Holy," *Journal of Philosophy*,
23 (1926) pp. 460-469; P. Tillich, "Die Kategorie des 'Heiligen' by
Rudolf Otto." *Theologische Blätter*, 2 (1923) pp. 11ff.; J. M. Moore,
Theories of Religious Experience (New York: Round Table Press, 1938),
especially pp. 75ff. Otto's book has attracted much attention and is
constantly quoted to dispose of the matter at hand, but it would be
difficult to rate it as a phenomenology of religion, for it limits itself to
the exploration of how the Holy is mirrored in consciousness. Religion
covers a range of phenomena that presupposes the encounter with the
Holy, and its intelligibility, but require separate phenomenological exploration.

which data are required as a point of departure, which answers are to be considered an adequate point of arrival, and which precepts more effectively lead to these answers. If the approach to the academic study of religion is to be phenomenological, this critical decision cannot be long in the making. It has, in fact, been made the moment the approach has called itself phenomenological,

For a more inclusive treatment see G. van der Leeuw, *Religion in Essence and Manifestation. A Study in Phenomenology*, trans. J. E. Turner (New York: Harper Torchbooks, 1963) 2 vols. The German original is unambiguously entitled *Phänomenologie der Religion* (Tübingen, 1933), but the work does not abide by a recognizable phenomenological technique in its description of the religious phenomenon. The phenomenological preoccupation emerges abruptly once the description is completed and takes the form of technical reflections on phenomenology and religion. See vol. II, pp. 671-701.

W. King, *Introduction to Religion: A Phenomenological Approach* (New York: Harper and Row, 1954; rev. ed., 1968); for a review of the revised edition cf. J. Boozer in *Journal of the American Academy of Religion*, 36 (1968) pp. 390-393. King describes his enterprise as "the observation of religion from a *detached withinness*," the detachment being from any particular religion, and the withinness being understood to mean "penetrating insight" and "sympathetic interpretation." Cf. p. 7.

E. J. Jurji, *The Phenomenology of Religion* (Philadelphia: The Westminster Press, 1963) defines itself as "an attempt to develop further Otto's thesis of the holy or numinous in all religions," (p. 3) "in a manner conducive to communication and coordination" (p. 5). In view of this the article in the title of the book is certainly pretentious.

J. Wach, once a student of Husserl and Scheler, has made some valuable contribution to the field. See *Types of Religious Experience* (Chicago: University of Chicago Press, 1951); *The Comparative Study of Religions* (New York: Columbia University Press, 1958), especially pp. 27-58 ("The Nature of Religious Experience").

On methodological issues see M. Eliade and J. Kitagawa, (eds.) *The History of Religions: Essays in Methodology* (Chicago: University of Chicago Press, 1959); L. Dupré, "Philosophy of Religion and Revelation," *International Philosophical Quarterly*, 4 (1964) pp. 499-513; G. Kaufman, "On the Meaning of God: Transcendence without Mythology," *Harvard Theological Review*, 59 (1966) pp. 105-132; J. E. Smith, *Experience and God* (New York: Oxford University Press, 1968; *Reason and God* (New Haven and London: Yale University Press, 1961).

for phenomenology pursues the intelligibility of experience. Thus intelligibility is the one-word definition of the finality of a phenomenological approach to the study of religion. The first task facing anyone who intends to explore religion phenomenologically is therefore to make a case for this single-minded dedication to the pursuit of the intelligibility of religion.

The case is not an easy one to make. If I interpret my classroom experience correctly, it says that the concern of students is initially oriented less toward the intelligibility of religion than toward the truth-content, the value, and the relevance of the same. They would experience no constraint were they invited to contribute their participation to an inquiry calculated to lead to the formation of judgments concerning religion's claim to truth, or the contribution of religion to the quality of man's existence in the word, or the attunement of religion to the moods and expectations of the times. And I for one feel somewhat on the defensive when the time comes to announce that the logically prior question, prior to the question of truth, value, and relevance is the intelligibility question. At that moment intelligibility rings in the room like a finality by decree, an act of academic imperialism controlled by the secret hope of evading the necessity to face up to the contention that religion is an illusion, unverifiable, unfalsifiable, yet false and doomed to perish. Freud's booklet *The Future of an Illusion* is an eloquent harangue in this direction, and here is a man who fails to pick up the challenge in order to pursue something as slippery as the intelligibility of religion.

The case for the logical priority of the intelligibility question needs to be made in this unfriendly courtroom. But it is a good case, for the intelligibility question is logically prior to the question of truth, value, and relevance since these questions are nonsensical to raise and impossible to answer unless the intelligibility question has been formally raised and a serious attempt made at achieving an answer to it. There simply is no way of evaluating the merits of man's experience of the sacred unless that experience has under scrutiny its own intelligibility. In the absence of intelligibility religious experience is an accumulation of raw data, a conglomeration of felt meanings, felt by others as opaque to the critic, saying nothing specific enough to be evaluated against the standards of truth, value, or relevance.

I am unable to tell how convincing this consideration is as mirrored in the consciousness of my students. As mirrored in their faces it appears to fall short of total success. But neither is it a total failure, for no matter how appealing may be the prospect of reaching a once-for-all determination as to what religion is worth, the desire to know what religion is survives the competition, and a case has been made for a shared venture, even though the shares are unequally distributed between teacher and students.

Once the intelligibility of religion has been established as the finality of the exploration, a discrimination can be made between adequate and inadequate data, and between suitable and unsuitable methods.

There is honorable perplexity among students of religion as to which phenomena qualify as religious. If the intelligibility of religion be the finality of the exploration, the perplexity can be ended by observing that the intelligibility being sought is that of religion as mirrored in the consciousness of the religious man. It is within consciousness that the experience of the sacred has a meaning, and the intelligibility of that meaning is what we aim to discover. This can be attempted on the basis of data that are in us and about us, in the people who do have a religion, who practice a religion, who do things that are called religious, who speak the language of a religious tradition, who experience the sacred as the source of moral imperatives, who organize themselves into religious communities. The history of religions enlarges this accumulation of readily available data considerably by contributing primitive and archaic counterparts of present-day religious experience, conceptualizations and dramatizations of that experience in myth and ritual, and so on. Wondering whether the accumulation of data be adequate, whether all the manifestations of religious experience have been included, whether among the manifestations included there be some that ought to be excluded, is not important enough for genuine agony, if religion is to be made intelligible as mirrored in consciousness. The question of intelligibility is the same whether it be raised on the basis of a small or large accumulation of data, and the answer to the question does not require any particular accumulation to be made any larger. In other words, the question, "What is religion?" is the same in the mind of a man who knows only his religious experience, and of the historian of religions who knows all religions from Animism to Zen. They are both prompted by the data to ask the same question: What sense does the affirmation of the sacred make to the consciousness that makes it?

Thus the point of departure of the phenomenological inquiry can be easily decided upon once the finality of the inquiry has been concretized under intelligibility. When we turn to the method whereby to seek the intelligibility of religion the choice is between definition and description, and definition is no choice after all. Attempts at defining religion have been made in great numbers by scholars with ingenuity to spare; symposia have been convened to pool ingenuities and produce a consensus, but to no avail. Religion much defined remains undefined. In addition, definition is not a proper instrument for the attainment of the intelligibility of the religious phenomenon, only for the standarization of language. Even assuming that a consensus could be reached as to what meaning the word "religion" ought to stand for, we would still have to ask how intelligible that meaning is to the man who exists within the phenomena so named.[3]

Description, then, is the only viable course of action. Here is perhaps where the phenomenological approach becomes difficult to put into words. What ought to be understood above all is that here description is instrumental to intelligibility. This means that the task at hand is to display man's experience of the sacred so that not only the experience itself becomes disclosed, but the intelligibility of it, and to anyone who is willing to look in the same direction. This is, then, a description of a special kind. It describes what appears in consciousness but so that the intelligibility of what is described comes through in the description itself. What is

3. See F. Ferré, *Basic Modern Philosophy of Religion* (New York: Charles Scribner's Sons, 1967) pp. 30-83.

described is religion, not intelligibility, yet it is the intelligibility of religion that becomes manifest to the one who follows the description and in virtue of that description itself.

I have come to the conclusion that to describe religion in order to disclose its intelligibility is the same as to erect a general theory of religion. The desire to describe for intelligibility is fulfilled by reducing the multiplicity of religious phenomena into a structure that is intelligible because it is a structure, and because each component within it is intelligible. The task of description for intelligibility becomes manageable in these terms. It is a matter of deciding first which component of religious experience is so logically prior to all the others that its intelligibility is presupposed to their intelligibility. This decision once made, this component is described first, and so described as to display whatever intelligibility can be discovered in it. Within the general theory of religion this component plays the role of foundation, logically prior to, and unconditioned by, other elements, and conditioning them. Next the description moves to the component that is immediately intelligible in terms of the component just described, and so on until the architecture is completed, or open-endedly if no capping stone can be found to arrest the upward thrust.

It may help if I try to show how this abstract blueprint in the order of intention looks at the level of execution. The initial step is the most crucial, for here a mistake is more than anyone can afford. When the Egyptians were building the great pyramids they made sure that the first course of stones was perfectly level-led, else whatever they would build on top of it would not be a pyramid. Here the problem is to isolate the experience that brings man to the threshold of the sacred, the point of intersection between the profane and the sacred sphere of experience. In other words, the first question is: What is man's religious premise? From a correct answer to this question the intelligibility of the whole religious phenomenon depends, just as the geometrical intelligibility of a pyramid depends on the correct level of that first course of stones.

Nor will it do to elicit the answer to the question from data derived exclusively from primitive or archaic religions and not observable in present-day civilization. Primitives may indeed have been led to the threshold of the transcendent by contemplating the majesty of the firmament, or blinking at the radiance of the sun, but what of contemporary man who knows that the firmament is an optical illusion? Hierophany, therefore, may well make primitive religion intelligible, but not the religious phenomenon at the highest level of generality. What then is the road by which man as man, not as primitive or as sophisticated, comes to the sacred any time, any place?

I have come to the conclusion that man comes to the sacred by experiencing the radical limitation, finitude, meaninglessness of the human situation. To put it differently: the sacred meets man as answer meets question, and the question is that which is raised by man's inability to make sense of his own situation in the world. This is not to say that the man who is led to the affirmation of the sacred by the affirmation of his own meaninglessness has in effect affirmed that meaninglessness to himself at the end of a dispassionate analysis of the human situation, or with the cogency of a conclusion emerging from premises. The affirmation of meaninglessness may well be nothing more than felt meaninglessness, a sense of alienation from one's own existence emerging from the facticity of the same, as it is held up to the possibilities for existence that can be imagined. The sense of alienation may in turn take many forms, depending on what the facticity of existence happens to be in any given case, and what possibilities are precluded by that facticity. I can, for example, well understand how a man, who defines the human situation as that of the intelligent subject driven by a desire of total intelligibility, may come to meet God as the transcendent response to that transcendent drive, that is to say, not as the last link in the great chain of being, nor the last explanation in the chain of explanations, but as the one who makes all inquiry intelligible to itself.[4] This is a sophisticated man who has achieved an equally sophisticated

4. See M. Novak, *Belief and Unbelief* (New York: Macmillan, 1965) p. 125.

grasp of his own situation as a man. His experience of radical limitation is contingent on the fact that he has lived under the control of the unconditioned desire to know, has realized the ultimacy of that desire, and his incapacity not only to fulfill it but to account for it.

For most people, I suppose, the meaninglessness of the human situation discloses itself at less sophisticated levels of experience and reflection: the experience of death, for example, or of our being-toward-death — death not only taking life away, but taking meaning away from life. It is also conceivable that a man who reads the human situation in terms of gratification might experience the meaninglessness of the same by realizing that gratification kills desire, and so life as gratification is absurd.

I have said that it is important not to misconstrue the first encounter with the sacred because this is the structuring moment in religion. A misinterpretation at this point vitiates the interpretation of the structure that man builds on it, beginning with the interpretation of the sacred itself. For if the sacred is affirmed as answer to the disclosure of absurdity it is bound to be mirrored in consciousness essentially as ultimately important meaning, for only an ultimately important meaning is the answer to the question of total absurdity. Religion will then consist in this constitutive moment in consciousness in the affirmation of an unconditionally important reality beyond the horizon of empirical experience: other, yet not so totally other, for it is correlated to it as the source of its meaning. This means that in its most radical and undiluted form the affirmation of the sacred is the state of a man who can no longer divorce his concern for the sacred from the concern for his own existence, since it is only in correlation to the sacred that his existence is fit for willing. In estrangement from the sacred, existence is not nothing, but it is not fit for willing; it is absurd.

The descriptive process moves at this point to the next structural component, next in the order of intelligibility. This is the religious man's quest for master symbols in terms of which he may specify to himself the felt meaning of the sacred. The man who exists in the state of affirmation and concern faces the ques-

tion: What is the sacred like? The creation of master symbols is
the answer to this question. Now the creation of symbols to
specify felt meaning occurs spontaneously, and precisely for this
reason the intelligibility of the process is hard to come by, and
harder to convey in words. The scholastics gave attention to
this process in their cerebrations about divine names and the analogy of proportionality, but they are less helpful here, perhaps,
than literary critics and students of poetic diction and depth
language, for they pick up the problem too far down the line.
They describe how divine names behave, whereas the problem
is how the *man* behaves who creates out of felt meaning both
divine names and the conceptions that are crystallized in them.
How does the religious man behave who symbolizes the felt
meaning of the sacred as impersonal power, unattached yet effective, or as a centered self that understands and wills and takes
initiatives that affect the functioning of nature and the unfolding of
history? These are the questions to which phenomenology addresses
itself in this second lap of the journey. To the extent to which it
discloses the intelligibility of the symbolization of the sacred it
makes a contribution to the problem of God.[5]

From symbolization and symbols the description moves on to

5. See P. Wheelwright, *The Burning Fountain: A Study in the Language
of Symbolism* (Bloomington, Ind.: Indiana University Press, 1968);
Metaphor and Reality (Bloomington, Ind.: Indiana University Press,
1962; PB 1968); O. Barfield, "Poetic Diction and Legal Fiction," in M.
Black (ed.), *The Importance of Language* (Englewood Cliffs, N.J.:
Prentice-Hall, 1962) pp. 51-71; P. Tillich, "Theology and Symbolism,"
in F. F. Johnson (ed.), *Religious Symbolism* (New York: Institute for
Religious and Social Studies, 1955) pp. 199ff.; *Theology of Culture*
(New York: Oxford University Press, 1964); "The Religious Symbol,"
in Rollo May (ed.), *Symbolism in Religion and Literature* (New York:
G. Braziller, 1960) pp. 75-98; D. Emmet, *The Nature of Metaphysical
Thinking* (London: Macmillan, 1946) pp. 94-114; R. Hart, *Unfinished
Man and the Imagination* (New York: Herder and Herder, 1968); E. T.
Gendlin, *Experiencing and the Creation of Meaning* (New York: The
Free Press of Glencoe, 1962); "Expressive Meanings," in J. M. Edie
(ed.), *An Invitation to Phenomenology* (Chicago: Quadrangle Books,
1965) pp. 240-251.

ritual, the third structural component of religion. Here the intelligibility question is brought to bear on the emergence of gesture from mere self-expressive behavior, the stylization of sequences, and the emergence of prescriptive sequences out of stylized but unrealized mannerisms. From prescriptive ritual in turn there emerge ritualism and formalism that belong already to the pathology of religion.[6]

The language of religion is being ardently discussed in our time. A descriptive theory of religion should include religious language, and this is perhaps the place to which the discussion belongs. Speech is already involved in symbolization and ritual, but the intelligibility of speech cannot be handled only in terms of symbol and ritual; it needs be handled also in terms of the speaker, for it is part of his behavior as a religious man. Here the task is to hold religion's speech up to that which it intends, namely up to the silent discourse within the believer's consciousness from which it emerges, and so discover the phenomenon of religious speech anew. This is strictly primary reflection, reflection on speech as speech, not as language.[7]

To put the confession bluntly, this.is as far as I have travelled in this attempt at building a general theory of religion. My yet unexamined impression is that a descriptive theory aimed at displaying the intelligibilty of religion is complete once the intelligibility of the faith option has been achieved, the sacred itself has been described as mirrored in consciousness, the process has

---

6. See S. Langer, *Philosophy in a New Key* (New York: Mentor Books, 1951) pp. 127-148; E. Underhill, *Worship* (New York: Harper, 1937).
7. See R. Kwant, *Phenomenology of Language* (Pittsburgh: Duquesne University Press, 1965); M. Merleau-Ponty, *Signes* (Paris: Gallimard, 1960) pp. 105-122 ("Sur la phénomenologie du langage"); R. W. Funk, *Language, Hermeneutic and the Word of God* (New York: Harper and Row, 1966 pp. 224-249; I. G. Barbour (ed.), *Science and Religion* (New Row, 1966) pp. 224-249; I. G. Barbour (ed.), *Science and Religion* (New York: Harper and Row, 1968), especially D. D. Evans, "Differences between Scientific and Religious Assertions," pp. 101-133; I. G. Barbour, *Issues in Science and Religion* (Englewood Cliffs, N.J.: Prentice-Hall, 1966), especially pp. 151ff., 238-251.

been described whereby the master symbols are created, and the
odd behavior of the religious speaker has been looked into and
the oddity explained. We then have a structure that is intelligible
as structure, and no essential elements are missing for the stability
of it.

This is not to say that the religious phenomenon, in the broader
sense of the word, is adequately mirrored in the theory. The
theory is descriptive, not prescriptive. It is designed to deliver the
intelligibility of the phenomenon as mirrored in consciousness,
not to list all of religion's normative holdings. The study of religion,
then, needs to be continued. Among the areas to be explored there
is, for example, religion's impact on the constitution of the moral
imperative (the question of a theonomous ethics), and the capacity
of religion to intersect creatively or critically with other areas of
man's spiritual, social, and cultural experience. But, as these examples show, here it is no longer the intelligibility of religion that is
being explored, but its potency, namely its capacity to condition
and control man as he goes about the business of being himself
in non-religious areas of experience. This, then, is the point where
the university catalogues should list the "Religion and . . ." courses:
Religion and Society, Religion and Culture, Religion and Politics,
etc.

In brief this is what I would consider a phenomenological
approach to the academic study of religion. How valid is this
approach? Held up to the silent discourse from which it emerges
this question appears to be two questions: (1) How valid is the
phenomenological approach in itself, as approach? (2) How valid
is the phenomenological approach as an alternative to existing
approaches?

The answer to the first question is by distinction. There is
little doubt that the phenomenological approach, as approach,
can make a good case for itself. The pursuit of intelligibility is a
legitimate intellectual endeavor, whether it addresses itself to
religious experience or to other varieties of experience. It emerges
from the desire to know, and fulfills that desire, and this desire
is unconditioned. This pretty much takes care of the problem.

The question arises anew in relation to the theory advanced

here to display the intelligibility of religion. The theory is certainly material for legitimate scrutiny and questions. It can be looked into in terms of coherence, simplicity, relation to data. The most relevant test, however, is whether the intelligibility that accrues to religion, when reduced to the proposed structure, can be reproduced self-identically in more than one consciousness. In other words, does anyone willing to take the proposed description seriously find religion intelligible because of that description? I realize, of course, that this kind of testing requires that the theory be displayed in full.

The second question does not concern validity, strictly speaking, but advantage. Does phenomenology as approach fulfill promises left unfulfilled by other approaches, or does it perhaps deliver benefits yet unpromised? In the absence of comparative material the question is difficult to answer, not to say impossible. Does anyone know what the academic study of religion aims to achieve, what benefits are being expected from it, and for whom? Does anyone know how successfully proposed objectives are being attained? I am speaking of the academic study of religion as carried out in the classrooms of the country, not in symposia, conventions, or learned journals. If there are answers to these questions they are not accessible to me, which makes it impossible for me to produce a comparative evaluation of merits.

It seems, therefore, as if the phenomenological approach will have to make a case for its merits against a competition it does not know. This can be done if we turn our attention to the students for whom it is meant. For one needs not teach religion long to realize that religion is true to its definition even when it is turned into an object of inquiry. It is man's concern for God, and remains itself an object of personal concern even when explored for intelligibility by people who propose to function as knowers and objective observers. The study of religion is self-involving. One studies both oneself and religion when studying religion, just as one speaks of oneself and of God when speaking of God. Because the quest for the intelligibility of religion is self-involving it takes on the mannerism of a dialogue between the student of religion and the religious dimension in his own experience. As religion emerges into consciousness as intelligible structure, the intelligibility of the structure engenders either self-understanding, or the understanding of one's prior inability to understand oneself as religious. Either way the student is a participant in the action, not only as a knower but as a person.

This participation of the total self is important in view of the social origins of religion. Our students had religion built into their fabrics during their formative years together with, and as part of, those definitions of reality that are handed to people as they make their way out of childhood and into the community. Thus their encounter with the sacred was not engineered by existence reflecting upon itself and disclosing its own absurdity, but by the social engineers who shouldered the responsibility for the production of their social selves. The consequence of this is that religion came into existence in them in the form of a plausibility structure, a legitimating definition that underlies the shape of things and the management of existence.[8]

A phenomenological approach to religion cuts through the social origins of the same and tries to read its intelligibility, not out of those origins, or in relation to social goals, but in terms of a confrontation between man, his existence, and the insufficiency of its meaning. And since the student participates in this reading, not only as a reader but as a person preoccupied with his own existence, the reading engenders self-understanding and self-evaluation. The student comes to know what it means to be a religious man, and by the application of this criterion he discovers how much or how little genuine religion there is in the religious allegiance that has been socialized into him. The opportunity for this kind of self-evaluation is an important benefit, and the phenomenological approach makes it available without deflecting for one moment from its own finality.

8. See P. L. Berger, and T. Luckmann, *The Social Construction of Reality: A Treatise in the Sociology of Knowledge* (Garden City, N.Y: Doubleday Anchor Books, 1967); *The Sacred Canopy* (Garden City, N.Y.: Doubleday, 1967); *The Precarious Vision* (Garden City, N.Y.: Doubleday, 1961); *A Rumor of Angels* (Garden City, N.Y.: Doubleday, 1969).

Many of our young people are inclined to see their chief responsibility to reside no longer in bringing their lives into conformity with pre-existing patterns and structures, but in bringing patterns and structures encountered as facticities face to face with their own normative intelligibility. In this climate religion can hardly survive on whatever intelligibility comes to it from its social origins and usefulness. It must learn to survive on the strength of its own intelligibility.

SISTER ANNA BARBARA BRADY, S.L.

12 Religious Education in the Church Tomorrow

A pill has finally been discovered which is able to cure the serious diseases afflicting the Catholic Church: suffocation of authoritarianism, paralysis of legalistic structures, wide-spread anemia. "The Pill" will so radically change the complexion of the Church that the Catholic school system, our multi-vitamin formula which is supposed to ward off attacks from a hostile environment, is bound to become unnecessary; religious education will be much more invisible because it will be taken in our everyday natural diet instead of in capsule form.

The event of the pill encompassing the Commission, the long period of Papal silence, the Encyclical, the reaction to the Encyclical, the reaction to the reaction — could never have done its job without the psychological preparation afforded the "patient" by the theology of Vatican II. An ecumenical spirit which respected rather than feared the world beyond the Catholic Church, a redefinition of the Church as the People of God, and a dynamic view of revelation as process rather than deposit all contributed to the mind-set which makes the cure a possibility.

These theological trends are no more in isolation, of course, than is the pill event itself. Theologians — even the Ivory Tower type — breathe a common air with the rest of twentieth century mankind and developments of theological thought are reflections of the world in which we live, a world which challenges traditional values, which calls for person over institution and demands participatory decision-making.

All this simply goes to say that the pill incident dramatically captured the theological and cultural currents of our times and has become both symbol and cause of the future of religious education.

I would like to look at two aspects of the incident which have peculiar significance for religious education of the future: (1) The problem of freedom, responsibility and authority; and (2) Emphasis upon humanization of civilization rather than upon doctrinal disputes.

1. Freedom, Responsibility, Authority

When you deal with college age youth today and try to imagine what they will be like as the future religious educators you know that they will not be able to force or entice a new generation into religious commitment. They won't want to! Many college students with whom I work — and this seems to be in direct proportion to the amount of formalized religious instruction they have received — resent having been "conned" into belief. They find themselves brainwashed and guilt-ridden and are reacting violently against a system which does not present alternatives.

Now my suggestions for facing this situation are not original. The first obvious suggestion for the future is much less formalized religious instruction for youth. In fact, I am ready to go down on record pleading for *no* formalized religious instruction at all if it ever vaguely resembles indoctrination.

So far I have been talking about religious education in a vague, undefined generality. (And accepting education in Dr. Westerhoff's terms justifies such an approach.) For the sake of clarity, however, let's call religious education a formalized, systematic study of religion, or of ultimate value. The broader aspect, the continual growth in Christ demanded of every Christian, could be called the educational mission of the Church. In the past the religious educator has been asked to do the whole job and to have a formed Christian ready to graduate from high school. Impossible! Not only is the high school student only beginning to make the sort of commitment demanded of Christian life, but even more significantly, to try to form Christians in an educational system abuses the most basic notion of education. The educational process must be an open, probing searching for truth wherever it is to be found and it cannot be used to feed the party line — not even the American dream.

I will return to the role of the educator later but first let's look at the broader aspect, that continual never-ending growth demanded of Christian life. That sort of growth is dependent more upon values and attitudes than it is upon factual knowledge. Parents do a better job of shaping values and attitudes than they ever dream. Here, too, the notion of freedom and responsibility is operative. Parents should be confident enough about their own values to allow children the possibility of meeting alternative systems. When parents encourage children into diverse, rich and challenging experiences they are sometimes surprised at the result. But the children can continue to respect their parents' values even if they don't "buy" all of them because those values have been offered to them freely. I don't have to knock a gift box of candy out of your hand if you offer it to me for my inspection. But I might if you start ramming it down my throat.

So I'd say, "No parochial schools, no CCD classes, no parents trying to have a religion 'class' on Saturday evening!" Instead let's give our children full, rich human experiences, and you never can tell; maybe the Spirit of Jesus is still alive and operative in our world and just maybe some of our children will be grabbed by that spirit without being grabbed by a catechist.

Is there then any role for the religious educator as such, the teacher of religion? Yes, but I'd like to see him teaching within the public school system so that he will be forced into an non-propagandizing position. Religion would be a "sociological" study or the phenomenological study of religion as students experience it in their life and their culture (and hopefully in that revolutionary form so ably described by Dr. Westerhoff). If psychologists insist that I learn who I am by becoming aware of my strengths and weaknesses in constant interaction with others, will I not learn who I am as a Christian by interaction with others who differ from me?

So far, we've been talking about children. Adult education is another matter; it fits more properly in the broader aspect which

I was calling the mission of the Church, rather than in religious education. Mary Perkins Ryan, Gabriel Moran, Joseph Dillon, other leaders in religious education have been saying for years that we need an adult-centered Christianity and some few dioceses have already begun to put this notion into practice. But no one seems to have found any magical solutions to the problem.

One avenue which has hardly been used is the Sunday Obligation and the loyalty which our adult generation has to the Eucharist. Of course, we would have to look much more radically at our parish structure, at our mass meetings scheduled at 1½ hour intervals with parking lot complications. If the obligation to worship could be spread out over two weeks' time we could have smaller worshipping communities who gather to experientially discover what it means to be an adult Christian. We cannot even begin to experiment in this area as long as money and personnel are being poured into one school system. There is much remedial work to be done with our present adult community: they need to be untaught and retaught to respect and trust their human, creative experiences.

And that takes me finally to the second point made so evident by the event of the pill.

2. The Emphasis upon the Humanization of Civilization Rather than upon Doctrinal Disputes

The overwhelming problems of over-population, mass starvation and hunger make in-group fighting over past authoritative (not infallible of course!) statements appear ridiculous, to say the least. But the whole thrust of Vatican II theology with its critical approach to Scripture, its appreciation of incarnation and redemption as essentially concerned with the historical process, its attempt to see *all* history as a dynamic, revelatory dialogue between God and man forces us to view the humanization of civilization as a more significantly Christian task than analyzing an encyclical.

If you just glance at any of the new religion texts being published you see that this trend is already upon us. Students are asked to look at the world around them, to examine their literature, their films, their songs, their growing experiences. Students are asked to live and grow as integrated human persons confident in the creative power present in themselves as redeemed Christians. They are being asked to be involved in the needed reformation of political, economic and social structures. Whether you call this religious instruction or not is irrelevant. It will have been most successful when it has been so internalized, so well blended into the mix of everyday life that it will be invisible.

And what do we do with college students today who want to be "religious educators?" We must help to decide whether they want to be teachers of religion or ministers of the Church. They must see these as two different tasks. The first implies examining religious truth wherever it is to be found in an open-ended way. The second implies being involved in the total human experience of some specific Christian community and trying to make Christian sense out of it.

In conclusion I'd like to say that college theology teachers will have made a significant contribution to religious education of the future when they have helped to graduate students who: (1) See their "religious life" as integrally interwoven into their lives as free, responsible human beings; (2) Live as (in the words of Michael Novak) " 'Secular Saints': radically committed to a vision of human brotherhood, personal integrity, openness to the future, justice, and peace"; and who (3) Work with all men of good faith to find the creative process operative in our chaotic world, with no divisions between Christians and non-Christians, Believers and non-Believers. "It is through the whole of creation that the one Father of creation speaks to all of us" (Gabriel Moran).

Therefore, the Catholic school system has succeeded when it has put itself, and "religious education" in its present form, out of business.

SISTER MARGUERITE GREEN, R.S.C.J. AND ELLEN
DOUGHERTY

13 Interdisciplinary Courses and Theology

This chapter is based on certain premises which arise from our understanding, first, of the nature and purpose of theologizing, or, more literally, the speaking of the Word which explains God to man; second, from our understanding of the function and purpose of the educational process; third, from our experience as participating members of interdisciplinary instructional teams; and finally, from our experience in our own disciplines, literature and history respectively.

1. The Nature and Purpose of Theologizing

It is clear that modern man has generally accepted Tillich's emphasis on God experienced as depth, as "the ground of being." [1] Gregory Baum, in a recent article published in the *St. Louis Review,* observes with Tillich that "in the past, our religious imagination presented us with a God outside of human life, whom we found when we turned away from our environment to him. To listen to God and to address ourselves to him, we separated ourselves from our situation, we left behind us the experiences of every day.... It seems to me that the change in human consciousness at this time has affected our religious imagination. Our religious imagination today proposes to us a God who is present in

---

1. Paul Tillich, *Systematic Theology,* Vol. 1 (Chicago: University of Chicago Press, 1951) p. 156.

human life, whom we find when we are in touch with the deep
meaning of our ordinary experiences. To listen to God and to
address ourselves to him, we cannot afford to separate ourselves
from the situation in which we live, we cannot afford to forget
the many things that move us deeply. On the contrary, it is in the
meaning of ordinary life that God addresses us." [2]

M. V. C. Jeffreys, similarly addressing himself to Tillich's emphasis, comments simply: "Religious truth is normal experience
understood at full depth." [3] More recently still, Colin Alves has
written: "To explore life and to understand it in depth is to come
face to face with God." [4] In view of this common emphasis on God
experienced as the deep meaning of our lives, we understand the
goal of theologizing to be that of helping man to understand, within
the larger context of revelation, the meaning of his normal, human
experience. Tillich has spoken well to this context of revelation:
"The many different meanings of the term 'Word' are all united
in one meaning, namely 'God manifest' — manifest in himself, in
creation, in the history of revelation, in the final revelation, in
the Bible, in the words of the Church and her members. 'God
manifest' — the mystery of the divine abyss expressing itself
through the divine Logos — this is the meaning of the symbol,
the 'Word of God.'" [5] Gregory Baum, adapting the methodology
of Professor Donald Evans, suggests that it is the function of theology to discover whether the Christian message, the word of God
manifest, has anything to say to man's depth experiences. The
theologian, Baum contends, must always and honestly be asking
the question, "Does this revelation *explain* his depth experiences
to man, does it *purify* those experiences, and finally does it

2. Gregory Baum, "Changes in Man Bring New Ideas on Prayer," *St.
   Louis Review,* November, 1968.
3. Quoted by Colin Alves in "The Overall Significance of Ronald Goldman
   for Religious Education," *Religious Education,* LXIII, 6 (November-
   December, 1968) p. 420.
4. Alves, *Religious Education,* LXIII, p. 420.
5. Tillich, *Systematic Theology,* 1, p. 159.

multiply his depth experiences?" [6] For clearly, out of the theologian's own reflecting comes his best service to men. With Alves, we note that "we are indebted to the Bishop of Woolwich for emphasizing the truth that religion is an unceasing search in depth rather than a body of fact to be learned without question." [7]

2. The Function and Purpose of Education

This brings us to an expression of our understanding of the goal of the larger educational process which we see as that of initiating and fostering the process of defining for oneself a substance of belief in all disciplines and the system of values by which one lives. We do not see it as the imposition or placing of clearly (and prior) defined, almost static bodies of truth and systems of moral values. Education, ideally, is question — rather than answer — oriented.

3. Interdisciplinary Study

The third premise on which this chapter is based arises from our experience as participating members of interdisciplinary instructional teams. Basically we value the interdisciplinary approach to study because it corresponds more nearly to man's actual experience which is one of *complexity*. Instead of reducing this experience to the artificial simplicity of merely linear study, interdisciplinary exploration suggests a significantly different method of ordering, one which not only acknowledges complexity but which seeks precisely to increase the student's awareness of the complex relations or juxtapositions which exist among his disparate experiences, in this way more really exploring in depth the *meaning* of those experiences.

6. Gregory Baum, *Faith and Doctrine* (New York: Paulist Newman Press, 1969) pp. 59 and 68.
7. Alves, *Religious Education*, LXIII, p. 420.

4. Particular Disciplines: Literature

Finally, we are basing our remarks on our experience in our own particular disciplines — literature and history respectively. Literature is the created Word which reveals man to himself. Art in general (and word-art in particular) may be defined as the translation of reality as the artist experiences it into a new formal structure defined by the medium (media) within which he chooses to work for the sake of bringing joy to man through his experience of integrity.

One must ask, then, at the outset, of this consideration of inter-disciplinary possibilities, "What has literature to offer to theology?" The answer, it would seem, falls quite naturally into two parts. First, it offers an acute sensitivity to and awareness of human experience. In an essay entitled "The Spirit of Place," D. H. Lawrence wrote: "Art-speech is the only truth. An artist is usually a damned liar, but his art, if it be art, will tell you the truth of his day. And that is all that matters." [8] The artist can only be an artist if he brings to his experiencing an extraordinary sensitivity. Because his art is rather a translating of experience than an explaining of it, he may seem at times to be speaking in his art a language which his contemporaries do not understand, or as Eliot has put it, a language which communicates before it is understood.[9] The experience of the waste-land world which Eliot himself presented in his early poetry seemed to men a kind of prophecy rather than a reflection of common experience.

In one sense, this reaction to the artist as prophet is understandable — not because he is, in fact, prophesying the future, but simply because he is more deeply sensitive, faster, to the actual shape of his experience and often re-presents it before his less sensitive audience has become aware of its own experiencing. In the second place, the artist brings to the theologian an aware-

---

8. D. H. Lawrence, "The Spirit of Place," *Studies in Classic American Literature* (New York: Viking Press, Inc., 1964) p. 2.
9. T. S. Eliot, "Dante," *Selected Essays* (New York: Harcourt, Brace and World, Inc., 1950) p. 200.

ness of the power and function of *relation,* that is, of contrast and opposition as the source of meaning. The work of the artist is precisely that of arranging parts, of setting them into a series of relations which create a totally new and unique, often non-logical, meaning. He is particularly aware of the fact that meaning arises from contrast; that a sense of absence, for example, can only be defined convincingly in the context — however this is invoked — of presence. His work, in fine, consists largely of setting elements into a relation of opposition so that the new formal structure which is the art-product may discover to the beholder its own unique integrity.

Both of these skills which belong properly to the artist — first, his exceptional sensitivity to and ability to reflect his experience, and second, his power to engage in "the relational activity that focuses meaning," [10] that is, to relate elements to one another in a way which allows new meaning to discover itself to the beholder — are valuable to the theologian. For it is the theologian's own proper function to explain to man the meaning of human experience and further, to be in his own right an expert in *relation* which even in the most traditional theology is the name given to the Spirit of Love who is himself, as Tillich puts it, "the answer to the question implied in man's finitude." [11]

On the other hand, one must also ask the question, "What has theology to offer literature?" for the possibility of real reciprocity among disciplines is essential to the success of interdisciplinary study. First, it seems clear that it can offer an explanation and a deeper understanding of the significance of those experiences which are re-presented by the artist in his art, experiences which are common to all men in varying degrees of intensity. This increased understanding of those experiences out of which the artist creates — pre-literary though it is — makes possible for man a deeper experience of artistic integrity. Secondly, theology

10. John J. McDermott, "To Be Human is to Humanize," *American Philosophy in the Future,* ed. Michael Novak (New York: Charles Scribner's Sons, 1968) p. 32.
11. Tillich, *Systematic Theology,* 1, p. 211

can offer, in its turn, an awareness of the power of relation to create the deep meaning of our lives where we discover God face to face, present and sustaining us in being and in hope. Certainly this awareness is valuable to the artist and his audience because in some sense artistic integrity is a living reflection of ideal oneness — whether of man's personal sense of wholeness and integrity or of that union among men toward which we strive in the Spirit.

5. Particular Disciplines: History

In reflecting upon the unique experience of interdisciplinary studies, our concern is directed to three interrelated aspects of the work: student attitudes, the role of the historian as teacher and, finally, questions posed by an historian to theologians.

Any teacher, sensitive to recent developments, cannot help but recognize that students are reacting and learning out of a significantly different social consciousness. This is the consciousness of complexity which has already been identified. Their world is, in a very real way, the "global village" which McLuhan has described. As individuals, whether they live in the midst of our great cities or not, they are bombarded with the information from a world in a constant state of low grade or high grade emergency.[12] They live with a sense of crowding, a pressing-in of mass civilization; and finally, they have a feeling for the fragility and vulnerability of life. Education must fit these students for world citizenship, yet like no generation before them they are cynical in their attitude toward publicity and pretense, vitally conscious of the ambiguities of enormous power. They are sophisticated enough to see their world as a kind of chessboard, whether they are observing the maneuvers of international politics played in Paris or Prague or Saigon; or whether they are watching the game of party or city politics as played in Chicago or New York. Besides the shrinking world of the global village and the game of inter-

12. Paul Goodman, *Like a Conquered Province* (New York: Random House, 1968) p. 345.

national power, our students are all too aware that they live in a computerized civilization, one in which the great achievements of science and technology both exalt man to greatness and reduce him to powerlessness.

Before this student enters the college classroom he has observed that his generation challenges the "Establishment," whether it be government or university, Church or family. The one real religious experience of his life may have been a profound sense of his own complicity in evil, as Michael Novak has suggested.[13] His efforts to understand or exorcize that evil may have already led him to drugs or demonstrations or violence in the streets and in the schools. It would be difficult and perhaps pointless to try to convince him of the relevance of the dogma of original sin by lecturing on the exegesis of Holy Scripture.

The foregoing brief description of changing social consciousness in our students provides the framework for further interdisciplinary considerations. What does the historian have to say to the theologian? If one searches out social truth in a special way, what has this to do with God's revelation?

Historians are deeply conscious of one overriding change in the position of man in the world: that which is marked by a progression from the condition of being subject to nature (in the age of primitive societies) through that of being a student of nature (in the age of reason and of science) to that of becoming in reality the very lord of nature. Man has discovered secrets of power so vast that no innocence or ignorance can save him from living with the social consequences of his knowledge. It is indeed the knowledge of good and evil that modern man possesses. Guardini once wrote: "The core of the new epoch's intellectual task will be to integrate power into life in such a way that man can employ power without forfeiting his humanity. For he will have only two choices: to match the greatness of his power with the strength of his humanity, or to surrender his humanity to power and perish." [14] In the light of this warning, it is disconcerting to read in a recent critique of American society by Paul Goodman, that Americans tend to regard technology as an autonomous cause of history and urbanization as a new Law of Nature.[15]

In his efforts to educate the young person for social responsibility, the historian must be present — and future — oriented. He cannot glorify the past, nor should he present it as one-dimensional. He tries to cultivate a reverence for reality. He tries to penetrate the various levels of man's social experience, especially conscious that man grasps at reality with great convulsive efforts toward creativity or destruction. You may recall Hannah Arendt's indictment of the banality of middle class evil in her unforgettable portrait of Eichmann, or Ernst Cassirer's analysis of that *Myth of the State* which has fascinated and so often trapped western man. More relevant to our present moment in history are the creative and destructive forces at work in the lives of so many exploited peoples and expressed by a deep social rage; they compel us to reexamine our racism and our propensity to solve awkward international (and urban) problems by military means.

When the historian examines man's social experience he has a very particular task. He is not simply a scientist. The natural scientist opens up a new field of knowledge by uncovering what lies hidden in nature. His work is not a creation of anything new; in coming to know nature the scientist is "re-thinking God's thoughts." [16] But if, on the other hand, through the critical work of the social scientist (and indeed the theologian too) the human mind comes to know itself better, there is an historical development in human nature itself. Human nature comes to operate in new and different ways. This brings to consciousness a "new man" and causes further moral and political and social problems. I would suggest that just as Crèvecoeur celebrated the individualistic

14. Romano Guardini, (trans. E. C. Briefs) *Power and Responsibility* (New York: Regnery, 1961) p. xii.

15. Goodman, *Like a Conquered Province*, pp. 316-317.

16. R. G. Collingwood, *The Idea of History* (Oxford: Clarendon Press, 1946) p. 84.

American of the nineteenth century as a new man, so today the Vietnamese or the American Black Man must be acknowledged as a "new man." This, Sartre feels, is a man created by violence.

Perhaps these thoughts indicate that the task of human creation is carried on in our streets and in our schools (even in our prisons) more adequately than in our churches. Michael Novak describes the "secular saint" as one whose quest for radical religious values has moved outside the churches.[17] Are not leaders like Gandhi, Malcolm X and Dan Berrigan more acceptable as the real moral and religious teachers of our students than are any churchmen?

However this concerns the churches, certainly in our colleges and our universities we engage in this difficult task of bringing man to a consciousness of what he has been, what he is and what he can become. If our students are sensitive to reality in a different way, then new educational approaches are essential. It is a time for diversity and not dogma. We are only beginning to understand as educators the immense possibilities available to us in a confrontation among persons skilled in various disciplines.

In an educational context, where does the young person confront theological problems most intensely? Is there more need for theologizing in an interdisciplinary situation than in the scientific presentation of theology? More than the historian or the sociologist or the man of letters, should not the theologian be the critic of society? In a society whose competitive pressures penalize spontaneity and instinct,[18] should not the theologian challenge the principalities and powers of technologies? If, as some responsible educators hold, we are doing as much in our schools to destroy the creative imagination of our students as we are doing to educate them to responsible citizenship, what is the role of the theologian here? Should he minister to man's docility or his creativity? The answers to these questions may appear obvious, but I suggest that they are best faced in those

17. Novak, *Center Magazine*, 51.
18. Goodman, *Like a Conquered Province*, p. 350.

classrooms where the historians and theologians together genuinely confront the issues of freedom, power, responsible judgment
and Christian love.

Conclusion.

In conclusion we would like to offer some practical observa-
tions on the initiative and process of interdisciplinary study. First
of all, it seems important to us that a *team* of instructors — each
expert in a single discipline — rather than a kind of Renaissance
man who is adept at changing his hat — be involved in the interdisciplinary presentations. We have found that artists and historians, for example, respond differently to the same realities, that
their modes of perception are basically different, and that it is
precisely this difference, this contrast, if you will, that brings
their vision of reality and experience into the kind of relational
context from which new understanding derives.

Secondly, we would strongly recommend that the specific matter of a given interdisciplinary course arise from the skills of
an instructional team which has already experienced its own
compatibility. That ease of exchange which is fostered by genuine
liking and respect for a given instructor and his discipline seems
the greatest single factor in creating fruitful interdisciplinary exploration. It is better, we think, for instructors who would like
to work together to ask themselves "What topic or topics can
we explore well and skillfully together?" than for a team to be
arbitrarily assigned a given topic without enough attention having
been paid to the abrasive atmosphere which might prevail throughout their mutual questioning.

Thirdly, we suggest that the potential team members be willing
and eager to ask live questions, that they be genuinely committed
to searching out the new understanding of their own and others'
disciplines that will inevitably result from deep questioning in a
new and wider context; for we believe that the best answer to the
last question is precisely the next question. Finally, it seems to us
that each instructor must be so jealous of his own discipline that
he will resist on the part of his co-instructors exploitation as op-

posed to exploration. It is not enough for the theologian or the historian, for example, to *use* the matter of literature for his own purposes; or for the artist, on the other hand, to *use* the explanations of history or theology merely as a tool for deepening an experience of artistic integrity. Each discipline can only contribute to a more serious understanding of its counterpart if its own identity is maintained and genuinely respected.

EVERETT L. DIEDERICH, S.J.

14   Liturgical Worship in the College

1.   Introduction

Let it be stated at once that when we qualify college liturgical worship as authentic, effective, and true, we are attempting to delimit a task by sharpening a goal, a task which has to be pursued collectively by those of us who are concerned with college worship. We are not designating a reality for which we can obtain a ready made blueprint or program, much less is it a reality whose existence we insure in our midst by scheduling it into the school's daily events. Liturgical worship on college campuses which is authentic, effective, and true is no more the result of a kind of nonchalant, casual, unplanned and unexamined effort than are any of the other important ingredients and events in college life. The very fact that a rather significant number of people's lives intersect in worship, in other words the fact that worship is public, the fact that worship is an action involving a complexity of modes of human expression, the fact that this complexus is sacramental, that is, that it is a visible, tangible, audible, affective, symbolic whole, mediating the primary faith reality of the Christian community, all this should alert us to the price-tag of a consistently good college liturgy.

I am not sure that all of us have yet weighed what that cost or that investment is going to be. What must we do to bring it about that the college worship for which we are responsible and in which we share is celebrated in an atmosphere which is open, creative, patiently and perseveringly critical and evaluative in regard to these celebrations? One thing is certain, such an atmosphere will not result unless there is a significant sharing of effort. Again

I am not sure whether many of us are willing or for that matter
even trust one another to make such a shared effort. Ironically
enough, in some instances, college liturgical worship has become
divisive and simply provides us with a sharper instrument than we
have hitherto possessed to cut us apart from one another. It is
going to take immense effort in some places to reverse what has
become almost a trend toward this splintering. This effort is going
to have to be collective. Individually we do not have the resources to pick up the tab for consistently good liturgical celebrations.

It seems to me of some importance at the outset to identify
the concrete liturgical experience upon which I am reflecting, the
one which is rather consistently nudging me and those with me
in our questioning, the one to which we are returning to validate
our conclusions, the experience in other words that furnishes us
with enough continuity that we can begin to speak of our liturgical
life, that we can identify a kind of faith which transpires during
the liturgy and which has such a vitality that it more or less anchors
much of what we want to say about the liturgy.

This liturgical experience centers around two kinds of celebrations in which I share. The one consists of weekday celebrations, occurring at twelve noon, Monday through Friday,
attended by a cross-section of our student body, half of them
coming from the School of Divinity, the other half from the
College of Arts and Sciences and the other schools of the North
campus of Saint Louis University. Joined to these are office
personnel from the University and from the midtown office buildings in the area. There are also faculty members present — religious, clerics, and lay. The number varies from two hundred to
three hundred and fifty. The other celebrations are four Sunday
Masses. Those present at the midnight Mass are almost entirely
students, from seven to eight hundred of them. Attendance at the
Sunday daytime Masses varies from three hundred and fifty at
the noon Mass to five and six hundred at the mid-morning and
late afternoon Masses. About half of the persons attending these
daytime Sunday Masses are students. The other half consists of
families from outside the parish, some of them faculty members,

others not a part of the University but simply searching for good celebrations.

All these celebrations are carefully planned by teams which include priest-celebrants and students — clerics, religious and lay, the majority of them coming from the School of Divinity and the College of Arts and Sciences. The weekday celebrations are evaluated in a weekly meeting attended by the heads of the planning groups. The Sunday celebrations and all that is connected with them are the subject of a weekly meeting of the University chaplain, the pastor of the parish in whose lower church these celebrations take place, the coordinator of the campus liturgy, the priest-celebrants responsible for each of the Sunday Eucharists, and the student representatives who handle the finances. All of these celebrations take place in a recently renovated lower church.

Having identified the liturgical experience, I can proceed now to the reflections issuing from it. I want to propose these in three steps: first I want to reflect upon the fellowship and the expectations shared by those who gather for the worship; secondly upon the liturgical setting for our celebrations; finally, upon the liturgical action itself, its overall shape, tone, style, and drift, trying to identify the kind of faith experience which the celebration is mediating to those who share it.

2. The Fellowship and Expectations Shared by Those Gathered for Worship

It is good for us from time to time to stand away from the persons who gather to celebrate the liturgy and reflect upon the reality of the fellowship in faith, as well as identify as nearly as we can the real life experience in which this fellowship is situated. There are times when the tone of our liturgical celebration really falls short of this reality which we are trying to express. We are limited persons, and we perhaps only in rare moments touch the depths of our own personal centers either individually or collectively. Because this does not happen often, our personal presence does not have the quality which communicates that we are really alive and in touch with one another and the rest of reality. If we are really to live during the celebration of the Eucharist, we must be in touch with ourselves before it begins. We come to the Eucharist as persons who are already living, already believers, believers in the Lord.

In fact, the primary reality which surfaces in our reflection upon the Christian community is the kind of fellowship that it is. It is the reality of us as we are by reason of our belief in Jesus Christ and the resulting willingness to come to him continuously to have life and have it to the full. Even though we come with the willingness to have life, we come realizing that we possess life and power already at our very personal centers. Life has been laid into us with the gift of the Spirit, life and power. It is this Spirit which makes us seek the Lord, and seek fuller life from him. It is ultimately this Spirit which lets us see ever so little into the personal centers of each other and recognize that the same Spirit is at work within us, not only opening the heart and lips of each of us individually to confess that Jesus is his Lord and that the Father of Jesus is his Father too, but also opening us out to each other with a deeply felt need to say *our* Lord and *our* Father. In short, we are persons who are in the deepest sense seekers after life to the full, and our instinct both by nature and the Spirit is that life is not found in its full richness except in fellowship, in a fellowship which, as John says, is with the Father and his Son Jesus Christ (I Jn. 1, 3) but a fellowship which John also designates as *our* fellowship, a fellowship which we share with one another. The Spirit, which is the most intimate and individual possession of each of us, is also dynamic, strongly yet gently moving us to seek the company and the visibility and the support of one another as we seek a significant meeting with the source and center of our personal existence.

It is unlikely that a conscious reflection such as we have just expressed is going to the surface in us at the very moment in which we are gathering for worship. It is necessary, however, that it surface at some time in our reflection upon worship. Because it has surfaced, it is a part of what we qualitatively are at the moment of worship. There are moments of depth in one's living, which are what they are precisely because they are lived. We *live* our truth in worship, we do not necessarily consciously conceptualize or verbalize the whole of it. Some of the superficiality, some of the self-conscious and awkward attempt to be casual, thereby hoping to establish more of a continuity with life during the liturgical celebration, even some of the rather exaggerated and artificial efforts to establish a horizontal bond during the liturgy result from our failure to reflect upon the quality of our Christian community. Sometimes we forget when we face a group who comes to celebrate the liturgy, particularly on weekdays, that these persons *do* believe in the Lord and are expecting deeper grounding in this belief. We shall return to this point after we have reflected a little upon what we might call our secular experience of life, particularly experiences which could relate to the liturgy.

Highly competent sociologists, psychologists, anthropologists, and other qualified commentators are speaking and writing a great deal about contemporary man. It is wearying if not impossible to read and hear it all. Yet we who are concerned with worship must continue trying to make their data, their conclusions and hypotheses work for us. It will be a gain for us and for the people whom we are serving if this data at least makes us concerned to be more explicit, as well as more realistic, about what our personal, shared, concrete, human condition is at this time in our history. But it will not be enough simply to make a litany of our present joys and sorrows, successes and frustrations, loves and hatreds, fears and hopes. We, who are interested in the primary reality of worship, which is ourselves already alive in the Spirit, coming to affirm this life and to seek it in greater fullness, must try to shape up our life's experience outside the liturgy so that it will be open for what we seek. This means sorting out our experiences, perhaps finding a way of letting those surface which are more relevant to the thrust of worship. Then perhaps we can anchor the experience of worship in them and let them serve as landmarks and points of reference. What might the experiences be which would give continuity to living outside and within worship? I shall try to identify some in a general sort of way. Some of them positive, some negative.

Among the positive experiences, there would be first of all the experience of tasks pursued with purpose and dedication, tasks which have a future, are thrusting toward some kind of goal and call for an investment of energy, demand persevering effort and a sustained vision. Included here would also be the experience of tasks thus pursued through collective effort.

What would such experiences have to do with worship? What is proposed above is an experience of intense living, which derives its intensity in part from the fact that it is an experience of purposeful living, an experience in which we might judge whether or not we are alive, or in what degree we are alive during the celebration of the liturgy. It could make it possible to ask whether we come to the liturgy, expecting it to be an experience of purposeful activity with a future. In other words it might furnish us with the possibility of experiencing worship as somewhat continuous with the rest of the time-line thrusting toward the future, the time-line which is our experience of life in this world. It might help us to avoid a view of the liturgy which makes of it a kind of timeless interval inserted into the line as a kind of dutiful nod or acknowldgement of the existence of a transcendental reality wholly other than ourselves.

A second experience, which is, in fact, involved in the one just described, are the moments when deep and inclusive values, hopes, and life meaning are actually experienced as shared. These also are moments of intense living. They are most likely the moments when the activity described above as purposeful becomes consciously reflective.

We can appreciate the density of such moments. The density has its own dynamic, thrusting us forward and upward. Such moments happen in love, in friendship, fellowship and brotherhood. They may be the moments when intense individual or collective struggle is realizing its goal and values, when hopes and life meaning are concretized, are actually lived.

Once more we can place the question as to what such experiences have to do with worship. The answer is that the comparatively short time which Christian communities spend in celebrating the liturgy is in reality very dense because it is in the period when Christian values, hopes, and meaning are most effectively concentrated, pursued, and communicated. It is the time in which the community is moved by the Spirit and challenged by the scriptural and sacramental word to search its human and Christian being deeply in order to move from a sphere of the anonymous, the ambiguous, the implicit regarding its relationship to the Father, to each other and to the world to the sphere of identity, clarity, and explicitness which has been revealed in Christ and laid into the community in the gift of the Spirit. The experiences of shared value and meaning which might have preceded the liturgy even when these are secular can serve to sharpen our expectancy that deeper moments will transpire during the celebration, and so open us to receive greater fullness of life from the Lord, greater identity, clarity, and meaning.

All these are positive experiences which we might want to surface in our conscious awareness sometime in relationship to worship, which we might even want to have surface during the worship itself and which might help us come more alive during the celebration. There are other experiences in life outside the liturgy which also pertain to the faith experience of worship. They are more negative in character. These are all the experiences which make life seem so precarious and threatened, crippled and twisted, sometimes muddled, even drowned or smothered. Such moments are experiences of misunderstandings, of alienation from others, of our own and others' insensitivity, our own and others' self-consciousness, which limits our sharing with each other, the prejudices and preconceptions which close our hearts and minds to one another, all the experience of isolation, loneliness, weariness, aimlessness. It would be the experience of having life drained out of us, of drying up inside, without a future, without a love. It would also be the experience of collective selfishness, shallowness, even hypocrisy and downright cruelty.

Again we can place the question as to what these negative experiences have to do with worship. The answer seems to be quite obvious. It is precisely experiences such as these which cluster, become more or less enduring, and constitute a really lived experience of a milieu which is weakness, darkness, bondage, fruitless struggle, hopelessness, lovelessness, absurdity, anonymity, hollowness, ultimately defeat and death. All of this constitutes a lived experience of what we call sin, not just personal sin but a whole milieu of sin. And it is with such an experience that we hear the message of a breakthrough in Jesus Christ, a breakthrough to life, a breakthrough that involved the sharing in the human condition described above, with Jesus like us in all things save sin. It is a breakthrough that is for us, a breakthrough which we have already laid hold of, and which we want to ground with greater firmness and fruitfulness in the celebration. As a matter of fact, our life experiences, both secular and faith, are a mixture of both positive and negative experiences. Both form the context in which we struggle towards maturity as human persons and as members of the Lord's risen body.

If I have dwelt on these experiences in this first section of this chapter, it is because I would wish our liturgical celebrations to have some of the seriousness, some of the depth, some of the realism which I feel life in our world has today. I am not always sure that our liturgy resonates resoundingly to the life which it is supposed to signify and communicate, whether this life be qualified as secular or of faith. I admit that there are still large numbers of apathetic, drifting, unconcerned students and faculty members on our campuses. But I hardly look to these when searching for models in reflecting upon life's experiences and asking what the liturgy is to be. I think I am more inclined to look to those students and faculty members who are moving out from anonymity, from aimless drifting, from cherishing a bundle of unexamined values, to some kind of explicit, clear statement and action concerned with a rather concrete goal. In other words I think some of us are living, while others of us are simply existing. We have to know through experience what it is to live before we can know what it is to celebrate the mystery of the death and new life of the Lord and of ourselves. Frankly, I am quite pained at times by what I can only characterize as a kind of escapism in the planning and execution of the liturgy. But this takes me into the next two sections of this chapter.

3. The Liturgical Setting

The remodeling and rearranging of the physical setting for worship has probably passed through its period of maximum activity. If we have not yet made a definitive step toward such designing and furnishing of the area for worship or if we still have further steps to make, then we ought to be a bit more explicit about what we want to achieve.

It seems rather obvious that the design and arrangement of the furnishings should be shaped to the persons who gather and support them in the actions with which they express their worship. The persons gathered have top priority and it is they who must come through in the setting. Therefore, it is important that they are not overwhelmed by its elaborateness, nor awed by its monumentality. It must be quite apparent to all that the place really needs persons worshipping to bring it to life. Without them it is not exactly cold and unlovely, but it is empty, empty like a family room when the family is not there, empty like a theater without players and spectators. It can have a beauty and warmth which pleases and inspires. But it should be possible for the persons gathered to look upon this beauty and still appreciate that it is really they who are the *Domus Dei*, that they are the living stones built into the spiritual house to offer spiritual sacrifices acceptable to God through Jesus Christ (cf. I Pt. 2:5). The setting should, when artistic talent is available, be beautiful while at the same time leaving something unsaid so that initiative is possible to the worshippers, giving them the feeling that they can outdo their setting. In short the setting welcomes them, invites them to their action, even helps them know what this action is to be, but lets them also know that what happens ultimately depends upon the persons who gather there.

It is altogether possible that such a setting can be multi-purpose. There are surely artistic creations and furnishings as well as ways of arranging spatial areas all of which could admit of greater flexibility in their use. Perhaps we could afford something far more significant by way of a worship area if we thought of the many purposes to which it might be put. While admitting of the possibility of a multi-purpose setting for worship, we should still make an effort to supply a well defined and accessible room for reserving the Blessed Sacrament and one which is designed to help people come and pray and reflect alone. Just as the worship area is designed to invite people to action, so this space should be designed to invite people to quiet and contemplation.

4.   The Liturgical Action

Reflecting upon the liturgical action we will be limited to the consideration of various questions which have to do with what seem to be more crucial aspects of the liturgical action and also which seem to raise what we might call current liturgical issues.

The first of these questions concerning the liturgical action has to do with the number and size of liturgical celebrations which we try to support on our college campuses. It seems that the trend in the past few years has been to multiply celebrations of the Eucharist in order that the time and place of celebration may be more convenient and also that the number of worshippers may be less. It has not been easy to find support for a liturgy which would be attended by significant numbers of students or faculty. I would like to question this trend, trying to weigh it against other projects in which students mobilize, as well as considering it in light of the kind of expertise and skills which good celebrations of the liturgy demand. Finally I would like to examine it in the light of the kind of orientation we are giving to our students as to their presence in the wider community of the Church and the world.

First of all, as I watch student action on our campuses, I am impressed that it is aimed at mobilizing significant numbers of students and giving visibility and expression to the numbers thus mobilized. I think that many of our students are keen enough to recognize that a milieu and structures have to be effected before there is anything significant accomplished in changing what they think must be changed. If the celebration of the liturgy is going to make an impression upon alert students and make a bid for their support, it is going to have to be thought of in a way that makes it seem good that rather significant numbers of persons gather for it. If we continue to foster a great number of small group celebrations on our campuses, we are heightening an aura of subjectivity about the liturgy. We are making it more difficult to think of it as a public action where our lives intersect and interact with others.

Secondly, liturgical planning makes demands which cannot be met unless we are able to mobilize and consolidate our expertise and skills. First there is that matter of music. How many competent musicians do we have to select, direct, and accompany the singing which we do? Then there is the matter of multi-media presentations during the liturgy. This not only calls for rather sophisticated equipment by way of tape-recorders, slide projectors, well-positioned and adequate screens, but it also demands long hours of viewing and careful selection of slides, listening to and re-recording musical excerpts. How many persons are capable of putting together a multi-media presentation for use in the liturgy? There are the less specialized, but no less important skills such as that required for giving an effective homily. Most priests at a university or college have a fulltime job in administration or teaching. They can perhaps find time to prepare well for one homily a week, but to expect *five* of them very often means a very hasty preparation and a kind of hit-and-miss effectiveness. The same can be said of the planners of the liturgy. A group can very well plan one celebration every fourth Sunday, or a group can plan a week of celebrations every eighth week. How many can plan for *every* Sunday and for *every* week? Most of our planners are also full time students and teachers and administrators. There is also the matter of rather long-term goals to be achieved in the liturgical planning, such as the acquiring of a respectable musical repertoire, finding an adequate instrument or procedure for ascertaining the effectiveness of the liturgical adaptation which we are doing. There is the all-important element of critical evaluation of the efforts being made so that we are able to learn from what we have tried, learn what is good, and insure that we have more of the same.

A final consideration in trying to assess the desirability of multiplying small celebrations of the Eucharist, rather than trying to consolidate them into celebrations involving greater numbers, has to do with the kind of orientation we are giving our students as to their presence in the wider community of the Church and the world. Our time in history is one of broad horizons and large issues, issues whose outcome demands that many persons of widely different cultural and racial backgrounds become concerned. It is difficult to know how the Church is to mobilize herself toward the issues which press upon the families of nations. But again we see our young people taking the big issues to heart, having the daring to think that they can stop such an evil as war, for example, even though they have seen the efforts at the level of high government representatives come to nought. Whatever we may say about what the Church's presence to the world is to be today, we must surely admit that the evils which threaten the world are those for which large groups of people must take responsibility and against which equally large numbers must take action. The evils which threaten us are vast. The transformation which is to overcome them must be equally vast. This is a time when there has to be a veritable mobilization of the moral and religious force of the world; it is a time for uniting rather than dividing. If the Eucharist is to be the hearth at which our moral force is warmed, the center around which we are focused, then we need consolidation rather than fragmentation of our celebrations.

There is a place for small celebrations of the liturgy. Giving priority and support to celebrations which are for larger numbers is not going to supplant these celebrations. It will rather support them, by providing a meaningful rhythm of small and large celebrations and by making it easier to insure that the small celebrations will be good by submitting them to something of the examination which they will surely undergo if they are celebrated by persons who are also a part of well planned larger celebrations.

A second question which has to do with the liturgical action regards the organizational structure required for its effective planning. This has to be such that it involves a representative cross-section of students and faculty. The talents and skills required for good celebrations make interdisciplinary cooperation a necessity. The persons involved from the various departments and schools in a college or university have to be grouped into planning teams. If these teams are planning for weekday celebrations, it is very desirable that they take a series of Masses in succession, for example, an entire week, in order that some rhythm of celebration and unity of theme be established.

Involved in the question of organizational structure is the rather sensitive matter of the relationship of the worshipping community of the college or university to the liturgical program and policy of the diocese as well as to the diocesan authority responsible for it. We are quite aware of the tensions and misunderstandings which arise. There are the resentments and suspicions which result either when the students living in the parishes give no support to the liturgy there, not even the support of their physical presence, or when others from the parish prefer the worship in the college or university to that in their parishes. One way in which we can achieve some degree of mutual trust and tolerance in this situation is by keeping the college or university liturgy in the public forum of the diocesan community and accepting the challenge of dialogue which is sure to result from thus keeping the celebrations above ground. We speak very much about dialogue, and most of us are engaged in it; but we have a great deal to learn about its use. One reason for opting for a more central celebration on a university or college campus is that it helps create a liturgical presence which can be identified by those who speak on its behalf. All of us like to know what we are speaking for. We need representative spokesmen from the college and university communities who can speak out the total picture of our particular pastoral liturgical needs to the national body of United States Bishops, just as we need spokesmen for the needs of the parishes, the high schools, and elementary schools. But we cannot instantaneously create an atmosphere in which such spokesmen arise. An important step toward this is made when a college or university begins to feel that it has a kind of liturgical focus or center or approach, can begin to identify and articulate it and so is able to dialogue with an ordinary or a liturgical commission about it. When such dialogue has taken place at many times and many places across the length and breadth of the United States, then our bishops too will have something in matters liturgical about which they can dialogue when they meet together. However, we must expect, as a consequence of the human condition of which we spoke earlier, that the dialogue between the spokesmen for the college liturgy and the diocesan authorities is going to succeed better in some places than in others, and the relative success or failure is going to depend upon both partners.

A third question or consideration concerning the liturgical action has to do directly with our faith-reflections upon it and the consequences of this reflection for our planning of the celebration. More specifically I am referring to the significance we are willing to attach to the multiple presence of the Lord in the celebration of the liturgy — his presence in the gathered assembly, his presence in the Word of God, his presence in the eucharistic prayer, his presence finally in the eucharistic bread and cup, the sacramental Body and Blood of Christ. It is only recently that we have come to qualify all these presences as real, and the acceptance of this qualification is probably more at the level of theological discourse than at that of lived faith experience. If there is validity to our distinguishing the different modalities of the Lord's presence, all of which qualify to be called real, then there must be different kinds of human activity in the celebration which are sacramentally mediating this presence. There is no difficulty in identifying these levels or kinds of human activity: gathering, praying and singing together; listening to words addressed to us in the scripture readings and the homily; sharing the sacramental food and drink. All these levels of human activity are sacramental in that they signify and bring about a holy reality. This reality is the Lord really with us, making us live in the Spirit. But he makes us live in and through the modality of the human experiences enumerated. It is one and the same Lord really with us at every point but with us as we can come to life through the particular liturgical sign which engages us.

There are two consequences for our liturgical celebration which flow from the faith-reflection. First of all, such reflection should incline us to give much more weight to the quality, wholeness and depth of our human actions in the liturgy. One might say that the modalities of the Lord's *real* presence are linked to our own *real* presence. In other words we can truly say that our human actions must come into their own as human experiences if they are to mediate the Lord's presence. Secondly, such reflection should incline us to strive for that delicacy and sensitivity of faith which leaves the total complexity of the celebration open to the Lord's presence. We should have the reverence and faith-expectancy to find Him *all through* the celebration, really present to us according to the particular liturgical form which engages us as the celebration unfolds. In diverse ways we are reaching out to his Father with him and in his Spirit as we engage in that one action which is the Eucharist. Such faith sensitivity and expectancy can do much to maintain an atmosphere of mystery in our celebrations, can insure that they are proclamations of faith, that we are announcing the death of the Lord until he comes.

If we are attentive to the manner in which the multiple presence of Christ is linked to our human experience, then the use of multimedia presentations will make more sense in the liturgy. Multimedia presentations are often very successful in evoking in us a very vivid, sharp, and shared human experience. It makes us alive perhaps more completely than we usually are in the celebration of the Liturgy of the Word, for example. But it is not enough simply to share a vivid and sharp human experience in the liturgy. The very vividness and sharpness of what is shared must move us to search for the way in which the Lord mediates his presence through it. We must probe with faith, must judge in the light of the Holy Spirit. If we are going to introduce more impressive sensoria into the celebration of the liturgy, then we must have a richer faith-expectancy with which to handle them. I think that taking seriously the multiple presence of the risen Lord in the celebration helps us toward such richness and fullness and even makes us want our liturgical celebrations to have these new communications media which are available to us.

It is worth reminding ourselves at this point that the person who bears the greatest responsibility in probing the vivid experience which the multi-media presentation may evoke is the homilist. The homilist must preview the material with his planners and with their help try to search them for the Lord's judging and saving presence, His own words must be modified by what he has seen and heard in the presentation just as surely as they must be modified by the scriptural Word of God. If he comes on in the homily as if the presentation had never been made, then little is achieved through the multi-media presentation. He must also have some awareness of how others are touched and moved by the presentation. It is for that reason that he has to preview the presentations with those who selected them and planned the celebration.

5. Conclusion

This discussion has not touched all that is involved in the liturgical worship on the college or university campus. A very obvious omission has been the celebration of Penance, which is a crucial matter in the lives of many students. Some of the principles proposed above will apply to the celebration of Penance, particularly to that kind of common preparation which is usually followed. This preparation parallels the celebration of the Liturgy of the Word. We ought to feel somewhat free, in planning such common celebration as preparation for the Sacrament of Penance, to use multi-media presentation. We ought also to realize that for such a celebration to be effective it must be well planned.

We ought to conclude our consideration of the liturgy on college and university campuses with a note of hope. We are coming to find ourselves in matters liturgical, have taken some firm steps toward liturgical identity in many places, an identity which makes us able to share what we are doing with others. Indeed many of us hope that we can soon have officially recognized centers of research for the liturgy based in academic centers but working with a cross section of the Church in any given area. In a word, the time is here in which the liturgical experience which we share can be put to a broader use so that we can begin to feel that what goes on in the liturgical life of the university and college faculty and students can help to reform and renew the worship of the entire People of God.

SISTER M. SHARON BURNS, R.S.M.

15   Problems of Faith : A New Approach

At the beginning of a new elective course in theology entitled "Problems of Faith," held first semester for twelve Junior and Senior college girls,[1] I found on the desk one day before class a piece of scrap paper, apparently left behind by another professor. As I crumpled the paper to throw it into the wastecan, I noticed typed words on the reverse side: "The more a professor knows, the more he knows that he does not know. In a properly conducted college, the faculty are simply the more mature students with a special responsibility for keeping the conversation going." As far as I know, this quote is quite anonymous. To me it was like a paragraph in proof of parapsychological findings — a message from "the beyond." For weeks I had been considering what kind of method I should use in presenting a course that I knew had limitless possibilities as far as content was concerned. That scrap paper pushed me into choosing a readings-and-discussion type approach. This choice piled on me the "responsibility for keeping the conversation going."

The course met with such success, that although this elective was not scheduled for second semester, twenty-three students insisted on having it offered again; the great majority of this group were the top-ranking psychology, English and math majors. Second semester was even more exciting than the first. I discovered that our three-day class schedule would be better employed by meeting just Mondays and Fridays, leaving Wednesdays free

1. Mount Saint Agnes College, Baltimore, Maryland.

for further opportunity to read and prepare for discussion. The discussions proved so lively that they continued in the halls and student lounges after classes were dismissed.

I would like to summarize the course before very briefly describing one of the class periods. The course is divided into four sections:

  I. Faith and Psychology
  II. Faith and Some of the Arts
  III. Faith and Philosophy (Existentialism)
  IV. Faith and Theology

The one text used throughout the course was *The Estranged God* by Anthony T. Padovano. Four five-page papers were assigned, each one corresponding to a section of the course. No written examinations were given.

Beginning with Psychology and Faith, with man as person, with man who is "man's way to God," we pursued the idea that faith requires openness, openness to each other, to life, to God. Along with short class lectures, we studied and discussed chapter three of *The Estranged God*, "Modern Man Not Only Seeks but Fears Some Genuine Values." Among other books and articles, we read for discussion *Captain Newman, M.D.* by Leo Rosten; *Restless Believers*, by J. Kirvan; Dag Hammarskjöld's *Markings*, and *Man's Search for Meaning* by Viktor Frankl. We also studied the theme of alienation in some of Ingmar Bergman's Films. (*Virgin Spring* was shown first semester and *Winter Light* second semester, as part of our college's Art Film Festival.)

This led us quite logically into the study of faith in literature and the film. With the conviction that an openness to history and literature is the best check on a closed system and a closed religion (Martin Marty, *Varieties of Unbelief*) we discovered how literature and the film can help us develop an openness to the *breadth* of human strivings, how the film and the novel can help us expand beyond our limited horizons by living vicariously the lives of other human beings. We began with the superb third chapter of *Irrational Man* by William Barrett, "The Testimony of Modern Art." All kinds of wonderful correlations could be made between literary works and art, such as James Joyce's *Ulysses* and Paul Klée's modern art, between Leon Bloy's writings and Georges Roualt's stained-glass window type of art. For the latter comparison we used Raissa Maritain's book *We Have Been Friends Together* as the peacemaker, just as she was between these two great men alienated from each other by their fidelity to their consciences. Using Arthur Miller's play *Death of a Salesman* (the film and the TV versions were familiar to almost all students in the class) we saw how the best plays and films reveal truths with a shock of recognition difficult to imitate in any other way. This gradually led us to the discovery that truth dwells in the depths and must be found and delivered to realization with some or much anguish. Padovano's second chapter, "The Literary Expression of Modern Man's Values and Problems," was a perfect aid to our study, and our previous handling of the psychology of man, an excellent beginning for better understanding the sufferings each author had to undergo to bring to the world the truth he had discovered — writers like Dostoevski, Kafka, Wolfe, Salinger and others. Toward the end of this article I intend to develop summarily one of my favorite lessons, the Grand Inquisitor scene (Dostoevski), and to show how we were able to correlate it with Viktor Frankl's book on Logotherapy, *Man's Search for Meaning.*

The section on Faith and Some of the Modern Arts seemed to provide a solid basis for an inductive approach to the study of belief and unbelief in relation to the philosophies of our day. Chapter one of *The Estranged God,* "Existentialism and Religious Belief: The Mood of the Age is Set," and *Irrational Man* (Barrett) were the basic readings the class used. (The students were Juniors and Seniors with a background in philosophy; however, all of them soon realized what a difference the study of philosophy makes when taken primarily in terms of religious belief). I used David E. Roberts' book *Existentialism and Religious Belief,* among other books, to keep to the subject of religious belief. We saw how an exploration of existentialism brings into sharp focus the basic struggle between contemporary Christianity and so-called "secularism," how existentialism, far from being a self-sufficient philosophy, has as its chief value that of being a corrective to abstraction, bringing us face to face with real problems of what it means to be a self, to be free, to be courageous enough to meet death. In this section, correlation amounted to fascination with me, for we were able effortlessly to see in our studies of some of the existentialists, from the most atheistic Jean-Paul Sartre to the Christian, Catholic, Gabriel Marcel, how their human lives, their psychological backgrounds, affected their philosophic and dramatic works, which in turn have affected the whole world and our individual lives. Even within this study of the existential philosophers, the students saw that all problems of faith are problems of the *whole* man, not just of the intellect. Ending with Marcel, as we did, the problems of faith were lifted to the realm of mystery where they truly reside.

The last section, Faith and Theology, would have been a terrible let-down, quite dull and boring, if we had followed only Padovano's last chapter, "God as the Catholic Church Understands Him." However, we dwelt more on the new theology of *Revelation* dealing with it as the testimony of persons, not evidence of propositions to be believed; with Tradition as dynamic, living, continually renewing and continually discovering the truths of faith in Christ. We discussed "Faith and Doubt" (Avery Dulles, *America,* March 11, 1967), the "Attraction of Atheism," (Michael Novak, *Belief and Unbelief*), and the possibility of Marxist-Christian Dialogue (Roger Garaudy, *From Anathema to Dialogue*). We found John Powell's essay, "The Ecclesial Dimension of Faith" to be a perfect conclusion to the course, summarizing for us, Catholics, the whole notion of faith as a "vital or living experience of encounter with God in Christ," and encountering Christ, here and now, the total Christ, in his sacraments, in his members, the Church. Again this article speaks to man as man eliciting the response of the whole person.

There were so many "favorite" lessons in this course that I find it difficult to choose any one that I might develop; however, the one that gave me the greatest thrill in research and reflection was the story of the "Grand Inquisitor" scene and its relevance to Viktor Frankl's book, and to our lives of real faith.

We had already studied and discussed at length *Man's Search for Meaning* and its implications in the life of faith. We had viewed, then verbalized our reactions to the film *Night and Fog,* a shocking documentary on the concentration camps. (This really brought up — on the "gut" level — the problem of a good God who could permit such evil in the world). The students had been assigned the reading of the Grand Inquisitor scene and I had given a short lecture on the life and background of Dostoevski. For my own background I used *Wrestlers with Christ,* K. Pfleger, and *Dostoevski, the Major Fiction,* E. Wasiolek.

One great author (John Middleton Murry) has said that "The whole clue to Dostoevski is in the Grand Inquisitor story." D. H. Lawrence and many other distinguished critics have taken the side of the Grand Inquisitor against Christ because his argument is so powerful and indeed unanswerable. Dostoevski himself knew only too well that "atheism never found such a powerful expression" as in *The Brothers Karamazov,* and that he himself therefore did not believe in Christ as a little child, but had said, "My hosanna has passed through the great purgatory of doubt" (*Pages from the Journal of an Author*).

In the Grand Inquisitor story we are concerned with *two ways of understanding man's nature* and they are discontinuous; one cannot stand in refutation by the other because there are no common assumptions. This will become clear by seeing and understanding the nature of the Grand Inquisitor's truth, which is consistent and complete and deep in its appeal. Christ had asked men to follow his example, the essence of which was contained in his rejection of Satan's three temptations in the wilderness: (1) to turn stones to bread, (2) to prove his divinity by performing a miracle, and (3) to agree to the worship of an earthly power. These three temptations are the three great limitations of a *free faith.* Christ's example is of a faith freely given, standing without the support of bread, miracles, or the need of collective earthly power. And Christ has asked men to believe in him with the same faith. But, according to the accusations of the Grand Inquisitor, Christ had cruelly misunderstood the nature of man, for fifteen centuries had proved that man by his very nature was incapable of what Christ asked. Men had always cried, and were crying in Dostoevski's time, "Feed us and then we will be virtuous," and men had always asked not for the anxiety and fear of choosing freely, but for the certainty of miracles, mystery, and authority, and they had always been afraid of being alone, craving always the comfort of approval of everyone else. Christ had asked men to be alone and unafraid in the presence of things unseen, supported only by the free movement of the heart. Fifteen centuries had proved that only a handful of men were strong enough to follow Christ's example, and that the rest could never follow it. It seems, then, that Christ had either misunderstood man's nature or understood it and visited needless sufferings upon man. Of course, even we of the twentieth century have not yet grown callous enough to prefer weakness to strength and slavery to freedom. But what the Grand Inquisitor shows is that it is not a question of what man would *like* to be but what he *is* and can be. It seems all of history has shown man to be as the Grand Inquisitor story has painted him, not as Christ had asked him to be. The Grand Inquisitor is not wrong because he sees man as weak and slavish, or because he is contemptuous of man. Nor does he contradict himself when he speaks of working for man's happiness, while seeing him as weak and slavish. He loves man for what he is, not for what he is not, and he accepts the melancholy fact of man's weakness because it is a fact. The Grand Inquisitor is wrong only if his view of human nature is wrong, and neither logic nor the facts of history are against him. The testimony of *things seen* are overwhelmingly on his side. But, Christ never based his truth on the testimony of things seen, but on the testimony of *things unseen*. Christ asks, though all men be against you, though history prove it impossible, choose what the heart says is possible, even though this choice will surely be in loneliness, anxiety and struggle, with no other guide than himself. This choice against logic and history and the example of the crowds, is Christ's freedom. A free faith for Dostoevski is a faith without conditions.

The Grand Inquisitor legend is the strongest piece of Dostoevski's writings that exhibits his faith in Christ, because Dostoevski had never before offered himself and his readers a choice so *stark,* because he had never granted so much to his antagonists before. In his previous works he had striven mightily to prove Christ right. This is Dostoevski's final statement against God. It is Dostoevski's confronting himself with the candor and courage to place everything he had built up into the balances again. It is his final confrontation with the testimony of things seen and with man's desolating weakness and infinite capacity for self-deception. Only the words he wrote from prison to a friend remain at the end to sustain him, as they had all his life: "If anyone proved to me that Christ was outside the truth and it really was so that the truth was outside Christ, then I should prefer to remain with Christ than with the truth."

After my presentation, similar to this, the students provided any insights they had from their reading of the Grand Inquisitor story. Then I elicited from them comparisons to the three temptations of Christ that were glaringly evident in some instances in the autobiographic sketch of the concentration camp life of Viktor Frankl. For example, they see immediately that Frankl believed — without bread. Among other incidents that could be recalled in reference to the need for miracles, there is the account Frankl gives of one of the prisoners who had come to him overjoyed with the dream he had of being freed from the camp by a specific date. Frankl knew this kind of reliance on a "sign" would prove fatal, and it did. As the dreamed-of day approached, the man became more and more discouraged, and on the day of the hoped-for "miracle" he died of despair. Yet Frankl, and other men with him, continued in faith without the certitude of miracle. Frankl tells us that his greatest difficulty was accepting the ugly treatment meted out to him and to his fellow prisoners, physicians, musicians, scientists, by Capos who, although far inferior culturally and intellectually, seemed to triumph because they were on the side of collective power. Yet, despite this greatest temptation to despair, Dr. Frankl believed, believed in the meaning and value of life and love and goodness. The students were able to make many connections from the Grand Inquisitor scene to the life of faith not only of Frankl but to their own lives as well.

An English theologian, H. E. Root, has said:

The best textbooks for contemporary natural theologians are
not the second-hand theological treatises but the living works
of artists who are in touch with the springs of creative imagination. This is only another way of saying that theologians cannot direct men's minds to God until they are themselves steeped
in God's world and in the imaginative productions of his most
sensitive and articulate creatures. That in turn is only another
way of saying that the enterprise of theology cannot come
to life until it takes to heart the principle of the Incarnation.[2]

This piercing judgment has hit the heart, I believe, of the
problem of contemporaneousness and relevance in college theology today. We must look to the poet, the novelist, dramatist, or
film producer, to bring theology for the twentieth century student
to *life*.

2. "Beginning All Over Again," in Alec Vidler, ed., *Soundings* (New York:
   Cambridge University Press, 1962) p. 18, quoted by Martin Marty,
   Varieties of Unbelief (New York: Holt, Rinehart and Winston, 1964)
   p. 200.

CATHLEEN M. GOING

16 Adult Theological Education

When we speak of adult education we are speaking of education as it pertains to ourselves. To some extent this is true of any area of education, under whatever circumstances; when one is concerned about university-level studies it is then fully true that in speaking of adult education we are talking of ways in which we ourselves might be helped to develop. It seems to me that this fact has to be taken as the test of everything we say or propose in this field. We can be so deceived in thinking always about the education of "those children" or "those young undergraduates": always "the others" who are to have something done to *them* by *us*.

Certainly graduate students are adults in university education but I am not thinking now of those interesting people: they have distinctive professional needs and they have not yet tested their futures in the way which I suppose of the persons I mean. Peace to defenders of the young! You sense that my spontaneous use of the world "adult" does not point directly to those seventeen-to-twenty-four-year-olds who move toward responsible university places precisely in the name of their adulthood. It would indeed be more sensitive to speak of "continuing education" and of "older adults." Understand, therefore, that it is these older adults I mean, add my expectation that special programming — more exciting and engrossing, not less — is appropriate for them, keep on the horizon in an important way the awkwardness problems of middle-age and the "disengagement" problems of the aging, and you have the context of what I say about adult education. It is not the context for every effort with adults — their needs are many.

Although the specialized context I mean is not shared by everyone whose work may be called adult education, I suggest that it always makes a difference to know what the possibilities are. Therefore I ask how approaches to the short-range needs of adults for refurbishing their vocabularies — in "contemporary theology," for example — might be different if shaped rather as extensions of what has been discovered possible with adults under better, more leisurely circumstances, than by a conception of the *whole* of adult education as remedial — as some liberal-arts equivalent of rapid technical upgrading.[1] I ask teachers of young undergraduates what difference it might make in what they do, if they were to think of the theological education of these young persons — even of their formal education under institutional auspices — as intentionally unfinished in view of further education that would be "continuing": dealing with the long-range questions of human life. (Realistically: the accounts given at my own institution about "adult differences" are being challenged by the appearance at its doors of young, intelligent, disgusted drop-outs from the college education designed for them; in a few months or years there will appear also some of the young people who will have just finished their court cases or prison sentences for having rioted or smashed computers at some neighboring institution.) I think therefore that a specialized approach may provide a suitable *focus* for other approaches to problems throughout a field.

What can be said about the theological education of adults? There is no theology *of* adult education, to go with "theology of revolution" and all the rest; there is so much yet to discover about concrete problems and results in adult learning. (Insufficient grasp of the concrete can probably be charged also to the theo-

---

1. Gabriel Moran has recently pointed out that in religious education it makes a great difference where one *begins* to focus one's thinking. Cf. *Vision and Tactics*: Toward an Adult Church (New York: Herder and Herder, 1968) pp. 12-13.

logian of revolution or of medical practice, though he certainly
must be on the scene learning, and shaping his words.) To replace
the "theologian of" continuing education, we might nominate a
patron or guide for the effort. Should it be C. G. Jung? He is not
the latest thing on the market; the nomination would be for his
ability to reflect on the second half of life, for his relating hopefully to the past, for his ability to help his patients be what they
could in line with their own histories, not with his.[2] Rather than
"theology of . . . ," I offer first some comments about a method
of education which seems appropriate to adults for much of
their education and especially for their theological education, then a
consideration of the suitability of the method to "the times."
You will find that it is impossible for me to focus on theology
by prescinding from a larger educational context. As I suggested
above, much has still to be thought out by way of proper ad-
justment to adult needs and possibilities; phrased technically:
so much work has yet to be done on learning theory, as this
concerns adults,[3] that one can hardly speak knowingly about
adult learning in theology by prescinding from this whole concern.

A method appropriate to adults and to their theological
education is reading-discussion. A brisk description of the setting

2. See C. G. Jung, *Memories, Dreams, Reflections* (New York: Vintage
   Books, 1963). Note especially p. 307: "I had an obscure feeling that
   by working on my book I would be answering the question that had
   been asked. It had been asked . . . by my spiritual forefathers, in the
   hope and expectation that they would learn what they had not been
   able to find out during their time on earth, since that answer had first
   to be created in the centuries that followed," and pp. 138-140.
3. Cf. *The Alerted Mind* by R. Eric O'Connor, S.J. (forthcoming): Work
   on learning theory is usually concerned with children; much that has
   been written about adult development has arisen from the problems of
   disturbed adults. The Thomas More Institute of Canada for Research
   in Adult Liberal Studies is presently working at the elaboration of
   learning theory as this concerns adults, relying on the experience of its
   related educational Institute which since 1945 has programmed specifically for adults.

as I think of it may prevent misunderstandings: the reading each week of a book centered on a course theme (or attendance at symphony, museum, film, theatre — according to the course); a two-hour discussion of that book (play, film) with the help of two experienced discussion leaders and the diverse collaboration of ten-to-thirty other persons — some pursuing a B.A. degree, others pursuing only the course-theme, some having one or more degrees already; books turn out to be unexpectedly significant in the light of neighboring readings; lectures set into such a course have unusual resonance; a course will fail unless the discussion leaders are themselves pursuing real questions of their own (clearly I am not speaking of sensitivity-training or of group therapy, much less of "bull-sessions").[4] As method, this seems to match the dynamics of human development at the level of adult need that the process be somewhat recognizable to oneself — and in so far as something called university education can assist. We all have our own names for the ways persons come to transcend themselves; let me suggest these:

— the opening up of questions and thereby of personal horizons;
— recognition and appreciation of historical styles as clarifying basic options;
— respect for heterogeneity in the backgrounds, insights, commitments of others;
— achievement of the objectivity of what has been called "the growing idea in the middle of the table";[5]
— gaining, by practice, perspective on one's own consciousness, i.e., increasing ability to distinguish one's images,

4. For a fuller description of discussion-method in theology, see C. M. Going, "Theology in Adult Liberal Education," *Thought*, XXXVIII, 151 (Winter 1963), pp. 547-557.
5. See Paul Byers, "The Idea in the Middle of the Table," *Columbia University Forum*, Summer 1967; the phrase comes to him from Margaret Mead.

feelings, insights, judgments, choices — with the corresponding possibility of control and of wisdom.[6]

(Can one responsibly hope for less than this as ongoing process in the adult educators also?) The *religious* names for the development which theology mirrors and theological education hopes to support seem to be: mystery luring us to openness by questions if not by suffering; the word of God spoken in human existence and receptivity for it (demanding of theology perspective on the elements within that receptivity [7]); hope, of course, with its courage for the long-range goals and its sharp eye for the present; freedom for the fully good; personal style in one's way of being a Christian; the love for God which involves radical self-transcendence toward the whole universe; the lure and support of community for all this, including the supportive communal task which is theology; theology itself as reflection on the quality of life.

Let me now remind you of some ways in which an education on adult terms and by intense participation (e.g., by "reading-discussion") might meet increasingly well the "temper of the times" and the related theological climate. The question will remain whether such an approach is fit to transform as well as to match that temper.

6. The work of B. J. F. Lonergan is fundamental to precise recognition of these moments and needs in human development. Cf. *Insight* (New York: Philosophical Library, 1958), the "moving viewpoint" in the presentation of the material of that book, and Lonergan's formulation of transcendental method in his current work on method in theology. Succinct statement of a differentiation crucial to maturing is contained in Gordon Allport's "Psychological Models for Guidance," *The Person in Psychology*: Selected Essays (Boston: Beacon Press, 1968) pp. 67-80: "tentativeness and commitment."

7. The theological area which should be most affected by what is known about the development of adults is Fundamental Theology (in its attempts these recent years to be something other than "apologetics"). I have tried structuring graduate courses in this area accordingly.

As to academic procedures: if students insist on being self-governed, surely they are also to be in some meaningful way self-taught; and if teachers must learn new styles of collaboration — with the passing of the "era of the lion" [8] — a way in which teachers (of course including teachers of theology) would again become publicly learners together with others, as discussion leaders do, would seem helpful.

Culture in crisis ensures a startling diversity of background, talent and aim in any group of persons assembled for education; if the materials are sufficiently rich, proceeding by questions and suggestions allows each to pick up a course at his own level and invites him to bring about a synthesis which he can test for himself. The way in which adults can find themselves relating very loosely to traditions which are yet well-known to them — and the smaller advantage for *their* maturing of learning a system — makes harmony with the pervasive talk of "interdisciplinary approach." In theology one can count on freshness emerging from a combination of theological traditions on a theme with the best insights one can have on that theme from other than theological approaches. One can, for example, see what fresh accounts of the meaning of the Eucharist (treasuring the most traditional phrases) will emerge from readings designed for reflection on the quality of one's life or, by identifying moments of self-transcendence in ordinary living and in a wide range of experiences, one might see what the phrase "love for God" would have to mean to be made deliberately part of his *own* tradition.[9]

Achievement of truly open continuing education would seem to be the one clear institutional force for closing that educational gap which assures the isolation of the aging; beyond opening immediate areas of interest, it can assist persons to build habits of *discerning flexibility,* for coming satisfactorily through the confusion of the new as well as for living freshly out of the past.

---

8. Cf. Charlotte Tansey, *A Lion on Every Hill*: Exploring Adult Teaching Roles (forthcoming).
9. Cf. the exposition of these insights in the book *The Quality of One's Life,* by C. M. Going (forthcoming).

What can we say about "priorities"; that is, which educational efforts should now catch the attention of persons competent in theological education specifically? Might Christian educators, of the Roman Catholic tradition, for example, be especially attracted to this field of work? The answers do not give clear directions. I find I can say only these things: *One*: Appreciation of the dynamics we have named in human development, and eagerness to assist in the process, might come from many sources; what *I* know of such appreciation has in fact come out of the inspiration of the Jewish and Christian traditions, that is, it has in fact been because of hope and sense of mystery and increasing self-transcendence and the rest, as formulated and valued in these religious traditions, that some people I know have seen the work of continuing education as an especially promising and fruitful field. *Two*: In adult education one can in many courses ask students to look at an important religious writing as they look attentively at other approaches to a contemporary theme ("silence," for example, or "patterns of commitment" or "the tensions of modern openness"); one can ask without embarrassment the question of *the ground*: one has to ask it. (So much is this the case that I have sometimes wondered whether to keep *courses* called theology in an adult curriculum.) *Three*: Has the theologian a place in adult education? Of course he has a place anywhere; he has to know this type of effort too, and some of his kind have to be in it. (It has been suggested to me that adult *discussion* in theology might be the best place for the theology professor who has taken on, as contributor, the confused character of his times, much as that character is represented to him by his young-undergraduate students; but there seems ultimately no adequate substitute for knowing what one is doing.) *Four*: I doubt that there can be something which would meaningfully be called Roman Catholic adult education, even in theology; I *would* know what it means to care that the important insights of the Roman Catholic tradition be kept alive within reflection. *Five*: The sense of "apostolate" for the Christian educator is in this work muted, indirect, clarified only by surprise: occasionally one learns that a graduate has changed his work to greater social responsibility; once in a dozen years a student, asking for more time with one of his essays, may state that he finds he must first come to terms with the Christian community before finishing his work on Augustine — or with his marriage before finishing his essay on hope. More consistently related to the Christian dream of having an apostolate is the possibility of bearing witness in this kind of education that closing of inquiry is least appropriate when it is of inexhaustible Mystery one is thinking.

I asked as a first orientation that you think, when we consider adult education, that it is ourselves we mean. What has struck me in starting to be in adult education all the time is this: in meeting the eyes only of adults I am meeting always persons who have taken a stand on nearly every serious human question that may arise in theology or in any other field of discussion. They may have understood badly or they may have chosen poorly, but they have already made a disposition of their lives on most of the important questions. Thinking of that, ask how one might help these people grow, enrich, perhaps see a need to revise, such serious lights and choices, and you will see why it is that we set before us the tasks of our own lives when we take up adult education; we have to do with what, as theologians, we might name the problems of continuity and conversion.

BERNARD J. COOKE, S.J.

17 Theologians as Teachers in the Church

The topics chosen for this volume are an obvious example of the heightened interest that the nature of authoritative teaching in the Church has aroused in Christian reflection these past few years. This is, of course, true of Vatican II where we had one of those unique examples of fully magisterial teaching which would not occur in the lives of most people. Interest has also clearly intensified because of decrees issued by various episcopacies and particularly by Rome, and it was brought to a head by the encyclical *Humanae vitae.*

There is no question but what we must undertake a thorough-going review of the meaning of the notion of *magisterium.* Obviously, one can use a word to denote anything he wishes, as long as he makes perfectly clear what he is doing. From that point of view one can limit *magisterium* to the teaching office of the episcopacy, or one can give it a broader interpretation. What is much more important, however, is that we re-examine the reality that is involved, and move away from the over-simplified view which sees all teaching in the Church as belonging to the episcopacy. Instead we must realize that what does exist is a process wherein the faith of the Christian people as a whole, the witness of the episcopacy, the instruction given by catechists and other religious educators, and the technical operation of theologians, all work together to teach all of us and to form the entire Church in its faith.

Vatican II made it perfectly clear that one must see a specific role proper to the episcopacy. At the same time, in the operational order, a good deal of the teaching that went on

at the Council was done by the *periti*. Moreover, it is becoming
increasingly clear that competent lay people in various areas can,
and should, contribute to the clarification of doctrinal issues by
the technical understanding and expertise they possess as well as
by the insights drawn from their own Christian life.

In this chapter our precise task is to examine the particular
contribution of the theologian to this process of nurturing the faith
of the Christian people. The theologian can, of course, be a
religious educator. As a matter of fact, he can be a bishop. But
the topic I wish to discuss is: when a person is acting properly
in the role of theologian, how does he or she participate in the
teaching that takes place in the Church? Before proceeding further,
I would like to suggest that we not try to define an "office" which
is proper to the theologian. The theologian may have a distinctive
role; but it distorts the reality of this role to view it as an office.
A theologian has his authority in proportion to his knowledge
and insight, insofar as his research and his theological exposition carefully follow the method proper to theology. He is
to be judged, as theologian, not on the basis of his personal
fidelity to Christian life, but rather on the basis of fidelity to his
methodology and of the fruitfulness of his application of that
method.

The episcopacy can pass a certain normative judgment upon
the theologian insofar as the theologian must use as his starting
point the tradition to which the college of bishops bears witness.
However, in his own proper area of procedure, the theologian
is to be evaluated by his peers. He does not come to conclusions
on the basis of obedience paid to those occupying institutional
office. Rather, he is bound rigorously by the demands of truth.
His assent is to evidence and not to pressures.

We have long recognized a certain force exerted by the consensus of theologians in the faith and life of the Church. At times,
this has been recognized quite formally and explicitly — as it
was in the fourteenth century. At other times we have used the
notion of theological consensus quite loosely and abstractly. As
a matter of fact, it is difficult to discover exactly what would
constitute theological consensus. Suppose that on a given question

one could list the opinion of twelve theologians, ten who answer affirmatively and two who answer negatively. Consensus would seem to be with the ten; but the two who answer negatively may be working independently and out of the intrinsic evidence, whereas the ten who answer affirmatively may all be somewhat uncritically copying from a common source. Again, theological consensus really functions as such only when there is question of genuine theology and not of sloganistic polemic — as has happened at certain times in the history of the Church.

When there is genuine agreement among competent theologians regarding the manner in which some element of Christian faith is to be understood, we can quite prudently accept the accuracy of the understanding which they express. While no particular charism is attached to their office, because it is questionable whether there is an office as such, I think one can say that the theologians, as Christians, share in the overall guidance of the Holy Spirit, and because of the educated formation of their faith, are able to verify the correctness of their insight.

However, one should not confine the contribution of theologians simply to the normative guidance of theological consensus. There is also an intrinsic authority, perhaps even greater, which is possessed by truly creative theological insight. Granted the possible difficulties in recognizing true creativeness, in distinguishing it from the eccentric or the outlandish, the future always belongs to those with creative ideas. Generally the keenest insights in any field, including theology, are not immediately recognized or accepted, even by professionals: here one thinks of St. Thomas Aquinas or of Matthias Scheeben. Most people feel rather safe at the mention of such names from the past, whereas they get uneasy when one refers to truly outstanding theologians of our own day.

One of the things that I think is important within the life of the Church is that the judgment on theological creativity be made by those who are competent to make it, that is to say, by truly professional theologians. Only those who are at least approximately as well prepared and who possess more or less parallel gifts of theological insight are really able to understand what a truly creative theologian is saying. For others, even if they occupy high office in the Church, to put themselves in judgment upon such men as theologians is injustice and arrogance. Office in the Church, even when it comes by priestly ordination or episcopal consecration, does not bring with it infused knowledge; yet it is not uncommon to hear those who occupy official positions glibly condemning theological opinions which they can neither understand nor evaluate.

What then, is the function of the theologian in the clarification of the understanding of faith? It would appear that it pertains, in general, to two areas: first, clarifying *statements* that have been made about the realities of faith, secondly, clarifying the understanding of those *realities* to which Christian faith is directed. First, with regard to statements about the realities of faith: There are several things that a theologian does in this regard which are indispensible in the life of the Church. In the course of the past two millennia many statements have been made about various aspects of Christian belief or practices. Some of these give clear and certain guidance, and others are of dubious value. Someone must, in technical fashion, ascertain the relative importance and certitude of different statements, and establish thereby the extent to which a Christian must assent to them by virtue of his membership in a community of Christian faith.

This, of course, is what the old thesis method of the theology manuals used to provide for, at least theoretically, in the so-called notes of the thesis. While at times this process was quite static, and oftentimes so complicated that it got out of hand, the desired objective was quite important. One can see in the Church today a real need to give clear evaluation to the various types of statements through which the faith is expressed. A classic instance of this need was the encyclical *Humanae vitae*. Leaving aside for the moment any evaluation of the intrinsic content of the encyclical, it was extremely important both for clarity of understanding and to avoid any unjust imposition of opinions on people's consciences, to point out the precise type of teaching that it was, and to indicate what kind of binding force this has on the consciences of people. It was necessary to point out that this was not a disciplinary decree, nor a question of Church law. Rather it was a question of fact and truth, and it is the professional role of the theologian to discover what is the relative importance and binding force of a given statement as an expression of truth.

Again, if one is to read any statement, but particularly a statement expressive of religious faith, with correct understanding, it is necessary to find out what really was intended when this statement was made. Any statement, at the time it is pronounced, is conditioned by an entire complex of circumstances: by the language in which it was spoken, by the questions or problematic to which it was addressed, by the disputes and discussions which preceded it, by the pressures that were perhaps exerted on the group of people who pronounced it, by the precise desires or hostilities of the group to which it was directed, etc. All of these elements, as we come to know them, help us appreciate exactly what was the experience of understanding that people had when those words were spoken. Thereby we grasp more exactly the faith that was meant to be enunciated by a given formulation.

Clearly, this is a technical and difficult task, and it is the role of the professional theologian to undertake this kind of careful textual and historical study, to ascertain as accurately as he can the meaning of a given statement, whether it be that of the bishop of Rome, or a council of the Church, of a local synod, or even of Scripture itself. In other words, the theologian has a moment in his methodology when he must be primarily an exegete, searching for that which is the objective of all such textual studies: the literal meaning of the text, the meaning which the author (or authors) intended.

However, having done this, the theologian must go a step further and try to distinguish within this statement, even as intended, two levels of understanding and communication: He must try to ascertain within a given statement those elements of understanding that witness to the basic faith of the one who speaks, those elements that reflect his belief in the reality to which his faith is directed. On the other hand, the theologian must strive to discover which elements in a statement are due to the author's attempt to give some amplification, some explanation, some rationalization of his faith.

Such careful distinctions are specially important when it is a question of the statements made by councils of the Church, for these bear the highest doctrinal impact. It is one thing for the Fathers of a council to witness to their faith in the mystery of Christ and human salvation; it is another thing for them to formulate that faith through anthropological and cosmological understandings that are proper to the particular historical period and cultural environment in which they find themselves.

Again, it is obvious that a group of experts must become involved in this, for it is a highly technical task of historical and textual work. Accuracy of understanding cannot come either through good will or through piety, but only through a very assiduously careful application of methods which are appropriate to the task. This painstaking effort may, at times, seem to be anything but the task of Christian dedication that it really is. To many it may seem to be a rather impious undertaking, for it always draws into question the over-simplified understanding of such statements which people may have held for many decades or even generations. Nothing so quickly hardens into what is mistaken for tradition than a popular understanding of some element of religion. The task of the theologian is that of constantly challenging such oversimplified and falsified understandings, in order to keep the faith of the Church free from both prejudice and superstition.

However, the role of the theologian is not just one of trying to clarify as scientifically as possible the meaning of statements that have already been made with regard to the mysteries of Christianity. His task is also the exciting and creative one of trying to provide some deepened understanding of the reality with which Christians deal in their life of faith. Here, the range of theological activity is much broader and less clearly defined than in the area we were just discussing, for it is possible under certain conditions to consider activities like artistic production or creative liturgy as being, in a sense, a theological function, if they truly utilize media other than the canonized language of faith itself to give some understanding to the mysteries of faith. My intent today is not to suggest the various areas in which theology might appropriately employ methodologies drawn from other fields, but to indicate the aspects of Christian existence to which the theologian must direct himself.

First of all there is an indispensible task of clarifying the exact nature of the experience of shared faith and life which makes up the Church's conscious existence. There is no other starting point from which the theologian, or any other Christian, can begin if he wishes to clarify his understanding of the faith. It is this shared consciousness of faith, this community constituted by the presence of the risen Lord and his Spirit which is the very medium of revelation. God the Father can only be known personally insofar as he reveals himself in Jesus Christ, and he can only reveal himself insofar as there is human consciousness into which his revelation is received. This means that the theologian, if he is to be truly such, must himself be a believer. The historian of religion, the anthropologist, the sociologist might as an uncommitted observer describe from the outside what it is that Christians do in their life and faith; but it is impossible for him to give an understanding of an experience which he himself does not share. The starting point of theology must be participation in the presently existing Church. We might just mention parenthetically that from the point of view of pedagogy this is also an excellent procedure. It is necessary to start from the point where people already are, and if one is attempting to educate their humanistic values or their personal view of life, it is essential that one work out of the experiences which people have already had or are undergoing at the moment. Thus if the theologian begins with the very experience of faith that people have at a given moment in the life of the Church, he can then more intelligently and significantly lead those people from that starting point to the insights he wishes to communicate.

Secondly, the theologian in the Church should be probing into the meaning of the redeeming action which is going on in and through the faith and life of the Christian people. This must, of course, remain within the ambit of that faith which he shares with his fellow Christians; but it must attempt to apply all the other disciplines of human knowledge — psychology, sociology, anthropology, philosophy — in order to give a deeper and richer understanding of the action of redemption. Since this level of investigation is clearly one which deals with the lives and awareness of people, all the developed disciplines of knowledge that deal with the meaning or the experience of man can be utilized by the theologian to amplify his understanding of God's action in the life of men.

Actually what the theologian is doing is investigating the "missions" of the second and third persons of the Blessed Trinity, the continuing and transforming presence of the risen Christ to his followers who are the Church, and the dynamic, vivifying presence of the Spirit that Christ and the Father share with men. Since these missions are the created expression of divine personal relatedness to men, they constitute a medium with which human understanding can deal, whose intelligibility can be probed by human insight and ordered by human logic. It is in these activities of the Son and the Spirit that their identity and the identity of the Father who sends them is discovered by the community of faith. However, it is extremely difficult to grasp with accuracy what it is that is happening within the community; to understand the redeeming activity that is taking place. It is even more difficult to make the kind of analogous extrapolation which produces some fairly accurate understanding of the identity of Father, Son and Spirit.

Here again, it is the task of theologians, utilizing a number of methodologies which, either as individuals or as groups, they must learn to master, to provide clear guidance for the believing community as it strives to understand its belief. Theologians must employ the analogy of faith and the analogy of reason, and both of these within the precise context of the analogous intelligibility of "person." Moreover, the methodologies of all the various disciplines which give insight into the human condition are meant to affect and control the level and accuracy of understanding which the theologian is able to possess with regard to his proper object, the God who is revealing himself in Jesus of Nazareth through the living Church.

Finally, the area of truth to which the theologian is directing himself in his research, and which he is clarifying for the understanding of his fellow believers, is not an abstract truth but one which is of the highest practical importance. The reality of the Father who gives himself in the sending of his Son and his Spirit and the reality of their action in the life of the Church are meant to be the most fundamental law governing human behavior. Faith, as has been increasingly stressed these past few decades, is not an acceptance of abstract credal formulations but a total personal response to God who gives himself in loving presence. It is God, revealing himself in Christ Jesus and in the Spirit, who is the demand laid upon us. That demand is spelled out in the living faith experience of the Christian community as it moves through different historical epochs and finds expression in different cultural contexts. This kind of law can never be formulated adequately in codified regulations; its demands must always find new expression as man encounters new circumstances of questioning and demand.

The theologian in the Church is not to be a legislator; that is not his function. Rather, as one who is to discover as adequately as possible the truth of the Christian condition, he is to provide insights into that law which is embodied in the very situation itself. For this reason, though he is not a law-giver, in certain circumstances he can and must pass judgment upon some who, occupying positions of authority in the Church, lay down human laws which do not faithfully reflect the true demands of the divine being and the divine activity. No one, because of a position of official authority, can legislate truth, either speculative or practical. He may provide guidance for translating the law of Christ to the practical circumstances of Christian life, but he can neither make nor unmake a code of morality — this is something which derives from the word of God in revelation and the response of sincere Christian conscience to this word. It is the purpose of the theologian in the life of the Church to provide that understanding of the word which conscience can then convert into truly operative Christian law.

This, then, seems to be the role of the theologian. The theologian is not a sacrament in the midst of the Church as is the episcopal college, nor is he necessarily the one who has the keenest awareness of the reality of the mystery of Christ nor the clearest dedication in response to Christ's presence. But it is the function of the theologian in the Church to clarify in orderly fashion the intelligibility of faith so that his fellow Christians can, with understanding and dignity, worship the God who is, rather than fall into idolatry, and so that they can translate into their own authentic conscience the demands laid upon them by their Christian vocation.

Contributors

GEORGE DEVINE (Editor) earned his Bachelor of Arts degree at the University of San Francisco and his Master of Arts degree in theology at Marquette University. Currently Assistant Professor of Theology at Seton Hall University, he now has four published titles to his credit, in additon to numerous articles in such periodicals as *Worship, U.S. Catholic, Catholic Digest* and *Christian Art.* Active in liturgical leadership on and off the campus, Professor Devine authors a liturgical music column in *The Advocate.* Appointed by Archbishop Thomas A. Boland to the Religious Education Advisory Council of the Archdiocese of Newark, he is a frequent lecturer in parish and diocesan religious education programs, and has appeared on numerous discussion programs, including those of the ABC and NBC networks.

ROGER BALDUCELLI, O.S.F.S., was born in Bologna, Italy, and educated at the University of Fribourg, the Angelicum in Rome, and the Pontifical Biblical Institute, which granted him a Licentiate in Sacred Scripture. He later earned an S.T.D. from the Catholic University of America. His teaching career in the United States first took him to DeSales Hall Seminary in Hyattsville, Maryland, and later to LaSalle College in Philadelphia. Since 1965, he has been on the faculty of the Graduate School of Arts and Sciences at the Catholic University of America, in the Department of Religious Education.

SISTER ANNA BARBARA BRADY, S.L., entered the congregation of Sisters of Loretto after one year of college at St. Mary's of Notre Dame, South Bend, Indiana. She received her A.B. degree from Webster College and her Master's in education at Loyola University, as well as a Diploma from the famed Lumen Vitae International Center for Religious Education in Brussels. Most recently, she was awarded a Master of Arts degree in theology by Marquette University. After a decade of teaching experience in St. Louis parish schools, she joined the faculty of Webster College, where she has taught theology, worked in the administration of the Teacher Preparation Program and directed the M.A.T. in Religious Studies curriculum from 1963 until the present.

SISTER M. SHARON BURNS, R.S.M., received her Master's degree in theology from the University of Notre Dame, and is presently engaged in the pursuit of a Ph.D. in religious education (with a minor in philosophy) at the Catholic University of America. She has taught in elementary and junior high school, and also conducted an art studio for children and teenagers. She has been able to gain experience with her "Problems of Faith" teaching approach at Mt. St. Agnes College in Baltimore, Maryland, where she has taught theology for several years, in addition to teaching art.

BERNARD J. COOKE, S.J., hardly requires an introduction in theological circles. Shortly after receiving his S.T.D. from the Institut Catholique de Paris, he returned to his native Wisconsin where he became chairman of the Department of Theology at Marquette University. Under Father Cooke's leadership Marquette's graduate theological programs have educated a great number of those now teaching theology in numerous colleges and universities. A popular lecturer and author, he has penned diverse articles in myriad journals, and his book *Christian Sacraments and Christian Personality* enjoys widespread and prestigious use in scores of universities and colleges. He is presently on leave from Marquette, and engaged in research at Yale University.

EVERETT L. DIEDERICH, S.J., did his undergraduate studies at Saint Louis University, and also got his M.A. in philosophy there. His S.T.D. is from the Gregorian University in Rome, which published his doctoral dissertation on Peter Aureolus' doctrine on habitual grace. Father Diederich later pursued post-doctoral studies under the theological faculty at Trier, and then taught at the Jesuit theologate at St. Mary's in Kansas. He has since been Associate Professor of Liturgy in the Divinity School of Saint Louis University, where he is also Chairman of the Department of Historical Theology. He is Associate Editor of *Review for Religious,* and has published articles in *The Yearbook of Liturgical Studies* and *The Way.*

ELLEN DOUGHERTY pursued her B.A. at Barat College of the Sacred Heart in Lake Forest, Illinois, and her M.A. in English at the San Francisco College for Women, later completing her doctorate in the same field at the Catholic University of America. Post-doctoral studies took her to Oxford, where she studied England from 1870 in an interdisciplinary program. She returned to Barat as Associate Professor of English, and there joined Sister Marguerite Green, R.S.C.J., in the experience of interdisciplinary teaching, including the theological enterprise of which the two tell us in this volume. Mrs. Dougherty is now on the English faculty of Coe College in Cedar Rapids, Iowa, and as a poet and critic has contributed to *America, The Commonweal* and *The Critic.* In addition, she has been represented in The Borestone Mountain Poetry Award Anthology *Best Poems of 1965.*

AVERY DULLES, S.J., attended college and law school at Harvard, then served as an officer in the U.S. Naval Reserve, prior to entering the Society of Jesus in 1946. He received his Ph.L. and S.T.L. from Woodstock College, and his S.T.D. from the Gregorian University in Rome. Father Dulles also spent a year in Münster, Germany, for ascetical and pastoral formation. Since 1960 he has been on the theology faculty of Woodstock College, where he is now a full Professor. His best-known book of late is probably *Apologetics and the Biblical Christ,* although he has authored several other books and contributed to an impressive array of periodicals in the theological field. He is a member of the Board of Trustees of Fordham University, and has received a variety of honors, including the French Croix de Guerre, and the honorary degree of Ll.D. from St. Joseph's College of Philadelphia.

ERNEST L. FORTIN, A.A., did baccalaureate studies at Assumption College in Worcester, Massachusetts, and later earned an S.T.L. from the University of St. Thomas and a doctorate in philosophy from the Sorbonne. He has also studied at the Institut Catholique de Paris, the Ecole Pratique des Hautes Etudes, and the University of Chicago. Presently Professor of Philosophy and Religion at Assumption College, he has also taught at Laval University and at the Catholic University of America. In 1967 he founded the Assumption College Ecumenical Institute of Religious Studies, which was the first program of its kind. Father Fortin has written *Christianisme et culture philosophique au cinquieme siecle* and co-edited *Medieval Political Philosophy: A Sourcebook.* His articles have appeared in such publications as *Augustinus Magister, The Bridge, Classical Folia, Cross Currents, Laval Theologique et Philosophique, The Review of Augustinian Studies, Studia Patristica* and *Theological Studies.*

CATHLEEN M. GOING earned her bachelor's degree at Albertus Magnus College in New Haven, Connecticut, and her Ph.D. at St. Mary's Graduate School of Theology in South Bend, Indiana. She also holds a Certificate in Philosophy from the Thomas More Institute of Montreal. She has taught at Trinity

College in Burlington, Vermont, Loyola College in Montreal, McMaster University in Hamilton, Ontario, and St. Mary's Graduate School of Theology. More recently, she has been a discussion leader and lecturer at Thomas More Institute for Adult Education, a degree-granting affiliate of the University of Montreal, and is a member of its Board of Directors. Dr. Going is also Secretary of the Thomas More Institute of Canada for Research in Adult Liberal Studies. She has contributed articles to numerous periodicals, including *Liturgical Arts Quarterly* and *Loyola Quodlibets*.

ANDREW M. GREELEY studied at St. Mary of the Lake Seminary in Illinois, where he earned his S.T.L., and at the University of Chicago, where he received his M.A. and Ph.D. He is presently a lecturer in the Department of Sociology at the University of Chicago, and also Program Director of the University's National Opinion Research Center. One of the best-known persons in contemporary American Catholic intellectual circles, Father Greeley has written virtually innumerable articles and many books. He is perhaps best known for his famous study, with Peter H. Rossi and Leonard J. Pinto, on The Social Effects of Catholic Education, published in 1966 by Aldine of Chicago as *The Education of Catholic Americans*. He also writes a weekly column which appears in a variety of newspapers and magazines.

SISTER MARGUERITE GREEN, R.S.C.J., received her A.B. at Barat College of the Sacred Heart in Lake Forest, Illinois, and her M.A. and Ph.D. in American History from the Catholic University of America. She has since become Chairman of the Department of History at her alma mater, and it is in the intimate and vital atmosphere of Barat College that she and her colleagues — including Ellen Dougherty — have been able to gain valuable experience with an interdisciplinary approach to college education, particularly as pertaining to theology, the subject of the chapter she co-authored with Mrs.

Dougherty. The Catholic University of America Press published Sister Marguerite's doctoral dissertation, *The National Civic Federation and the American Labor Movement.*

JOHN KELLEY, S.M., did undergraduate studies at the University of Dayton, and seminary and doctoral studies at the University of Fribourg. Since 1958 he has been at the University of Dayton, first in the Department of Theological Studies, and more recently in the Department of Philosophy. He is interim director of Bergamo Center for Christian Renewal, and a consultant in educational experimentation. Father Kelley is active in civil rights and social action causes, and is currently Coordinator of an ecumenical experimental ministry in adult education, called Malachi.

WILLIAM J. KELLY, S.J., underwent the educational preparation of the Wisconsin Province of the Society of Jesus, including M.A. work in Classics at St. Louis University and theological studies at St. Mary's College in Kansas. He then completed doctoral studies in theology at the Institut Catholique de Paris, and since then has been on the theology faculty of Marquette University. Father Kelly has also been secretary to the Provincial Superior of the Society of Jesus in Wisconsin, and has taught Latin and English at Saint Louis University High School while a scholastic. He is one of the editors of the well-known volume *The Church Teaches,* and has contributed articles and reviews to *The Reign, Review for Religious* and *Theological Studies.*

EDWARD D. O'CONNOR, C.S.C., graduated from the University of Notre Dame with a B.A. in philosophy, then undertook theological studies at Holy Cross College, Washington, D.C., in preparation for ordination. Graduate studies at the Institut Catholique de Paris earned him a licentiate in Sacred Theology. Later, he received his S.T.D. at Le Saulchoir in Paris. Thereafter, he joined the faculty of the University of Notre Dame in the Theology Department and the Institute of Medieval Studies, and has remained there except for three leaves of absence: as Director of Studies at Moreau Seminary (University of Notre Dame); as visiting lecturer at St. Michael's College (University of Toronto); and on a grant from the Hazen Foundation, when he went to Tübingen, Germany, for research on a book to be entitled *Sin and Grace: A Comparative Study of the Theologies of St. Augustine, St. Thomas Aquinas and Martin Luther.*

COSMAS RUBENCAMP, C.F.X., received his A.B. (*magna cum laude;* Phi Beta Kappa) from the Catholic University of America, where he majored in Greek and Latin. He then pursued graduate studies in education at the University of Maine, and in systematic theology at the Catholic University of America, where he was awarded his doctorate. His doctoral dissertation was on "Immortality in Seventh-day Adventist Eschatology." He spent five years teaching classics and religion in secondary schools, and then seven years on the faculty of Xaverian College in Silver Spring, Maryland, where he served as Chairman of the Department of Religious Studies. More recently, he has been Assistant Professor of Theology at Georgetown University.

EUGENE F. SHAW, S.J., received his Ph.D. in communications from Stanford University, and completed his contribution to this book while at Marquette University, where he served as Assistant Professor of sociology and journalism, and was deeply and actively involved in the eventful life of that Milwaukee campus. Presently, Father Shaw is Vice-chairman and Assistant Professor in the Department of Communication Arts, a rapidly-developing area at Fordham University in New York City.

GERARD A. VANDERHAAR, O.P., received his doctorate in theology at the University of St. Thomas in Rome (the Angelicum). He has taught at Christian Brothers College, Catherine Spalding College, Saint John's University, (New York City),

Providence College, Wesleyan University, and Wisconsin State University-Oshkosh. Presently, he is on the faculty of Ripon College in Wisconsin. For seven summers he was director of the graduate theology program at Catherine Spalding College, and is former chairman of the New England Region of the College Theology Society.

JOHN H. WESTERHOFF, III, is an ordained minister of the United Church of Christ, and a staff member of the Division of Christian Education, United Church Board for Homeland Ministries. Rev. Westerhoff also serves as a field education supervisor in church education, and as a consultant to the Dean of Harvard Divinity School. He is well-known as the editor of *Colloquy,* and is the author of a forthcoming Pilgrim Press book entitled *An Alternative Future for Education in the Church.*